London School of Economics
Monographs on Social Anthropology

Managing Editor: Peter Loizos

The Monographs on Social Anthropology were
established in 1940 and aim to publish results of
modern anthropological research of primary interest
to specialists.

The continuation of the series was made possible by
a grant in aid from the Wenner-Gren Foundation for
Anthropological Research, and more recently by a
further grant from the Governors of the London
School of Economics and Political Science. Income
from sales is returned to a revolving fund to assist
further publications.

The Monographs are under the direction of an
Editorial Board associated with the Department of
Anthropology of the London School of Economics
and Political Science.

London School of Economics
Monographs on Social Anthropology
No 63

André Béteille

Society and Politics in India:
Essays in a Comparative Perspective

OXFORD
UNIVERSITY PRESS

OXFORD
UNIVERSITY PRESS

YMCA Library Building, Jai Singh Road, New Delhi 110 001

Oxford University Press is a department of the University of Oxford. It furthers
University's objective of excellence in research, scholarship, and education
by publishing worldwide in

Oxford   New York

Athens   Auckland   Bangkok   Bogota   Buenos Aires   Calcutta
Cape Town   Chennai   Dar es Salaam   Delhi   Florence   Hong Kong   Istanbul
Karachi   Kuala Lumpur   Madrid   Melbourne   Mexico City   Mumbai
Nairobi   Paris   Sao Paulo   Singapore   Taipei   Tokyo   Toronto   Warsaw

with associated companies in   Berlin   Ibadan

Oxford is a registered trade mark of Oxford University Press
in the UK and in certain other countries

Published in India
By Oxford University Press, New Delhi

© André Béteille 1991

The moral rights of the author have been asserted
Database right Oxford University Press (maker)
First published by The Athlone Press 1991
First published in India 1992
Oxford India Paperbacks 1997
Third impression 1999

ISBN   019   564   1078
For sale only in India, Pakistan, Bangladesh,
Nepal, Bhutan, Sri Lanka and Myanmar

Printed by Saurabh Print-O-Pack, Noida, U.P.
Published by Manzar Khan, Oxford University Press
YMCA Library Building, Jai Singh Road, New Delhi 110 001

Contents

Acknowledgements

I have incurred many debts in writing the essays brought together in this volume. The first among these is to my students and colleagues in the Delhi School of Economics where I have taught since 1959. This collection may serve as a record and an acknowledgement of that long association. More recently, the Department of Anthropology of the London School of Economics has been a kind of second intellectual home for me, and I gratefully acknowledge the friendship and hospitality I have received there. The essays were put together while I was a Fellow at the Institute for Advanced Study in Berlin; I am grateful to the Institute for its congenial atmosphere and its excellent facilities.

Chapter 1: Race, caste and gender A first draft of this paper was prepared to be read at a number of American universities – Duke University, the University of Chicago and the University of California at Santa Barbara – whose hospitality I enjoyed as a Fulbright Distinguished Lecturer in May 1989; I would like to thank the US Educational Foundation in India for providing me with the opportunity to travel in the United States. The paper was revised for publication at the Wissenschaftskolleg zu Berlin where I was a Fellow in 1989–90; I would like to thank the Kolleg for its generous hospitality, and in particular Peter Burke, Robert Darnton and Esther Goody for their stimulating comments.

Chapter 2: Race, caste and ethnic identity I am grateful to my colleagues A. Sharma and S.C. Tiwari of the Department of Anthropology and M.S.A. Rao of the Department of Sociology, University of Delhi, for much help in the preparation of this chapter.

Chapter 3: The concept of tribe with special reference to India This paper was prepared for a seminar in the Department of Anthropology of the London School of Economics where I was an Academic Visitor during the Summer term of 1986.

I would like to thank all the members of the Department, and in particular Maurice Bloch, Chris Fuller, Alfie Gell and Johnny Parry for their friendship and their intellectual stimulation.

Chapter 5: The politics of 'non-antagonistic' strata An earlier version of this paper was prepared in May 1966 for a seminar at the Centre of Indian Studies at the École Pratique des Hautes Etudes. It appears here substantially revised and I am grateful to the Jawaharlal Nehru Memorial Fund for providing me with a Fellowship which gave me the time and leisure to prepare it for publication.

Chapter 7: the Future of the Backward Classes I am grateful to Professor M.N. Srinivas for having allowed me to make use of his unpublished Tagore Lectures from which some of the basic concepts employed here have been drawn. Although I have not made specific acknowledgements at every point, my debt to him will be recognized by anyone who is familiar with Indian sociology.

Chapter 9: Individualism and equality The argument of this essay was first presented to a small group at the University of Leiden in April 1984 and shortly thereafter to similar groups at Utrecht and Oxford. It was written up in roughly its present version for a seminar at the London School of Economics in May 1985, and the paper was presented later in the same month at Manchester and at Leeds. I am grateful to the members of my various audiences for their many helpful comments.

Acknowledgements are gratefully made for permission to republish copyright material: Chapters 1 and 6 first appeared in *Man*, in 1990 and 1964 respectively; Chapter 2 in *International Social Science Journal*, 1971; Chapter 3 in *European Journal of Sociology* [Archiv. europ. sociol] 1986; Chapter 4 in *Castes Old and New*, 1969, Asia Publishing House; Chapter 5 in *Contributions to Indian Sociology*, 1969; Chapter 7 in *Indian Journal of Public Administration*, 1965; Chapter 8 in *London School of Economics Quarterly*, 1986; Chapter 9 in *Current Anthropology*, 1986.

For M.N. Srinivas, on his seventy-fifth birthday

Introduction

The essays brought together in this collection were written or published between 1964 and 1990. A quarter-century is not a small span in the professional career of a single individual. In this case it was also a period of many changes in the disciplines of social anthropology and sociology, as well as in the social and political environment to whose understanding the essays are mainly devoted. I thought it might be of interest to use the work of a single individual to recall and recount some of these changes. Hence I have included some early essays even though the volume might have had an appearance of greater unity if I had put in their place some more recent ones not included here.

I would not like to claim for the collection any substantial unity in terms of theory, argument and conclusion. Perhaps to an even greater extent than in other such collections, this one has neither a beginning nor an end. The work that it reports upon was taken up in the middle of a growing discipline, and it continues in the middle of the effort to understand social and political processes in a state of flux. Such unity as the volume has derives from the selection of particular problems, and my responses to those problems as well as to other ways of looking at them. I have deliberately avoided arranging the essays in a chronological order since I believe that, although my answers to particular questions might have changed in some cases, the orientation to them remains basically the same.

Society and politics are subjects of continuous and animated discussion in contemporary India. Indians are eloquent speakers and there is a great deal of writing in newspapers, magazines and books about the past, present and future of Indian society and politics; it should be stressed that sociologists and social anthropologists, or even social theorists in the wider sense, are not the only ones who think and write on these subjects. A number of changes in the intellectual climate of India set in around 1977, leading more and more persons to question the value of existing theoretical approaches to the Indian reality and to search for alternative approaches to it. The anxieties of Indian intellectuals about their framework of understanding and explanation reflect to some extent their anxieties about society and politics in contemporary India.

It is impossible for a student of society and politics to live and work in India without responding at all to the changes in the general climate of opinion taking place in the country; and I have expressed myself periodically in articles in newspapers and magazines. But the essays here are not presented as instant political commentary or reflections on current affairs. I view them rather as contributions to a discussion that is shaped primarily by the demands of sociology and social anthropology as academic disciplines, with occasional excursions into related disciplinary domains such as political theory, law and history.

An important difference between what is offered as political commentary and the essays presented here is the extensive use of the comparative method, or at least of comparisons, in each one of the latter. I have commented briefly on the use and abuse of the comparative method in the essay on race, caste, and gender in this volume, and more extensively in a recent essay devoted to the subject but not included here.[1] Suffice it to say that although there are, and will continue to be, disagreements on the procedures to be used and the precautions to be taken in making comparisons, there is a more fundamental question of orientation. Here I derive my orientation from Durkheim who said, 'Comparative sociology is not a special branch of sociology; it is sociology itself'.[2] I do not believe that we should refrain from making comparisons or seeking illumination from them until the perfect method has been devised on whose soundness we will all be in full agreement.

A second important difference between commentaries on social and political processes and the approach adopted in these essays lies in the more or less consistent use I have tried to make of the concept of social structure. When I began my career as a social anthropologist, the notion still had a prominent, not to say a unique, place in social anthropology, particularly in the form given to it by Radcliffe-Brown, Fortes, and also Evans-Pritchard in his earlier writings. That concept had been greatly influenced by Durkheim's notion of social morphology. It has now gone out of fashion, having been largely superseded by other concepts of structure that derive more from Durkheim's views on collective representations than those on social morphology. But I have retained some attachment to the old idea, particularly as used in Evans-Pritchard's first book on the Nuer and in *African Political Systems*, partly out of inertia, but I hope not entirely out of a lack of good sense.

Social anthropology in the 1950s and 1960s was different in many ways from what it is today. Despite its fascination for the comparative method, the anthropology of Radcliffe-Brown – and also of Fortes and Evans-Pritchard – was firmly rooted in the study of primitive or pre-literate societies, or at least of societies that differed markedly from those to which the anthropologist belonged. In Britain and in Western countries generally, it was accepted by and large that if a scholar studied other societies and cultures, he was an anthropologist, whereas if he studied his own or his own type of society, he was a soci-ologist. This I regarded as a challenge and an opportunity, for I wanted to be a sociologist, although my intellectual equipment derived from the heritage of anthropologists such as Rivers, Lowie, Radcliffe-Brown, Malinowski and Evans-Pritchard.

Thirty years ago one could work from the assumption of the unity of sociology and social anthropology, if not as an estab-lished fact, at least as a realizable possibility. The relationship between the two disciplines now appears, at least to me, to be more problematic, for they have both changed. Anthropology as a whole is now concerned much more with the study of culture than of social structure, with the 'thought-out' rather than the 'lived-in' order; and the most prominent anthropologist of the 1970s and 1980s has reiterated the commitment of his discipline to 'the view from afar'.[3] Perhaps I have worried a little more than others in my position about the implications of this shift in perspective for the identity of the anthropologist engaged in the study of his own society.[4]

The unity of sociology and anthropology, the definition of social anthropology as comparative sociology, and the primacy of the concept of social structure were all more or less articles of faith in the new department of sociology that I joined in the University of Delhi in 1959.[5] These convictions were strongly held and expressed by M.N. Srinivas, the first professor in the department who had worked in Oxford with Radcliffe-Brown and Evans-Pritchard both of whom he admired equally.[6] He had already made a mark in the field of Indian studies, and his work played a large part in shaping the field in the 1960s.

Until the 1950s Indian anthropology was largely identified with tribal studies. In the four years that I spent as a student of anthropology in the University of Calcutta, I read innumerable monographs on tribes: the Todas, the Andaman Islanders, the tribes of Chotanagpur and those of the north east. There were, of course, notable exceptions,[7] but popular belief still viewed anthropology as 'the study of oddments by eccentrics'. I was determined to move away from the study of tribes and on to areas considered more central, although I have, through various routes, returned to their study from time to time, as can be seen from two of the essays in the present volume.

The new field that was opening up in Indian anthropology in the 1950s may be described as 'village studies' as against 'tribal studies'. Two important collections of essays were published in 1955, *India's Villages*, edited by M.N. Srinivas, and *Village India*, edited by McKim Marriott.[8] These and subsequent studies explored the different domains of Indian society, such as kinship, religion, economics and politics through the intensive study of single communities. I began with a case study of a village in Tanjore district in south India where the focus of attention was social stratification, till then not a subject of central concern among anthropologists.[9]

As the collection by Marriott in particular showed, an important shift had come about in the orientation of American anthropology which made a strong impact on Indian studies. The moving spirit behind it was Robert Redfield whose work opened the way for the anthropological study of civilizations through detailed investigations of peasant societies and cultures. Anthropologists could not only move out of tribal studies, but they had found a way of exploring very large and very complex systems through the kind of case study that they had made their own. Village studies began to be made all over the world, and these gave a new lease of life to anthropology in India.

Srinivas, who played a leading part in developing village studies in India, was on the whole sceptical of the approach of Redfield which he contrasted unfavourably with that of Radcliffe-Brown. He felt that Radcliffe-Brown's concept of structure was superior in clarity and rigour to Redfield's concept of culture, and that view (or prejudice) made its way into my work, as can be seen in several of the essays, particularly the earlier ones. However, analytical rigour was not Srinivas' strong suit; his strength lay rather in his sensitive imagination and his unerring instinct for the ambiguities in a social situation, or what he called its 'messiness'. My deep suspicion of the modern 'structuralist' approach, implicit or explicit in many of the essays here, derives partly from this and partly from my own experience of everyday life in the society in which I live and work.

Perhaps even more than the concept of social structure, Srinivas valued fieldwork as the basis for understanding society. Fieldwork is, of course, the trademark of the professional anthropologist, and its value was underlined for me even before I came to Delhi by my teachers of anthropology in Calcutta. There its exemplar was N.K. Bose who was a man of enormous intellectual vitality, largely self-taught, but with a command over an astonishing range of subjects. Later, I was able to see the difference between his approach to fieldwork – as to many other matters – and that of Srinivas. Srinivas' approach conformed more to the orthodoxy then prevalent in Britain, particularly Oxford, which required the anthropologist to spend twelve to eighteen months at a stretch in the intensive study of a single community. Bose did not feel obliged to conform to any orthodoxy, and developed an approach to fieldwork that may be called 'extensive' rather than 'intensive'.[10] He made brief but repeated visits to several communities, and did this throughout his career, collecting a large body of information from different parts of the country. He felt that this was a better strategy for the anthropologist engaged in the study of his own society which was in many ways more easily accessible to him than to an outsider.

Bose and Srinivas were both superb fieldworkers, but I, unfortunately, failed to become one. For Srinivas, fieldwork not only provided reliable information, it opened up a new view of society, and that was its most significant contribution. Srinivas, Bose, and others among my teachers were not only professional anthropologists, they were heirs to an intellectual tradition that reached far beyond Evans-Pritchard, Radcliffe-Brown, Malinowski and Rivers. They were proud of that tradition, but also reacted against it. The Brahminical tradition had many achievements in mathematics, logic and grammar, and in several branches of speculative thought; it had little to show for itself in history and geography, and in branches of learning that required careful observation and exact description. Both Srinivas and Bose felt that fieldwork was essential to correct the biases of their own intellectual tradition.

It is in this light that we must view the great significance of and the initial enthusiasm for the distinction proposed by Srinivas between the 'field-view' and the 'book-view' of Indian society. There were book-views of every major institution: of caste, of the joint family and of the village community. Srinivas attacked these views as being out of date, out of touch with reality, and mistaken. He argued for their replacement by accounts based on fieldwork that would reveal the dynamic tensions in their actual operation. As I have indicated, this was largely a reaction against the Brahminical bias for the 'thought-out' as against the 'lived-in' order; but the reaction was fuelled by the antipathy, derived from Radcliffe-Brown, towards 'conjectural history'.

I would like to underline the point made in the concluding section of the essay on race, caste and gender that the field-view entails more than the use of one's own fieldwork as the main basis of analysis. There are in any case strict limits to the extent to which that can be done in the study of Indian society. Indeed, it should be possible, at least in principle, to adopt that view in preference to the 'book-view' without oneself undertaking fieldwork in the strict sense. The field-view, as I understand it, is at bottom an orientation to the lived experiences of people, with all their inner tensions and contradictions, that one seeks to understand and interpret.

The basic orientation of the essays in this volume derives from the field-view in the extended sense that I have given to the term. Their focus of attention is the lived experience of Indians here and now: they are not views from afar. But, I must insist, they are not instant political commentary either. I have tried to apply certain methods and concepts developed in social theory to reach a clearer understanding of experiences that take shape in Indian society every day. And I have tried to compare them with experiences in other societies to make that understanding more complete.

The great wave of enthusiasm for the 'field-view' that had animated anthropological studies in India in the first two decades after independence began to decline towards the end of the 1960s. The focus of attention shifted away from the social and political processes of contemporary life to structures of thought and representation. For me this world-wide change in anthropological orientation was dramatized by the eclipse of Radcliffe-Brown (and likewise Redfield), and the ascendancy of Lévi-Strauss. It gradually made its impact on the anthropology of India. I was young enough to get some sense of the significance of the change when it was coming, but did not yield as readily to its temptation as did some others.

Radcliffe-Brown's concept of social structure, by which Srinivas had set so much store, was now replaced by a new and very different concept of structure.[11] This new concept drew its inspiration from linguistic analysis whereas the old one had been based on a biological metaphor. The earlier idea of social structure, which goes back to Durkheim's concept of social morphology, still retains some attraction for me, partly because of the great importance in Indian society of collective identities, and of the arrangements of groups that retain a degree of consistency and constancy. At the same time, the shift away from morphology was welcome as it brought the study of ideas and values, or of collective representations, to the centre of attention.

The new trend in the anthropological study of India was heralded by the work of Louis Dumont. Dumont had published an outstanding monograph in French on the Pramalai Kallar, but it did not make an immediate impact, partly because it was not available in English until recently.[12] But his book, *Homo hierarchious*, which first appeared in 1966, became soon available in English, and made an impact almost at once

(I wrote a very early response to Dumont's approach in a paper presented in Paris in 1966 which appears here as 'The politics of "non-antagonistic strata" '). Even more important in creating and sustaining an interest in Dumont's approach was the journal, *Contributions to Indian Sociology*, launched by him (in association with D.F. Pocock) in 1957.

It is through Dumont's work that the new concept of structure, as against the older one of 'social structure', made its appearance in the social anthropology of India. Dumont had been directly influenced by Lévi-Strauss, as is evident from the dedication of the monograph, *Hierarchy and Marriage Alliance in South Indian Kinship*[13] to him and the acknowledgement to Lévi-Strauss for his idea of structure in the opening pages of the monograph on the Pramalai Kallar,[14] both published in 1957. It took anthropologists of India, accustomed to the staple fare of British and American anthropology (whether inspired by Radcliffe-Brown or Redfield), a little time to realize that a major change of orientation had been introduced with the new concept of structure.

The early numbers of *Contributions to Indian Sociology*[15] defined the focus of study in terms of religion and kinship rather than economics and politics. They also called for a closer relationship between the sociology of India and Indology, as based on the study of classical texts. Thus, the book-view of society or the indological approach was reintroduced as an integral part of the study of Indian society. However, unlike in the past, this time it was informed by ethnographic fieldwork, sometimes of a very high quality. But, despite the very high value placed on fieldwork, it was from the structures of traditional Indian thought as described in the classical texts that this work appeared to take its orientation.

Like others before and after him, Dumont finds in the caste system the defining features of Indian society, but views it first and foremost as a system of ideas and values. Further, he argues that the principal task of identifying the systemic properties of caste had been performed two thousand and more years ago by the authors of the Hindu Dharmashastras, and that we should take their representation of the system as our point of departure.

Yet on certain points we shall take the liberty of completing and systematizing the indigenous and orthogenic theory of caste – not without employing empirical aspects in a secondary capacity – by postulating that men in society behave in a coherent and rational manner, especially in such an important matter, and that it is possible to recover the simple principle of their thought.[16]

It would be a serious mistake to regard Dumont as simple-minded, as might well appear from the quotation above. *Homo hierarchicus* is a magisterial work, impressive alike for its tone of authority and its richness of fact and argument. It made a great impact on European and American anthropologists of India, and gradually also on my own students and younger colleagues; but it did not alter very substantially the perceptions of Indian sociologists in the rest of the country. As for myself, I was more impressed than convinced by the body of Dumont's work.

Let me say at once that I find it impossible to believe that Indians, or any others, for the most part 'behave in a coherent or rational manner': life would be enormously more simple – and more dull – if they did so. Anyone looking at Indian society today is likely to believe that their manner of behaviour is closer to the opposite. It can of course be argued that Dumont's observations apply to traditional and not contemporary India. But I would find such an argument unconvincing, either because it cannot be easily proved true, or because, even if true for traditional India, it may not be relevant to contemporary India, or for both reasons.

Preoccupation with the Hindu categories of thought has figured prominently also in the recent writings of a number of American anthropologists of the University of Chicago, or trained in that university. Most influential among them is Professor Marriott whose ideas have made an impact as much through his own writings as through the work of his many able pupils.[17] Marriott began his work on India under the influence of Redfield, but subsequently changed its direction to address himself more specifically to the distinctive features of Hindu thought with special attention, as I understand it, to Hindu systems of classification. The term 'ethnosociology' has been used to characterize the work of the Chicago school of anthropologists.[18]

The preoccupation with modes of thought, systems of classification, and so on has been associated with the attempt to define the unique, invariant and unchanging properties of Hindu culture, with special emphasis on traditional Hindu culture. Such an attempt has had attractions, though not exactly of the same kind, for both Indian and Western scholars. But it has also had the unfortunate effect, at least from the sociological point of view, of exaggerating the contrast between contemporary India and other modern societies. India has emerged as the repository of unchanging cultural values in a world in which change is conspicuous everywhere. The method adopted is more a method of contrasts than the comparative method as I understand it.[19]

The anthropological approach has acquired a certain influence in contemporary intellectual life, but in the process it has shifted its attention somewhat from social structure, social institutions and social processes to modes of thought, systems of classification, and the symbolic order in general. Through this change, however, it has retained or even strengthened the definition of the object of its study as the Other.[20] This has led to a peculiar tension among anthropologists in India: their theoretical concerns tend to be determined by the general intellectual ambience of their discipline; at the same time, it is difficult to consistently play the part of 'the astronomer of the social sciences' while studying one's own society and culture.

Since I maintain that my position as a sociologist of India must be in some sense different from that of 'the astronomer of the social sciences', I must indicate, however briefly, the place I assign to moral judgements in my kind of work. I do not believe that sociology, as I view it, has much scope to become a 'policy science'; my tasks are mainly confined to description, comparison, interpretation and analysis, as against prescription.[21] There is, however, one essay, 'Equality as a right and as a policy', that touches upon questions of policy, but it is mainly an account of the social and political conditions out of which certain policies arise, and of their intended as well as actual consequences; it is an exercise in policy analysis rather than policy prescription.

It now remains for me to make a few brief comments on the essays included here in the light of the general observations made above. The first two essays on race and caste deal with the same subject, but not quite in the same way. (I was surprised to find how much they have in common, despite the interval of nearly twenty years in their writing.) They are both comparative in outlook, 'Race, caste and gender' being more self-consciously so than 'Race, caste and ethnic identity'. I have argued that much can be learnt about both caste and race by comparing the two, and I now believe that our insight into each and both can be deepened by a consideration of gender and its place in societies divided by race or by caste.

Caste and race are about inequality, a subject in which I have had a long-standing interest, but they are both also about collective identity. Collective identities are of great importance in India, and their place in society and the part they play in politics are recurrent themes in this collection. In the essay, 'Race, caste and ethnic identity', I try to give a brief account of the different forms taken by collective identities in India, using the morphological concept of structure as my point of departure; that approach figures as the point of departure in several other essays as well.

While groups having a 'high degree of consistency and constancy' are particularly salient features of the social morphology of India, it would be a mistake to regard them as being unique to it or as being absent from advanced industrial societies. Collective identities based on race and ethnicity are important features of many societies, and there is no doubt that some individuals suffer disadvantages while others enjoy advantages by virtue of their ascribed membership in particular groups in the United States as well as in India; the 'group-disadvantaging principle' and its basis in social morphology are very briefly discussed in 'Equality as a right and as a policy', a lecture delivered in the London School of Economics in the summer of 1986.

In the essay on 'The concept of tribe', prepared for a seminar, also in the London School of Economics in 1986, I examine the special significance of collective identities in the social morphology of India, past and present. The morphological approach has been used to good advantage in a recent work on Indian society and politics by a French social and political theorist.[22] My own approach in this paper is of somewhat older vintage. It draws its basic inspiration from a paper published in 1941 by N.K. Bose[23] who had devoted a considerable part of a lifetime to tribal studies; the point on which I depart from Bose is in the use of the comparative approach, but that, in my judgement, only confirms his basic insight.

'Caste and politics in Tamilnadu', written shortly after my monograph on a Tanjore village, is an attempt to interpret regional political processes in the light of my fieldwork experience. Political anthropology had dwelt largely on politics in small-scale societies or at the local level, whereas political science, with a different disciplinary orientation, had been concerned more with the state and its institutions. In my essay I sought to examine the linkages between processes at different levels of territorial organization. Collective identities were again important in examining problems of both distribution and process, and I argued that even the identities of caste did not remain the same from one political context to another, or from one territorial level to another.

'The politics of "non-antagonistic strata"' was written for and first presented to Professor Louis Dumont's seminar in Paris in May 1966. It sought to challenge the view that castes ceased to be castes when they organized themselves for competitive politics. I found that view to be out of tune with what was happening in India. Many Indians, of both liberal and radical persuasions, believed in the 1950s that caste was on its way out and that it would be swept away by economic development and democratic politics. By the 1960s it had become clear that caste had been given a new lease of life by electoral politics and was, in the process, undergoing important changes. While electoral politics had given a new turn to the relations between castes, I found it an unnecessary limitation of our view of traditional Indian society to exclude in principle any competition or conflict between its basic morphological constituents. As an extreme point of comparison, I asked how far we could reach in an understanding of Soviet society if we stopped short at the then official doctrine that the relations between the social strata that were its basic constituents were in principle 'non-antagonistic'.

The essay, 'Networks in Indian social structure', written jointly with Srinivas and published a year before my Tanjore monograph, sought to examine the limitations of a morphological approach in which attention was confined exclusively to enduring groups and the enduring relations between them. It drew attention to the limitations of such an approach in the study of a large, complex and changing society in which the choices available to the individual were steadily expanding, despite the continued existence of groups with more or less clear boundaries.

I have included in this selection two essays on the Backward Classes to whose study I have devoted much of my attention in recent years. There is a vast literature on the subject – descriptive, analytical and prescriptive – to which scholars in many disciplines have contributed. In my larger work, I have tried to use the resources of both legal and social theory to understand and interpret the changing place of this large and very important constituent of Indian society.

The essay on the future of the Backward Classes is one of the earliest, being concerned with the two related issues of social stratification and social mobility. The approach is directly sociological, showing in particular the influence of Max Weber in the basic distinction it makes between status and power, and in its analysis of the tensions between their respective demands. The second and much later essay, 'Equality as a right and as a policy', shows my more recent and still somewhat uncertain interest in legal theory. I had started with stratification or inequality, and its different forms or dimensions; it took me close to two decades to recognize that equality as well could be conceived in more ways than one, and that there were fundamental tensions between the different conceptions of equality.

The two last essays deal more with ideas, beliefs and values than social structure in the morphological sense. Equality is more an ideal than a fact; or, rather, it is a social fact in so far as it is collectively acknowledged as an ideal and a value. To the sociologist, what is interesting about equality is that it does not have the same force as a social ideal in all places or at all times. This has led some scholars to categorize whole societies as either egalitarian or hierarchical, a proceeding I have criticized in detail elsewhere.[24]

'Individualism and equality' deals with the relationship between the two values comparatively and historically. The focus of the essay is on equality, which I insist is a complex and not a simple idea. It is not enough to say that it goes hand in hand with individualism, for, as I argue, following Simmel, there is an 'individualism of inequality' as well as an 'individualism of equality'. At the same time, and with all its inherent tensions, equality is a powerful ideal in the contemporary world as a whole, and no longer only in the West. My essay evoked a sharp response from Professor Dumont who has written authoritatively on the subject; I have reproduced my reply to Dumont because in it I develop a little further the arguments presented in my original essay.

The focus in the last essay is not on equality or inequality, as in much of my other work, but on individual and person. These are difficult concepts whose meaning and significance have varied enormously from one society to another; yet the individual, at least as citizen, occupies an important place in all modern societies. My essay has two main objectives: (1) to point out how difficult it is to reach agreement on the significance of these ideas, rich in ambiguity as they are, when societies of different types are being compared; and (2) to question the conventional view that they have had little meaning or significance outside Western history and culture. I develop my argument through a critique of the celebrated essay on the person by Marcel Mauss. Thus, I end as I began, with the plea for a differentiated view of each and every society as a basis for the comparisons and contrasts we make between them.

1 Race, caste and gender

Any attempt today to bring together race and caste for comparison and contrast is likely to meet with a cold reception. Such an attempt invites the opprobrium specially reserved for positivism, empiricism and eclecticism by the theoretically well tuned. They will readily acknowledge the similarities between caste and race when they are pointed out; what they will deny is that these similarities can have much significance for the understanding at least of caste. It may be safely said that, although the subject of caste has been discussed threadbare by students of Indian society and culture, the comparison with race has hardly figured, if at all, in the last twenty to twenty-five years.

Yet the fruitfulness of comparing race with caste was taken for granted by American and other sociologists studying the 'Negro problem' in the United States in the 1930s, 1940s and 1950s. The pioneer in this regard was Lloyd Warner (1936) who wrote about caste and class in the United States, saying that it was more appropriate to describe blacks and whites as castes than as races or classes. Warner directed and inspired a number of monographic studies of what came to be known among sociologists as the problem of caste in the US South (Davis, Gardner and Gardner, 1941; Cayton and Drake, 1945). The psychologist John Dollard used Warner's conceptual scheme in his outstanding monograph, *Caste and Class in a Southern Town*.

The major work of the 1940s on the blacks in the United States was Gunnar Myrdal's *An American Dilemma*. Myrdal, too, used the same conceptual scheme as Warner, and justified the characterization of blacks and whites as castes rather than races on the ground that they were socially, and not biologically, defined categories. Monographic studies were accompanied by discussions in general and comparative terms. Kingsley Davis (1941) published a paper in which he contrasted the 'primarily physiognomic, usually chromatic' basis of the caste system of the United States with the 'purely socio-economic' basis of the caste system prevalent in India. None of these formulations was wholly satisfactory, although several of them illuminated interesting features of both systems. The point I wish to stress is that in all these writings 'caste' was used not merely as a metaphor but as a concept, and attempts were made, though never very successfully, to formulate the concept precisely.

Students of caste in India have drawn on insights from the study of race in two quite different ways. There were the earlier anthropologists, of whom Risley is perhaps the most notable example, who constructed elaborate arguments to prove that the caste system originated from the encounter of races (Risley, 1908; also Ghurye, 1969). I shall have nothing to say about the part played by racial difference in the origin of the Indian caste system. My concern is with the approach in which insights from the study of race in the United States and from the study of caste in India are used to illuminate each other. A good example of what I have in mind is the work of G.D. Berreman (1966; 1967; 1968). The approach adopted there showed promise when it first appeared, but it went into a decline after the 1960s[1] and has never really recovered its voice.

Berreman's essays and other studies which sought to present caste as a form of stratification were dismissed as examples of 'butterfly collection'[2] in which superficial similarities were allowed to conceal profound differences. It must at once be pointed out that those who introduced the concept of caste into the study of racial stratification in America were acutely aware of the differences between India and the United States, which some of them stressed to a degree that may not have been fully justified. Warner (1936) pointed out that caste in America differed from its Indian prototype because the former, presumably unlike the latter, existed not by itself but in conjunction with a system of classes. Myrdal (1944), in his turn, pointed out that, unlike in India, caste in the United States existed in a moral environment governed by the principle of equality.

Berreman (1960) brought his experience of life in Montgomery, Alabama in 1953-5 to the study of a village in Dehra Dun district in which he lived in 1957-8, and found that the first experience greatly illuminated the second. He noted in particular the deep resentment of the underprivileged groups in both cases even where they appeared to acquiesce in their social subordination. He went on to construct a formal typology of kin groups, local groups, castes and classes, summarizing their similarities and differences in a somewhat mechanical manner (Berreman, 1967; 1968). To make matters worse, he appeared to be arguing that the real objective of the comparative method was to reveal similarities between systems.

A change of attitude towards such studies came about in the mid-1960s reflecting to some extent a change of outlook and orientation among anthropologists in general. Behaviourism and empiricism came under attack, while a case was being made at the same time for redefining the whole field of sociology as the sociology of ideas. In Indian studies this meant a slow, often unperceived and generally unacknowledged shift from the 'field-view' to the 'book-view' of society, culminating in the assignment of a privileged position to traditional 'structure' over contemporary 'reality'.

What is of specific interest to the present argument is the redefinition of the aim of comparison, viewed now as being directed to 'typification' rather than 'classification' (Dumont, 1967). I would say that a fundamental shift of orientation came about in anthropology with the dominance of an intellectual style in which 'difference' became the primary object of attention. The major figure in this shift was, of course, Lévi-Strauss, and the same shift made its impact on studies of caste through the writings of Louis Dumont. Lévi-Strauss made his point about 'difference' most sharply while contrasting the aims of anthropology and history: 'It is true that a discipline whose main, if not sole, aim is to analyse and interpret differences evades all problems when it takes into account only similarities' (1963, p. 14). This seems a very arbitrary requirement that a discipline should either only interpret differences or only take similarities into account.

Like race in the United States, caste in India is perceived by millions of people today as a particularly rigid and oppressive form of inequality. Many practices, described in earlier text-books as integral to the normal functioning of caste, would now be considered invidious and discriminatory, and might invite

legal and political sanctions. Fifty years ago it might have made
sense to say that discrimination based on race was pathological
while discrimination based on caste was normal. To insist on the
same contrast would be misleading today.

When we consider caste and race together, we are struck at
once by the remarkable similarity in the contrasting attitudes
towards women of lower and higher ranks characteristic of men
in privileged positions in both systems. My argument is that
inequalities of caste are illuminated in the same way as those of
race by a consideration of gender. There are two aspects of the
problem. There is, firstly, the sexual use and abuse of women,
which is an aspect of the inequality of power, seen in its most
extreme form in the treatment of women of the lowest rank by
men of the highest; this is the aspect of the problem that has
received most attention. There is, in addition, the unremitting
concern with the purity of women at the top, associated with
ideas regarding bodily substance that have been discussed
separately in studies of American kinship (Schneider, 1968),
and of caste and kinship in India (Inden and Nicholas, 1977;
Marriott and Inden, 1980); we can deepen our understanding of
both caste and race by exploring these ideas more systematically
and in comparative terms.

If we believe that the position assigned in thought and life
to women is of crucial significance to the understanding of
both caste and race, we are much better placed today than
anthropologists were a generation ago to pursue the comparison
between the two in greater depth. The position of women
in society, particularly in modern or contemporary society,
received very little scholarly attention from sociologists and
social anthropologists in the decades when comparisons of
race and caste were most extensively made. It is true that
Dollard (1957) wrote about the 'sexual gain of caste' in the
U S South and Berreman (1960) later wrote about the sexual
exploitation of both black and untouchable women. But these
observations were either lost or ignored in the absence of an
adequate conceptual framework for the comparative study of
gender.

It may well be the case that such a framework does not
exist in a fully developed form even now. But there is no

doubt that the climate has altered vastly so that the plea for a serious consideration of these issues can no longer be as easily ignored as in the past. The advances achieved in women's studies in the last two decades have implications not only for a fuller understanding of the relations between the sexes, but also for a deeper insight into the general problem of inequality, of which caste and race are two particular forms. I am talking now not only about new facts but also about new ways of looking at facts that have long been taken for granted.

The sexual use of women of inferior rank by men of superior rank would not acquire its characteristic forms in societies divided by caste or race if the ordinary relations between men and women were not marked by asymmetry. The asymmetry characteristic of such relations in general is merely reinforced when the man belongs to a superior race (or caste) and the woman to an inferior one. The normal requirement of asymmetry would be seriously upset if the woman belonged to a superior and the man to an inferior rank. The stricter the demand for asymmetry in the ordinary relations between men and women, the more severe will be the sanctions against the reversal of roles. I would surmise that the distances required to be maintained between castes or between races are likely to vary directly with the disparities established between men and women in the society as a whole.

We have to be careful, however, to distinguish between relatively stable societies and those undergoing rapid change as a result of changes in the legal and political systems and in the general climate of opinion. Such changes have been marked in the last four or five decades not only in the United States, but also in India. In these changing conditions, small and gradual reductions in disparities are periodically met with sudden and violent reprisals which bring established patterns into sharp relief. It is difficult, when this is happening, to demonstrate or even to discern any clear direction of change.

The asymmetry inherent in the link between race and gender is nicely brought out in Dollard's study of Southerntown.

In simplest terms, we mean by a 'sexual gain' the fact that white men, by virtue of their caste position, have access to two classes of women, those of the white and Negro castes. The same condition is somewhat true of the Negro women, except that they are rather the objects of the gain than the choosers, though it is a fact that they have some degree of access to white men as well as to men of their own caste (Dollard, 1957 (1937), p. 135).

This asymmetry sustains and is sustained by contrasting images of the sexuality of black and white women of which exact parallels may be found in the contrasting images of lower and upper caste women in India.

Leaving aside the facts of interaction for the moment, we may turn very briefly to the logic of the asymmetry indicated above. That logic is articulated very well in the Hindu Dharmashastras. The traditional Hindu theory of marriage clearly reveals the dual subordination of inferior to superior *varnas* and of women to men in the distinction it maintains between *anuloma* and *pratiloma* unions. An *anuloma* union is one between a man of a superior and a woman of an inferior *varna*, and, subject to certain conditions, it is accepted. The rule in its broadest interpretation allows a Brahman man to take, in addition to a Brahman wife, a Kshatriya, a Vaishya and a Shudra wife; a Kshatriya man is allowed to take, over and above his Kshatriya wife, a Vaishya and a Shudra wife; a Vaishya man may take, in addition to a wife from his own *varna*, one also from the Shudra *varna*; a Shudra man has to be content with only a Shudra wife (Manu, 1964, p. 77). *Pratiloma*, on the other hand, is the union of a woman of a superior *varna* with a man of an inferior one, and it is condemned in the severest possible terms. The lowest of human beings, akin to beasts, are the Chandalas who are described as the offspring of *pratiloma* unions between Brahman women and Shudra men (Manu, 1964, p. 405).

It must be pointed out that scriptural authorities are by and large uneasy about *anuloma* even though they acknowledge its consequences. We may say that there is a norm of *anuloma* only in the sense that its consequences are acknowledged but not in the sense that the act itself is commended. Or, we may say that the act itself is viewed very differently from *pratiloma* which is clearly condemned. The contrasts here are strikingly similar to the contrasts encountered in the conventions governing unions between whites and blacks.

By its acceptance of polygyny, Hinduism gave itself room to construct an elaborate formal structure for defining the relations between men and women belonging to superior and inferior *varnas*. Protestantism, with its strict code of monogamy, left itself little room for elaborating a theory of hypergamy, but it gave a kind of piquancy to sexual relations between the races by making them in varying degrees unsanctioned. It must be remembered that in the US South *all* sexual unions between whites and blacks were extra-legal; but the extra-legal domain itself was not homogeneous, being differentiated according to recognized, if not well-defined, principles.

We must not make the mistake of believing that Indian practice adhered strictly to Hindu theory, and that all inter-caste unions were according to the recommendations of the Dharmashastras. We have seen that the Dharmashastras themselves were uneasy about unions between *varnas*. P.V. Kane (1974, pp. 449-52), our leading authority on the subject, suggests that *anuloma* unions came to be viewed with increasing disfavour by authors of legal digests and commentaries from around AD 900, although we know that such unions in various forms were legally recognized as marriages until our own time. What is germane to the issue is that, with or without *anuloma*, a large number of extra-legal unions took place between men and women of different castes everywhere and at all times, and that these unions were governed by the same unwritten rules which, according to Dollard and many others, governed extra-legal unions between the races.

A great deal has changed, in law as well as politics, in the last forty years, not only in the United States but also in India. The Hindu Marriage Act of 1955 has set itself against the theory of *anuloma* by allowing inter-caste marriage and disallowing plural marriage. But the asymmetry of which *anuloma* was the theoretical expression is still very much in evidence in social practice. Inter-caste marriages are infrequent if not rare, and it is difficult to make any categorical statement on the basis of the limited and rather uneven information available.

A great many sexual unions take place outside marriage, including some between persons of different castes. These range from permanent companionship at one end, through semi-permanent and casual liaison, to seduction and rape at the other. In the absence of detailed information collected systematically, one can go only by general impressions. Such impressions clearly indicate that there is a wide measure of tolerance of extra-marital relations between men of superior and women of inferior rank, particularly between men of landowning castes and women of landless, including untouchable, castes (Freeman, 1979), whereas the reverse relationship generally, though not invariably, meets with reprisal.

I would like in passing to point to an important change in the attitude of the courts in these matters as indicated in the judgement of the Calcutta High Court in Mongal Chandra versus Dhirendra Nath (AIR, 1976, p. 129). Mongal Chandra, the illegitimate son of a Shudra named Bhadreshwar by his Brahman concubine, Urmila Bala, claimed succession as a *dasiputra* (son of a female servant or slave) to a part of his father's estate. The arguments against him were twofold. Firstly, it was pointed out that the *dasiputra* had a recognized claim only among Shudras, i.e. it would hold only if he had been the illegitimate son of a Shudra by his Shudra concubine. Secondly, since the union of which he was the offspring was a *pratiloma* union, no claim could possibly arise. The High Court rejected both the arguments and upheld Mongal Chandra's claim to a share in his father's estate equal to half the share due to his legitimate half-brother.

Although it is difficult to be categorical, it would appear that upper caste men have less easy access to untouchable and tribal women than they did in the past. From this I am inclined to infer that material sanctions are more decisive than ritual ones in restricting such access. When the balance of political power made the risk of material sanctions relatively small, ritual sanctions were not very effective in preventing the sexual use of untouchable or tribal women by upper caste men. The balance of power has now changed, though perhaps not very radically, and this has altered not so much the attitudes of upper caste men as their horizon of possibilities. We have accounts of similar changes taking place in the US South in the 1930s.

Relations between castes are changing rapidly and these changes are accompanied by reports of caste violence, including atrocities against untouchables and tribals in many parts of the country. The new legal and political systems have not eliminated the traditional hierarchical order, but they challenge it at many points. Disputes lead to clashes between members of different castes. It is difficult to assess the extent of change, because caste clashes are now reported much more extensively than before although, clearly, not all such clashes are reported even now.

The disputes that lead to atrocities against untouchables and tribals arise from many causes. Some of them clearly are engineered by interested political parties. There are many others that arise from the conditions of land tenure and of agricultural work. But there can be no doubt that there has been an increase in the clashes that arise out of attempts to control and use the sexuality of lower caste women. It is a sign of the changing times that annual statistics of atrocities against untouchables and tribals, including atrocities against their women, are now officially published in India.[3] These statistics are defective on many points, but they are illuminated to some extent by reports of increasing violence against women in general.[4]

It is clear that there is some pattern in the use and abuse of the sexuality of lower caste women, even though the pattern is changing. This has to be seen in conjunction with the jealous attitude towards and strict control over the sexual and reproductive capacities of upper caste women. The jealous concern of white men for the purity of their own women has been noted by most students of race and stratification in the United States (and also South Africa). The purity of women has of course been long recognized as the cornerstone of the Hindu theory of caste and kinship. We are now in a position to compare the two systems at a deeper level as a result of advances recently made by cultural anthropologists, mainly American, in the study of ideas regarding bodily substance in the United States as well as in India.

When we compare caste and race at a deeper level, we find

in both systems a prevalence of values and symbols relating to blood and natural substance, and beliefs regarding the strong constraints imposed by them on human character and conduct. These beliefs, values and symbols are deeper in the sense that they remain relatively unaltered even when the asymmetries described earlier change due to changes in law and politics. Hindus regard differences of caste as being in some sense differences of substance, and believe that these latter impel members of different castes to act differently. There are, as I shall show, parallel beliefs that differences of race express differences of natural substance which constrain character as well as conduct. One might still contrast caste and race by arguing that ideas about natural substance and the constraint imposed by it on social conduct are central to Hindu culture and peripheral to American culture, but I doubt that such an argument can be easily sustained.

I would like to enter here into a brief discussion of Schneider's account of American kinship (Schneider, 1968). It has stimulated a body of work on caste and kinship in India, and the authors of an important essay on caste systems have acknowledged its seminal influence on their work (Marriott and Inden, 1980).

Schneider describes American kinship as a part of American culture, which for him is a system of symbols and their corresponding meanings. There are two symbolic features, described for short as substance and code, which singly or in combination define the domain of kinship in American culture. Americans think of kinship in terms of shared biogenetic substance, typically blood; they think of it also in terms of a distinctive moral code, expressive of diffuse enduring solidarity, or love. Father, mother, brother, sister, son, daughter, etc. are relatives in the full sense of the term because they share the same blood and also because they love each other or ought to do so. In-laws, step-children and foster-parents are also relatives but not in the fullest sense because, although there is love between them, they do not have the same blood; husband and wife constitute a special case because although, like in-laws, they are brought together by marriage rather than blood, there is nevertheless a transmission of substance between them. Natural relatives (e.g. genitor and illegitimate offspring) are the obverse of in-laws because between them there is no recognized code, or so Schneider would have it, although there is shared substance.

According to Schneider, Americans believe that 'relationship as substance' belongs to the natural order whereas 'relationship as code' belongs to the social order. The natural order has its own compulsions as does the social order, although the two compulsions are not of the same kind. The interpenetration of the 'natural' and the 'social' orders within the domain of American kinship is a subject of crucial importance on which, unfortunately, Schneider's account does not throw much light.

The significance of Schneider's work is that it has drawn attention to a fundamental feature of American, indeed Western, culture as a whole. It is true that in one sense kinship is to a large extent segregated from other aspects of American culture, but in another sense the dichotomy between substance and code is of general significance. Clearly, the pivot on which the relation between race and stratification turns is the question of rightful kinship, i.e. with whom one may rightfully have kinship, with whom one may not, and for what reasons. It goes without saying that 'rightful' is not the same thing as 'legal' or 'by law' or even 'legitimate'; unfortunately, these distinctions are obscured rather than clarified by Schneider's manner of exposition.

The intimate, though negative, relationship between race and kinship is nicely brought out by Everett Hughes. After drawing attention to the highly flexible nature of American marriage and the kin ties arising from it, he goes on to say:

> 'But on one point of difference the grandly flexible system is hard and unyielding. The essence of the race line in North America is that no person identified as Negro will be admitted as effectively social kin of any person classified as white' (Hughes, 1965, p. 1136).

I must, however, point to the asymmetry which is not brought out with sufficient clarity by Hughes. The risk of being kinless does not weigh equally with all children of racially-mixed unions; it is likely to weigh much more where the genitor is a black than where he is a white.

The ethnography of the US South to which I have already alluded provides fairly detailed information on extra-marital sex, concubinage, and illegitimate offspring which may be used for re-examining the place of substance and code in American culture. The one point that is stressed above all others is the strict governance of the relations between whites and blacks by the rule of endogamy. This is the reason given most frequently for choosing the term 'caste' for the system. The same literature also points out with unfailing regularity that, although marriage was by definition confined within the caste, sexual unions commonly took place across it. This at once raises the question of the social position of the concubine or mistress and of the natural children borne by her.

There is ample evidence of the presence in many cases, though by no means in all, of bonds of affection – perhaps even of love – between a man and his mistress, and between him and his natural children. Davis, Gardner and Gardner recount the story of a white man who stood by as the house of his black mistress was burning down. Unable to bear the sight any longer, he rushed into the house, calling out, 'Let me in to save my children', and earning permanent ostracism from his own community (Davis, Gardner and Gardner, 1941, p. 31). Summing up their observations, our authors state:

> Furthermore, the white man accepts the children as part of the relationship; he cares for them and exhibits much the same affection as if they were legitimate. Thus there is formed a family group which, at least within the home, ignores caste restrictions (Davis, Gardner and Gardner, 1941, p. 38).

Here we see the great significance of the distinction between the 'politico-jural' and the 'domestic' domains; what has to be denied in the former may nevertheless be acknowledged in the latter.

Settlements were made of house and other property, and sometimes even of land, for the maintenance of the concubine and, less frequently, for the upkeep and future well-being of the natural child (Davis, Gardner and Gardner, 1941; Dollard, 1957). The ownership of a black plantation could on occasion be traced to a gift from a white landowner who had fathered a coloured child.[5] One can see that a black mistress and her children might claim an obligation on the part of the white husband-father to give them protection and patronage. But why should the white man acknowledge a claim that had no basis whatever in the law? The answer seems to me to be obvious. The very fact that American culture places a high value on 'biogenetic substance' means that there is some obligation towards one's own substance, even when that substance is generated clearly outside the law. One is compelled by American culture to acknowledge a part of oneself in one's natural child.

The flaw in Schneider's argument, it seems to me, lies in his belief that code can be completely separated from substance within the framework of American culture. The two may indeed be considered separately for many purposes and in many contexts, but only up to a point and within certain limits. A father cannot disown his son – or a son his father – however much he may be socially embarrassed by him, precisely because son and father are of the same substance. 'Owning' here means owning an obligation which can only be expressed in social terms and which does not cease to be social simply by being outside the law. Other codes may be violated or disowned; but in American culture, and I suspect in Indo-European culture generally, it is impossible to disown completely the code that is inherent in an immediate relationship by blood.

I have argued that the distinction between 'legal' and 'extra-legal' is by no means simple, at least so far as kinship by blood is concerned. The extra-legal not only has its own code, but is itself internally differentiated. I may illustrate the point by adapting the distinction, formulated by Fortes, between 'illegitimate' and 'illicit' (Fortes, 1969, p. 252). Only the children of legally-wedded spouses of the same colour-caste are 'legitimate' in the restricted sense of having full legal title. The child of a white man and his black commonlaw wife is illegitimate; but neither the union nor its fruit is illicit; the mother can transmit status to the child. A sexual union between a black man and a white woman would be in a wholly different category; like incest, it would be illicit, and neither parent could transmit status to the offspring.

Schneider's mistake has been magnified by some of those who have carried his conceptual scheme into the study of Hindu caste and kinship. I will take as an example the account of kinship in Bengali culture by Inden and Nicholas which begins with a handsome acknowledgement of indebtedness to Schneider. Substance and code, according to the authors, are fundamental features of Bengali kinship, but their mutual relationship is quite different in Bengali culture from what it is in American culture. This is so because the premise of Bengali culture is altogether different from that of the American:

> As a consequence of this cultural premise, no distinction is made, as in American culture, between an order of "nature", defined by shared biogenetic substance, and an order of "law", defined by code for conduct (Inden and Nicholas, 1977, p. xiv).

The authors proceed to underline 'the inseparable relationship of code and substance in Bengali culture' (Inden and Nicholas, 1977, p. xiv), suggesting clearly their separability in American culture.

I have already indicated, and will try to show by further illustration, that the assumption of the radical separability of substance and code in American culture is open to question. We have seen that in American culture some social obligations are entailed in the natural kinship between father and illegitimate child. We must now ask whether Bengalis – or Hindus in general – are able to distinguish between 'artificial' and 'real' kinship, and the answer to that question will show that there are circumstances under which they are able and willing to treat substance and code as separate.

I shall avoid the obvious trap of adoption, because in Hindu law adoption was governed traditionally by strict conditions, including the condition that adoptor and adoptee be of the same caste – a point in favour of the argument by Inden and Nicholas.[6] The ties of kinship may, however, be extended artificially in other ways than by adoption. There is, firstly, what is broadly described as ritual kinship. Adrian Mayer tells us: 'There are several ways in which people of different castes can be linked as kin through ritual acts' (1960, p. 139); and, further, 'there is no great feeling that ties should be made inside or outside the caste' (1960, p. 142). Then there is 'village kinship', through which terms and some forms of courtesy are extended to co-villagers. Obviously, the strength of these ties varies greatly.

Mayer himself classifies kin ties into three kinds according to their strength. The strongest are real ties and certain kinds of ritual ties where 'there are definite obligations with a minimal amount to be fulfilled on pain of general public disapproval' (Mayer, 1960, p. 146). Then there are 'minor ritual kin ties (*rakhi*) and strong friendships which have become expressed in a kinship idiom' (Mayer, 1960, p. 146); these too entail definite obligations, though not of the same kind or the same strength as in the first case. Finally, there is 'village kinship' where the idiom of kinship is extended mainly as a form of courtesy.

I would like to stress the point, to which Mayer has also alluded, that kin terms and corresponding modes of behaviour are commonly extended, sometimes across caste, in a highly differentiated manner. This means that a certain person may be treated as mother's brother and another person as father's sister even though they both belong to castes other than one's own. It is difficult to see how this could happen if code and substance stood in an 'inseparable relationship' in Hindu culture.

Marriott has used Schneider's unit ideas of substance and code to formulate an elaborate and complex argument about the 'transactional and transformational culture of India' (Marriott, 1976, p. 111). This argument may be viewed as a first step in an ethnosociology of Indian culture which will lead to the construction of a more informed general sociology free from the distortions inherent in the use of categories derived from one civilization for the study of all civilizations. This first step, however, entails an accentuation of the contrast between Indian and Western thought and culture. It is with this accentuation of the contrast, rather than with other aspects of Marriott's important essay, that I am concerned, since it impinges directly on the comparative study of caste and race.

Turning back for a moment to the example of 'artificial' kinship, it can certainly be argued that a man may well treat a person as mother's brother or father's sister, but he will surely not eat food cooked by either if these 'artificial' kin both belong to an inferior caste. Thus, the code of kinship may be extended artificially up to a point, but not beyond that point, for there is also a code of food transactions with which it has to be congruent. Extending the sentiment of kinship may

not go very far, it may be argued, if it runs counter to the code
of food transactions.

We have to be careful in dealing with such an argument for
it does indeed point to a very important part of Hindu culture.
There is no doubt about the general importance of food transactions in traditional India and about their specific importance
in the operation of kinship and caste. But a number of further
points need to be made. The code of food transactions was never
observed with the same strictness in all parts of India, and it is
now undergoing change to such an extent that ethnographic data
become rapidly out of date. Undoubtedly, the traditional code of
food transactions was unusually elaborate, but the elaborateness
of a code is not the same thing as its social significance. It is
not at all clear how far the structure of caste (or of kinship)
is dependent for its continued existence on the survival of the
traditional code of food transactions. There are now thousands,
if not millions, of Indians who ignore or repudiate the traditional
code in both principle and practice, but that certainly does not
mean that they have given up caste.

Marriott is surely right in asserting that Hindu thinking denies
the 'easy separability' of substance and code, and of actor and
action. But I am not sure that Hindus are quite unique in that.
It is true that the separability of actor and action is much
more in tune with modern capitalist that with traditional Hindu
culture. But there is at least one significant area of American
life, concerned with race, where it is precisely this separability
that is widely denied, implicitly if not explicitly.

The doctrine of the separability of substance and code and,
more generally, of actor and action is a liberal doctrine whose
importance in modern Western culture cannot be denied. But
this does not mean that the doctrine is never disregarded in
either theory or practice. Nor is it the case that the *in*separability
of substance and code, of actor and action, is affirmed only in
the context of race. The attitude towards the destitute in early
nineteenth-century England was not wholly dissimilar to the
attitude towards the blacks in early twentieth-century America.
It was a common argument, familiar to every reader of Dickens,
that the destitute were unthrifty and improvident *by nature* and
not due to circumstance, and that charity, whether private or

public, would only harden their nature and not alter their conduct. Echoes of the same kind of argument are heard today in the debate about gender; but that is too large a subject for me to enter into here.

Although attitudes to race in the United States vary greatly among both whites and blacks, the ethnographic literature on the US South reveals the persistent belief that whites and blacks are different *by nature*: there are beliefs of inherent difference in regard to every conceivable attribute, from size of genitals to aptitude for music. Moreover, whatever white men may believe about the separability of substance and code, they do not apply that belief uniformly to themselves and to others.

The explanation of 'Negro conduct' in terms of an unvarying, indeed unalterable, 'Negro nature' is commonly reported in the ethnography of the 1930s and 1940s. It is true that racial stereotypes are now less commonly and less crudely expressed, at least in public, and perhaps also less widely held. To some extent this is parallcled in India by the fact that caste stereotypes are out, at least on the public platform, although they are widely held and frequently expressed in private. There can be little doubt that the upper caste Hindu typically believes that untouchables perform poorly at school and at work – which in fact they do – because they are made of an inferior substance. This is surely paralleled by the American belief that the poor scholastic achievement of the black is due to his inherently inferior intelligence.[7]

As pervasive as, and perhaps deeper than, ideas about black intelligence are white ideas – and fears – about black sexuality. The idea that black men are governed by untamed and untamable natural sexual urges and that black women are sexually 'hot' and white women 'cold' is a commonplace of southern literature (Dollard, 1957). These ideas, being consistent with the asymmetry of power between the races and between the sexes, no doubt served to maintain that asymmetry. But it would be an oversimplification to treat them merely as rationalizations designed to justify and maintain an unequal structure of power.

The idea of substance manifests itself most insistently in the context of miscegenation. It is true that miscegenation has taken place extensively in the United States, as also in India, but in both cases it has occurred largely outside the law. In each case the fact of miscegenation brings out deep-rooted fears about its effect on the purity of race or caste. Myrdal has discussed in detail the fear of miscegenation or amalgamation, and the arguments against it. 'The basic role of the fear of amalgamation in white attitudes to the race problem is indicated by the popular magical concept of "blood"' (Myrdal, 1944, p. 587). He also tells us that the standard response of the man on the street to the plea for racial equality was the presumably unanswerable question: 'Would you like to have your daughter marry a Negro?' Myrdal is quick to show us where his own sympathies lie. But in the light of the discussion now available on American kinship, we cannot as easily dismiss the popular American concept of blood as 'magical'. That concept is of fundamental importance for understanding not only kinship but also race and stratification in the United States.

Myrdal's own liberal presuppositions prevent him from seeing in full the real contradiction between the American Creed and the American attitude to 'blood'. For him, there is a liberal view of race and a conservative, or even a reactionary, view of it. The liberal view, which is also his own view, is the rational one; it has gained ground steadily and is bound to prevail in the end. In the meantime, the conservative view, arising out of the 'popular magical concept of "blood"', is still entrenched in the South which, in any case, is known to be backward, although it is showing definite signs of progress. This view may not be wholly wrong, but it is superficial and can be misleading.

My reading of Schneider, which differs somewhat from that of Parsons (1975), tells me that American attitudes to race are pervasive and enduring because they are tied up with American ideas about blood which are deep and fundamental. This does not, of course, mean that these ideas are unalterable, but only that their rhythms of change are not the same as the rhythms of change in what is popularly described as political ideology. All aspects of a society do not change at the same rate or even in the same direction. There is abundant evidence of a change in the relationship between race and the occupational structure which is a central part of the American system of stratification (Freeman, 1976; also Pinkney, 1985). But it would be a mistake to read that evidence to mean that there has been a corresponding change in the American attitude to miscegenation, which belongs to a different domain of culture.

All the evidence suggests that, by and large, Americans continue to adhere to the belief that race is a biological fact. Why should this be so when every undergraduate student of anthropology knows, or ought to know, that race is a cultural and *not* a biological fact? (Montagu, 1974). It is impossible, in the face of this evidence, to agree with Marriott (1976) that 'biological substantialism' is a peculiarity only of the Hindus.

I am now in position to return to the original objective of this paper. That objective was not to reach any definite conclusion about caste or about race, or about the similarities and differences between them. My purpose was to raise certain questions about attitudes towards the comparative method held by influential students of Indian society and culture; and, at the same time, to enter a claim for the validity of limited comparisons, when made systematically and with an open mind.

Comparisons between caste and race have been all but banished from the field of Indian studies for the last twenty-five years on the ground that, since Indian and Western civilizations are so radically different, such comparisons cannot be fruitful and must be either superficial or misleading (Dumont, 1964; 1966). It is a part of this argument that caste is 'normal' in India whereas race is 'pathological' in America (Dumont, 1961). Such an argument is itself misleading because in a rapidly changing world it is difficult, if not impossible, to determine what is normal and what is pathological; and it introduces evaluations that cannot be defended and are not really necessary.

The marked stress on 'difference' and 'contrast' prominent in anthropological writings on Indian society and culture in the last two decades is associated with a return to the Indological approach, or, as I indicated at the beginning of this essay, to the 'book-view' as against the 'field-view' of Indian society. I do not mean by this that the anthropologists who have contributed most to this return – whether Dumont or Marriott – have ever denied the importance of fieldwork; indeed the fieldwork done in the 1950s by each of these anthropologists was outstanding, if not exemplary.[8] It is none the less true that they have increasingly taken their orientation from Hindu thought rather than Indian life, however crude that distinction might sound. Moreover, the growing preoccupation with thought rather than action has led them, and their followers, to go back to the past and to locate its basic elements in classical Hinduism and its religious and philosophical literature.

The book-view or Indological approach assigns a privileged position to the past as compared to the present. Obviously, a great deal of fieldwork has gone into the anthropological writings to which I have been referring. But we have to consider not merely the *quantum* of fieldwork but also its *orientation*; not just how much fieldwork one does but also where one sets one's sights. It hardly needs to be argued that in anthropological fieldwork what one observes and what one sets out to observe are never wholly unrelated. In particular, there is a marked tendency in the anthropological writing which has emerged from the fieldwork to which I refer to push to the margins whatever is distinctive of modern or contemporary Indian life.

All this has meant that the predominant anthropological representation of Indian society and culture over the last twenty years or so has had a certain timeless character. Attention has shifted away from technology, politics and law and has been focused on ritual, ceremony and religious thought. It is maintained, directly or indirectly, explicitly or implicitly, that the changes taking place in India now are confused and confusing, that they affect the surface of Indian life without touching its core. If in my discussion of race in the United States I have used mainly the ethnography of the 1930s and 1940s this is in part deliberate, since we have to believe that some things in America remain relatively fixed even though many things change, just as some things in India change even though many things remain unchanged.

What emerges from the literature that I have criticized is a 'structural' view of Hindu culture against the backdrop of a 'historical' view of Western civilization. This fits in very well with the emphasis on 'difference' and 'contrast' to which I have drawn attention. My view is that if we are to develop the study of Indian society and culture within the framework of comparative sociology, we must put back the Indological approach where it properly belongs. I mean by this not that we should ignore the past or treat it as unimportant, but simply that the present and not the past should be the point of departure in the sociology of India as it is, or ought to be, in the sociology of any society. A sociology of India that has its orientation to the past and disregards or devalues the present is bound to be unfruitful and in the end self-defeating.

It is, of course, the most difficult thing, in applying the comparative method, to maintain a proper balance between comparison and contrast. One must try nevertheless to be faithful to the facts and fair to scholars with a different intellectual orientation from one's own. Perhaps there may be genuine differences of orientation between sociologists devoted to the study of their own society and those devoted to the study of other cultures. I would not, however, push that point too far, because implicit in it is the presumption that societies or civilizations (India and the West in the present case) are somehow like substances and, as such, mutually impenetrable; such a presumption itself becomes an obstacle to comparison.

Those who adopt the 'typifying' or the 'distinctive features' approach do not renounce comparison in either principle or practice. It is true all the same that their approach leads to a sharpening of contrasts in the short run if only because they hope thereby to make their comparisons more fruitful in the long run. For what does it mean to typify if not to engage in 'one-sided accentuation' (Shils and Finch, 1949, p. 90) for establishing clear contrasts? We know how effectively that technique was used by Max Weber for constructing ideal types of great analytical value.

However, it is one thing to engage in 'one-sided accentuation' for constructing ideal types of, say, economic action or legitimate authority, and quite another to accentuate in a one-sided way the peculiarities of a whole nation or a whole civilization. In the former case it is easy to keep in mind the fact that 'market rationality' or 'charismatic authority', as the case may be, is a construction that we have made for a particular analytical purpose. In the latter, it is easy to lose sight of the distinction between the construct and the reality, for it is useless to pretend that human beings - including anthropologists and philosophers – can be persuaded to regard India, France, Europe, America or the West in the same way as, or with the same detachment with which, they might regard 'market rationality' or 'charismatic authority'. It is here that the 'typifying' or the 'distinctive features' approach, with its inclination for 'one-sided accentuation', may become a source not only of intellectual error but also of political mischief.

2 Race, caste and ethnic identity

The attempt to view race and caste within the same framework of understanding could take us in two different directions. In the first place, we might consider to what extent systems of stratification based on caste (as in India) and on colour (as in the Southern United States) can be regarded as analogous in structure; this is a problem in comparative sociology. In the second place, we might ask how far in India caste distinctions correspond to differences in physical or racial type; this problem is of more special interest to students of Indian society and history.[1]

When American social anthropologists, mainly under the influence of Lloyd Warner, began to study the Deep South of the United States in the 1930s, they found it useful to speak of a caste system in representing the cleavages between blacks and whites in rural and urban communities there.[2] Gunnar Myrdal employed similar terms and categories in his classic study of the American Negro made at about the same time.[3] The metaphor of caste has since then been widely used in describing multi-racial societies in other parts of the world, notably South Africa.[4]

There are certain obvious parallels between the Indian caste system and the system of stratification based on colour, whether in the US South or in South Africa. In studying the US South both Warner and Myrdal were struck by the rigid distinctions maintained between blacks and whites which seemed to them to be in marked contrast with the more flexible pattern of relations in a class system. Their purpose in labelling as 'caste' the system of stratification based on colour was not so much to explore its similarity with the Indian system as to emphasize its difference from the class system in America and other Western societies.

It might be useful to explore a little further the similarities between the Indian caste system and what I shall call for short the colour-caste system. In both systems the component units are differentiated from each other by clearly defined boundaries. Differences between castes are reinforced by a measure of homogeneity within the caste.

Caste systems may be described as systems of cumulative inequality. Advantages of status tend to be combined with advantages of wealth and power, and those who are socially underprivileged also tend to be at the bottom of the economic and political scales. There are many exceptions to this in the colour-caste system where poor whites co-exist with well-to-do blacks,[5] but exceptions of the same kind have existed in Indian society for a long time.[6]

In both systems the component units maintain their social identity through strict rules of endogamy. In a class system individuals tend to marry within their own class but there are no prescribed rules which require them to do so. In the US South marriages between blacks and whites were strictly forbidden and this is still the case in South Africa. In India the principle of endogamy was in certain areas mitigated by the practice of hypergamy (*anuloma*) by which a man from a higher caste could under prescribed conditions marry a girl from a lower caste. It must be emphasized that traditionally the practice of hypergamy was governed by strict rules which recognized the distinctions between castes as well as their hierarchical order; and, as Mrs Karve has pointed out, it 'is found in certain parts of India among only certain castes and is not a general practice in any region'.[7] Those who define systems of stratification in terms of the rigidity of marriage rules are bound to be struck by the similarity between the Indian and the colour-caste systems.

Closely associated with the rules regulating marriage are certain attitudes towards women characteristic of both types of society. A very high value is placed on the purity of women belonging to the upper strata and they are protected from sexual contamination by men of the lower strata by sanctions of the most stringent kind.[8] On the other hand, there is a strong element of 'sexual exploitation' in the relations between men of the upper strata and women of the lower. Berreman notes that the 'sexual advantage' enjoyed by high caste men in an Indian village studied by him are similar even in their details to those enjoyed by white men in the town studied by Dollard in the US South.[9]

We might at this stage sum up the characteristics of castes by saying that they are hierarchically ranked groups or categories based on hereditary membership which maintain their social identity by strict rules of endogamy. The fact of hereditary membership is of great importance. It fixes the social status of the individual at birth and prevents his movement from one group or category to another. In spite of many exceptions, these factors combine to fit the social divisions in a caste society into an uncommonly rigid mould.

If I began by considering the similarities between the two types of social stratification, this was not to imply that I consider these to be in some sense more fundamental than their differences. Opinion is sharply divided on the significance to be attached to these similarities and differences,[10] and scholars like Dumont[11] and Leach[12] would consider it misleading to describe systems of stratification based on colour as caste. For them, the institution of caste in the true sense of the term is a unique feature of the pan-Indian civilization.

The differences between the two types of caste system – using the same term for convenience – are obvious enough, but it has not proved easy to sum them up in a formula. Some would draw the distinction by saying that one represents a 'cultural model' and the other a 'biological model'.[13] The caste system in India is certainly a cultural phenomenon, but is it adequate to represent the colour-caste system in the US South (or in South Africa) simply in biological terms? Both Warner[14] and Myrdal[15] had first considered and then rejected the view that the groups they were studying be described as races. A quick look at their argument will throw some light on the complex relations between race, culture and society and help us to probe a little deeper into the subject of our study.

Warner insists that in the stratification system of the Deep South the categories black and white are socially and not biologically defined. Persons who are socially defined as blacks might be biologically classified as white and people who are regarded as blacks in one society might in another society be viewed as whites.[16] Myrdal's position is similar. He points out, first, that 'the "Negro race" is defined in America by the white people' and second, that 'this definition of the Negro race in the United States is at variance with that held in the rest of the American continent.'[17] What is significant is not merely the presence of physical distinctions but also the manner in which they are socially recognized which is essentially conventional. Neither blacks nor whites in the US South can be regarded as races in the strictly biological sense of the term.

Kingsley Davis sought to characterize the distinction which we are considering as being between 'racial' and 'non-racial' caste systems.

> A non-racial caste system, such as the Hindu, is one in which the criterion of caste status is primarily descent symbolised in purely socio-economic terms; while a racial system is one in which the criterion is primarily physiognomic, usually chromatic, with socio-economic differences implied.[18]

We have just seen why it is not wholly satisfactory to describe the caste system in the United States as racial; and it is not entirely clear that the chromatic differences there are more fundamental than the socio-economic ones as Davis would seem to suggest. Nor is it wholly satisfactory in this context to view 'race' and 'descent' in opposition for in both cases we are concerned with the cultural definition of biological processes.

It is true, none the less, that *visible* physical differences are much more conspicuous in the colour-caste system than in the Indian. An outsider in the US South will not have much difficulty in deciding in the majority of cases who belongs to which caste merely from appearance. In India he will find it difficult, if not impossible, to do this beyond a certain point. But this in itself would not establish the absence of more fundamental genetic differences between castes in Indian society. Indeed, their complete absence would be surprising in view of the fact that members of most castes are believed to have practised strict endogamy for countless generations.

Those who emphasize the differences between the Indian and the American systems would base their argument on the uniqueness of Hindu cultural values. In fact, one might distinguish between the 'structural' view of caste which draws attention to broad similarities and the 'cultural' view which regards the caste system in India as unique.[19] There is no doubt that in India caste is embedded in a system of religious values which has no counterpart either in the US South or in South Africa.

Western scholars have been struck by the importance of hierarchy in the Hindu scheme of values.[20] Central to this are the notions of *dharma* and *karma*.[21] These are both complex, philosophical notions and it is difficult to put them in a nutshell. Very briefly, *dharma* implies right conduct in accordance with one's station in life, defined largely by one's caste; *karma* explains – and justified – one's birth in a particular station in terms of one's actions in a previous life. In other words, moral rules and standards of worth would differ from one caste to another. Most Western observers have been struck by the iniquity of the system, but scholars like Leach would point out that it ensured a measure of material and psychological security to all sections of society, particularly to those at the bottom of the hierarchy.[22]

In contrast to the values of traditional India, the American creed has always placed the highest social value on the equality of men. Thus, the moral environment in which rigid social distinctions exist in America is quite different from the moral environment in India. One may say that the American system is disharmonic; inequalities exist in fact although rejected by the normative order. The traditional Indian system was, by contrast, harmonic; rigid social distinctions not only existed but were generally accepted as legitimate. If this argument is correct, then the two types of system would show very different patterns of tension and conflict.

The values of a society are not easy to describe in an objective way. They are often ambiguous and made up of conflicting elements. It is difficult to believe that hierarchical values were accepted in the same way by all strata of Indian society. Most of what we know about traditional Indian values is based on texts written by people who belonged to the top of the hierarchical system. Perhaps we will never know in quite the same detail how the order of caste was perceived by people at the bottom of the hierarchy.

Berreman, who, unlike most students of Indian society, has studied a village community by living with the lower castes, would contend that there are sharp differences of perspective between the lower and the upper strata.[23] Others also have noted the presence of tensions and conflicts between castes which would not be expected if everyone accepted without question the position assigned to him within the hierarchical order.[24] However, most of these tendencies have been recorded within the past twenty years and their emergence in contemporary India would not contradict the assertion that traditionally the Indian caste system approximated to the harmonic type.

Berreman also rejects the view that the American value system can be defined unambiguously in terms of its emphasis on equality.[25] He quotes Spiro's critique of Myrdal to support his argument:

> The assumption of egalitarian culture norms is untenable unless one adopts an idealist conception of ideal norms which are irrelevant to human behaviour and aspirations. Actually discrimination against the Negro is not in violation of southern ideal norms; it is in conformity with them.[26]

There is also the question of the colour-caste system in South Africa. Can we say, perhaps, that here we have a normative order which accepts the existing structure of inequality between groups as legitimate?

Differences between the colour-caste system and the Indian system are not confined to the realm of values. There are important differences in the structure and composition of the groups which constitute the two types of system. In the US South there are only two principal castes, blacks and whites; in South Africa there are four, Africans, whites, coloureds and Asians.[27] In India the caste system comprises a large number of groups whose mutual relations are of an extremely complex nature.

In India it is not at all uncommon for a single village to have as many as twenty or thirty castes.[28] Each linguistic region in the country has between 200 and 300 castes. Many of these are divided into sub-castes which might in turn be further subdivided.[29] If we leave the village and take a larger territorial unit, it becomes impossible even to determine the exact number of castes in it. The distinctions between caste, sub-caste and sub-sub-caste become blurred. The same caste might be called by different names and different castes by the same name.

There is no single rank order for all the castes and sub-castes which applies in every region. Perhaps all that can be said very firmly for the country as a whole is that Brahmins rank at the top and Harijans at the bottom. There is a great deal of ambiguity in the middle region. The different cultivating castes make competing claims to superior status. The Brahmins (like the Harijans) are themselves divided into a number of castes and sub-castes whose mutual ranks are by no means easy to determine.[30] All this is not to deny that a certain measure of consensus in regard to caste ranking does exist within the local community.[31] This consensus was probably stronger in the past than it is today.

It can be argued that structurally there is a basic difference between a dichotomous system and a system of gradation in which there are many terms. Once again, the two types of system are likely to display very different patterns of social conflict. Theories of social class and of conflict assign a crucial significance to the dichotomous division of society.[32] Where the contending parties are two in number, the conflict tends to be intense; where they are many, a shifting pattern of coalitions reduces the intensity of conflict. The same theory can be extended to caste. Where the community is divided into blacks and whites, the conflict is likely to be sharp; where it is divided into twenty or thirty groups, no particular conflict is likely to absorb the energies of the community as a whole.

Next we shall try to see if any relationship can be established between caste distinctions and physical differences in the Indian population. It might be said at the outset that if such a relationship exists it is not likely to be either simple or direct. Physical differences are not polarized in India but are spread over a continuum. The population cannot be readily divided into races or even into clearly recognizable physical types. The caste system in its turn is a system of great complexity. It is divided and subdivided into innumerable groups and a consideration of these might provide a convenient point of departure.

The word 'caste' is used in India to refer to groups and categories of very different kinds. Two types of distinctions are particularly important. The first is between *varna* and *jati* and the second is between caste and sub-caste. The difference between *varna* and *jati* can be briefly described as the difference between a model or a conceptual scheme on the one hand and a set of real social groups or categories on the other. There are only four *varnas* which are arranged in a particular order whereas *jatis* are many and their rank order is both more ambiguous and more flexible.[33] *Jatis* should not be viewed as having grown out of divisions and subdivisions within a set of four original *varnas*. Rather, as Mrs Karve has argued, *varna* and *jati* have co-existed as two different but related systems for at least 2,000 years.[34]

The distinction between caste and sub-caste is of a different kind. Both are real social divisions, but one is more inclusive than the other. If we take potters or carpenters as examples of castes, we will find that in any given region there are two or three different kinds of potters or of carpenters, differentiated according to technique or provenance or sect or some other less tangible factor. These different divisions we might refer to as sub-castes. They are similar in structure to the more inclusive groupings and are generally endogamous. Scholars like Ghurye would maintain that the different types of potters are sub-castes, being products of segmentation within the potter caste.[35] Mrs Karve, on the other hand, has argued that the different types of potters are often unrelated and that each should be called a caste and the potters as a whole a 'caste cluster'.[36] Her argument is important in this context because she has tried to support it with anthropometric data.[37]

Sometimes there are several levels of differentiation and not just two. Thus, the Tamil Brahmins are of three main kinds: (1) temple priests; (2) domestic priests for the non-Brahmins; and (3) scholars and landowners. The last are divided into Smartha and Shri Vaishnava. Smartha Brahmins, in their turn, are further subdivided into Vadama, Brihacharanam, Astasahashram and Vattima. The Vadama, finally, are divided into Vadadesha and Chozhadesha Vadama.[38] This kind of differentiation makes it useful to view caste as a segmentary or structural system.[39] For even though each segment is endogamous, the social distance between segments is variable. Thus, the social distance between Vadama and Brihacharanam is smaller than the distance between Vadama and a Shri Vaishnava segment which in turn is smaller than that between any Brahmin segment and any non-Brahmin segment. This way of viewing the system leads us to ask if there is any relationship between social distance and racial distance.

Most anthropologists who have analysed caste from the biological point of view would concede that some physical differences do exist between castes. But they are sharply divided on the significance they attach to these differences. On the whole, earlier scholars emphasized the differences in physical type they observed between castes. Contemporary scholars are more inclined to stress the fact that most castes are more or less heterogeneous in their physical composition and that variations within the caste are sometimes greater than variations between castes.

It is not enough to know that castes differ from each other in their biological make up. We would like to know in addition whether the extent to which they differ in this regard is related to their social distance. Castes which are socially adjacent might be quite different in their biological composition while those which are at opposite ends of the social scale might show very little difference biologically. To answer this kind of question satisfactorily we will need a great deal of systematic empirical material. The evidence that we now have is scanty and does not all point in the same direction.

The first serious effort to study physical or racial differences between castes in a systematic way was made towards the end of the last century by Sir Herbert Risley.[40] Risley not only believed that such differences existed but argued that they were systematically related to differences of social rank between castes:

If we take a series of castes in Bengal, Bihar, the United Provinces of Agra and Oudh, or Madras, and arrange them in the order of the average nasal index so that the caste with the finest nose shall be at the top, and that with the coarsest at the bottom of the list, it will be found that this order substantially corresponds with the accepted order of social precedence.[41]

Risley was also struck by the fact that the upper castes were in general lighter skinned than the lower and drew attention to a number of local proverbs in which this distinction was given recognition.

Risley developed an elaborate theory to explain the social ranking of castes. He argued that the caste system was the outcome of the encounter between two distinct racial groups, one representing a light-skinned, narrow-nosed, 'Aryan' type, and the other, a dark-skinned, broad-nosed, 'non-Aryan' type. The Aryans, according to the theory, were not only the dominant group but also adopted the practice of hypergamy. This practice led to the formation of a series of intermediate groups whose social rank varied directly with their amount of Aryan blood. Risley sought to support his arguments with anthropometric data. His conclusions were challenged by later scholars who found fault with both his data and his methods.[42]

Ghurye criticized Risley's work but did not reject his argument altogether. He emphasized the importance of regional variations and noted that a caste which ranked very high in one area might closely resemble in its physical features a caste which ranked very low in an adjacent area. He pointed out that in many parts of the country there was no clear relationship of the kind which Risley had sought to demonstrate: 'Outside Hindustan in each of the linguistic areas we find that the physical type of the population is mixed, and does not conform in its gradation to the scale of social precedence of the various castes'.[43]

But Ghurye agreed that in the Hindi speaking area itself there was a close correspondence between the 'physical hierarchy' and the 'social hierarchy'. Here the Brahmins were long-headed and narrow-nosed, and very low castes like the Chamar and Pasi were broad-headed and broad-nosed. On the basis of such evidence, Ghurye was prepared to conclude that here, at least, 'Restrictions on marriage of a fundamentally endogamous nature were thus racial in origin'.[44]

The most comprehensive single investigation so far carried out is the anthropometric study of Bengal made jointly by an anthropologist, D.N. Majumdar and a statistician, C.R. Rao.[45] The data were collected from a defined cultural region, Bengal, comprising both West Bengal and Bangladesh. Sixty-seven groups were investigated, including Muslims, Christians, a few tribal groups and a large number of Hindu castes. These groups were studied with regard to sixteen basic anthropometric characters and a number of indices derived from them. Some serological data were collected in addition. The anthropometric data were analysed by means of rigorous and sophisticated statistical tests.

In spite of many qualifications, Majumdar concluded that there was some clustering of groups according to their social proximity. The tribal and semi-tribal groups tended to be clustered at one end and at the other end were the higher castes such as Brahmin, Baidya and Kayastha.[46] Majumdar pointed out that these data confirmed the observations made by him in two other areas in India, Gujarat and Uttar Pradesh. 'In all the three surveys, it has been found that some correlation exists between the order of social precedence in a state or region, and the ethnic constellations based on anthropometric data.'[47] It must be emphasized, however, that the relationships which emerge from the study by Majumdar and Rao are of a far more complex nature than the one which Risley believed he had established.

Studies made more recently do not all support Majumdar's conclusions. Karve and Malhotra have published the results of a detailed comparison between eight Brahmin 'sub-castes' in Maharashtra, taking anthropometric, somatoscopic and serological data into account.[48] Their data show the existence of significant differences among some of the Brahmin 'sub-castes'. Comparing their findings with those of other scholars, they conclude that there is no necessary relationship between social distance and physical distance. Thus there is no justification for assuming that the distance between the Brahmin 'castes' under investigation is less than the distance between a Brahmin 'caste' and a non-Brahmin 'caste', for some Brahmins are closer to members of other 'castes' than to each other.[49] It would appear that the more closely we look at the system the less firm we can be about the linkage between caste and race.

The shift from morphological to genetical indicators would seem to confirm the view that the linkage between social and physical distance is tenuous and uncertain. As my last example I shall take a study by Sanghvi and Khanolkar which examines the distribution of seven genetical traits among six endogamous groups in Bombay.[50] Of the six groups, four are Brahmins; one is a high non-Brahmin caste, Chandraseniya Kayashth Prabhu (CKP), ranking next only to the Brahmins; and the other is a Cultivating caste, Maratha (MK), belonging to the middle level of the hierarchy. As the authors point out, all these groups have been regarded by earlier anthropologists as being of the same physical type.

The results of the analysis show a rather complex pattern of variations. Some of the Brahmin groups are quite close to each other, and one of them is very similar in its genetical composition to the non-Brahmin Marathas. The Koknasth Brahman (KB) are, on the other hand, quite distinctive in their genetical composition as are also the Chandraseniya Kayasth Prabhu (CKP). Moreover, these two groups are markedly different from each other. 'The magnitude of differences between the groups KB and CKP for each one of the seven genetical characters is more or less similar to that between American whites and American Negroes.'[51] Although the Chandraseniya Kayasth Prabhu are non-Brahmins, they rank very high and might be regarded as being socially proximate to the Koknasth Brahman.

This leads us to a consideration of the social significance of genotypical as opposed to phenotypical differences. Earlier anthropologists such as Risley sought to establish a relationship between the social rank of a caste and the physical appearance of its members. They were encouraged in their pursuit by beliefs widely held in Indian society about the existence of such a relationship.[52] Upper castes are universally believed to be light-skinned and narrow-nosed and lower castes to be dark-skinned and broad-nosed. It would now appear that two socially adjacent castes whose members are very similar in their physical appearance might nevertheless be quite different in their genetical composition.

Genetical differences are likely to acquire social significance only if their existence is widely known or if they are reflected in clear differences in physical type. As I have indicated, certain broad differences in appearance exist between castes at opposite ends of the hierarchy in many parts of the country and equally significant are the beliefs and stereotypes regarding these differences which persist in spite of much evidence to the contrary. Beliefs which are technically wrong or inconsistent sometimes assume crucial significance in social life. As Passin has argued,

> The relation of caste to race is not simply a question of whether the groups are in fact racially different, but rather that there seems to be some disposition to attribute racial difference to even the most marginal cues in caste and caste-like situations.[53]

This is particularly true in the Indian context where in some languages the same word is used to denote both caste and race.[54]

What is important in social life is the sense of solidarity which people feel when they belong to the same community and the feeling of distance which separates members who belong to different communities. The sense of community is often based on the feeling that its members have a common origin. This feeling may be vague or it may be consciously formulated in an ideology. It may be strengthened if the community is marked out by distinctive physical features, but this is not a necessary condition for its existence. Sometimes a strong sense of community can exist even in the absence of visible physical indicators. This leads us to a consideration of ethnic groups and identities.

The systematic use of the concept of ethnicity is of relatively recent origin in sociology and social anthropology although the presence of ethnic groups in the United States has been widely discussed for many years.

> An ethnic group is a distinct category of the population in a larger society whose culture is usually different from its own. The members of such a group are, or feel themselves, or are thought to be bound together by common ties of race or nationality or culture.[55]

As this description suggests, there is no single criterion by which ethnic groups can be defined.

In the United States the term 'ethnic group' came into use to describe immigrants from the different parts of the world. Examples of these would be the Irish, the Italians and the Poles who settled in the country in successive waves of migration. These groups were not all differentiated by visible physical indicators. Initially there were major differences of language, culture and religion among the groups. As some of these differences began to diminish among second- and third-generation immigrants, it was felt that a culturally homogeneous population would emerge out of the melting pot of American society. But in spite of a high degree of mobility, both horizontal and vertical, and a certain amount of intermarriage between groups, ethnic identities have proved to be remarkably persistent in American society.[56]

The presence of ethnic groups is of course not a unique feature of American society. They exist in all societies where cultural differences are given a particular meaning and are organised in a particular way. Ethnic differentiation has been a conspicuous feature of the so-called plural societies of South and South-East Asia.[57] Sometimes this differentiation is associated with the presence of large groups, such as the Chinese and the Indians in Malaysia, which differ markedly from each other in language, religion and provenance. The co-existence of such disparate groups is likely to generate tensions and conflicts which might, in the extreme case, threaten the integrity of the political framework itself.

Ethnic identities might persist even when ethnic groups are not visibly different or politically organized. In a recent collection of papers Barth and his colleagues have argued persuasively that ethnic identities do not depend for their survival on any particular aggregate of cultural traits. 'It is important to recognise that although ethnic categories take cultural differences into account, we can assume no simple one-to-one relationship between ethnic units and cultural similarities and differences.'[58] Eidheim gives a graphic account of the manner in which an ethnic boundary is maintained between Lapps and Norwegians even in the absence of any readily visible physical or cultural differences between them.[59]

Ethnic groups are generally endogamous and in that sense they tend to be biologically self-perpetuating.[60] Even in the complete absence of diacritical distinctions endogamy could of course serve to keep ethnic boundaries intact. When all marriages do not take place within the group, ethnic boundaries might still be maintained if intermarriage is governed by the rule of hypergamy; the practice of hypergamy acts as an important boundary maintaining mechanism among certain sections of the hill Rajputs in India.[61] Far from dissolving ethnic boundaries altogether, intermarriage might under certain conditions serve to bring these boundaries into sharper relief.

Thus, the concept of ethnic group is somewhat broader in its scope than that of race. Ethnic differences might be based at least partly on race as in the case of Malays, Chinese and Indians in Malaysia or of blacks, Indians and whites in the Caribbean. They might also exist in a society which is racially more or less homogeneous as in the case of the Pathans in West Pakistan and Afghanistan or of some of the multi-tribal systems in East Africa.

The caste system, in its turn, may be viewed as a particular case of ethnic differentiation. Whether or not 'racial' differences exist between castes, they are often differentiated from each other culturally, in their dress, diet and rituals. Where even these distinctions are feeble or absent, the boundaries between castes are maintained by the rules of endogamy and hypergamy. However, even if we regard caste as a system of ethnic groups, it is a system in which the different groups are all integrated within a hierarchical order. Ethnic groups are not necessarily arranged in a hierarchy and they are not always integrated within a unitary system.

We notice a close similarity between caste in India and ethnic groups in the United States when we examine the part they play in the political process.[62] In the United States ethnic solidarities are widely used for mobilizing political support and ethnic rivalries have to be taken into account in formulating electoral strategies.[63] In India caste enters into the political process in a number of ways.[64] Caste associations have not only acted as pressure groups but, in at least one area, have transformed themselves into political parties.[65] Rivalries between parties are sometimes heightened when they base their support on mutually antagonistic castes.[66] However, in both India and the United States the relationship between caste or ethnic identity and the political process is complex and ambiguous. The political process brings out not only the cleavages between such groups but also the possibilities of coalitions among them.

The Harijans provide a particular example of solidarity based on caste or ethnic identity. In the past the barrier of pollution kept them segregated from many areas of social life. These barriers have now been legally abolished but the Harijans retain much of their traditional stigma and continue to be socially and economically underprivileged. But they are now provided with opportunities to organize themselves politically.[67] This has enabled them to gain some advantages but it has also brought them into confrontation with the upper castes whose members are not always in a mood to accept them as equals. The situation of the Harijans in contemporary India – like that of the blacks in the United States – reveals a paradox. The lessening of cultural distance has in both cases been accompanied not by a decrease but by an increase in tension and conflict.

India has not only a Harijan problem, there is also an Adivasi or tribal problem. Harijans and Adivasis are officially grouped together as the Backward Classes and their separate identity is given constitutional recognition.[68] The tribal people numbered about thirty million at the 1961 census and they constituted over 6 per cent of the Indian population. They are divided into a large number of separate tribes, differing in race, language and culture. They are concentrated in particular areas in the country which tend to be geographically isolated but there is no policy of keeping them in reservations.

The tribal population of India does not belong to any single racial or physical type. The differences between the 'Veddoid' type common among certain tribes in central and south India and the 'Palaeo-Mongoloid' type found in the north-east hill areas might be greater than the differences between the tribal people and their non-tribal neighbours in any particular area. But Furer-Haimendorf has rightly pointed out that differences of the latter kind also exist[69] and Majumdar's anthropometric data seem to point in the same direction.[70]

After drawing attention to differences in physical type between the tribal and the non-tribal population, Furer-Haimendorf says, 'It is all the more remarkable that despite racial differences no less fundamental than those found in countries with acute race problems, there have never been any cases of racial tension in India'.[71] One important factor is the very great variety of physical types which has prevented a polarization of the population along racial lines. This does not mean that differences do not exist or are not socially recognized. In fact, tribal solidarity is perhaps being given a new lease of life by democratic politics. But the conflict is transferred on to a different plane where the cleavage between tribals and non-tribals becomes one among a number of politically relevant ethnic distinctions.

We have so far considered ethnic differentiation among groups which are hierarchically arranged, for, although the Adivasis are in the strict sense outside the caste system, they are almost everywhere ranked below the caste Hindus. We may now turn to ethnic differentiation between groups which are not hierarchically arranged, such as those based on religion or on language. In some sense these provide the most fundamental cleavages in contemporary Indian society. When one talks about 'national integration' in India one has primarily in mind the problems of holding together the different religious and linguistic communities. While one can distinguish analytically between ethnic identities of different kinds – hierarchical and non-hierarchical – in reality these often tend to become confused.

India has been described as a multi-religious nation. The Hindus are in an overwhelming majority, accounting for around 80 per cent of the population; the Muslims constitute a significant minority with a little more than 10 per cent of the population. There are other religious groups which are of significance in particular regions, such as the Sikhs in the Punjab and the Christians in Kerala. But for the country as a whole the cleavage which has greatest significance is the one between Hindus and Muslims. If there is a 'communal' problem in the country its prototype is the one which grows out of the relations between these two communities.[72]

Hindus and Muslims in India do not belong to separate

races. In fact, they are both racially very mixed. This is only to be expected since the majority of Indian Muslims are the descendants of converts from Hinduism. Spear argues that there were two main types of conversion: clan or group conversion as a consequence of which castes such as Rajputs, Jats and Gujjars in north India have Hindu as well as Muslim sections; and mass conversions through which low-caste Hindus, particularly in Bengal, embraced Islam.[73] The last point finds confirmation in Majumdar's anthropometric data referred to above; the low-caste Namasudras are closer in their physical appearance to the Muslims than they are to the upper caste Hindus.[74]

Hindus and Muslims have co-existed as communities in different parts of India for a millennium. Religious differences have been associated with a host of other differences in ways of life. These differences have not always been the same, but the fact of difference has remained, heightened at times and sub-dued at others. Hindus and Muslims might not differ in physical type but religious ideology has provided each community with a basis for consciously organizing its identity in opposition to the other. Over the centuries the two communities have borrowed much from each other and during the last few decades they have been exposed to similar forces of change. But this has not erased the boundaries between them. In fact, the pattern of Hindu-Muslim relations in recent Indian history would seem to show that groups might become more conscious of their opposed identities precisely at a time when external differences between them are being reduced.

The population of India is also divided on the basis of language. The divisions of language and religion generally cut across and do not reinforce each other as they do to a large extent in countries like Malaysia and Sri Lanka. This, in addition to the fact that both linguistic and religious groups are many and not two each, tends to make the conflict between communities diffused rather than polarized.

Over a dozen major languages are spoken in India but there is none which is the mother tongue of a majority of the people. The speakers of the different languages are not randomly distributed throughout the country. Each language has its 'homeland' so that linguistic differences largely coincide with regional differences.

The different states which constitute the Union of India are in effect linguistic units. This means that the ethnic identity provided by language has both a cultural basis and a political organization.

Differences between linguistic groups can give rise to two kinds of tensions. At one level are the disputes between the different linguistic states over particular issues, for instance the question of boundaries or the distribution of river water.[75] At another level one encounters the problem of linguistic minorities in practically every state; these problems are likely to be particularly acute in large metropolitan cities like Bombay or Calcutta which attract people from all over the country. Ethnic boundaries based on language are in a way crucial; they restrict communication between people in the literal sense of the term.

Differences of language have in reality very little to do with differences of race although in one important case linguistic differences have been represented in a racial idiom. The different languages of India belong to two major families, the Indo-Aryan languages spoken in the north by about three-quarters of the population and the Dravidian languages spoken in the four southern states by about a quarter of the population. People in the southern states have, particularly since independence, sometimes expressed a fear of domination by the north[76] and a separatist political movement developed there although its influence has been confined almost wholly to one state, Tamilnad.[77] One of the arguments advanced by leaders of this movement was that South Indians, being Dravidians, had a separate identity in race, language and culture and should free themselves from the domination of the Aryan North Indians.[78] Tamil separatism has now become subdued and one no longer hears the racial argument very frequently but language barriers are in other respects no less significant than they were before.

We have moved a long distance from a consideration of racial differences to differences of quite another kind which are at times expressed in a racial idiom. Ethnic identity must not be thought of as something which defines the character of one group in opposition to another for all time. In India the same individual has a number of different identities according to caste, religion and language and any one of these might become more important than the others, depending upon context and situation. It is not enough to know that boundaries exist between groups, one must also examine the situations under which some boundaries are ignored and others become significant. Thus, in one context Tamil speaking Hindus and Muslims might unite to defend themselves against 'Aryan' domination; in another context Hindus from both north and south India might regard Muslims as aliens among them.

Although ethnic differences have a bearing on social conflict, a knowledge of the former is not enough to predict the pattern of the latter. In order to understand the scale and intensity of conflicts between ethnic groups we have to take a number of factors into account. These are (1) the objective differences between them; (2) the social awareness of these differences; and (3) the political organization of this awareness.

As we have seen, the objective differences themselves are of many kinds. They may be roughly grouped together as physical or cultural. Cultural differences in turn can be based on religion, language or region. There is no direct relationship between the degree of these differences and the extent to which people are aware of them. Differences of colour might exist to the same degree in two societies and yet people might be acutely aware of them in one society and not in the other. Cultural differences are more difficult to measure. And, in any case, there are no satisfactory criteria by which one can compare the awareness of, say, religious differences with that of linguistic differences.

People might be highly conscious of their differences, whether physical or cultural, without their consciousness acquiring a political form. In traditional Indian society there were not only differences between castes, but people were universally aware of these differences. Yet castes were not always organized into mutually antagonistic groups. They began to organize themselves into associations at a time when people were beginning to feel that caste consciousness would fade away. The course of political conflict remains unpredictable. There is no general theory which can enable us to delineate in exact terms the relationship between cultural differences and their organization into mutually antagonistic groups.

3 The concept of tribe with special reference to India

Anthropologists have been from the very beginning engaged in the study of tribes, and it is in some sense to this study that their discipline owes its distinctive identity. When historians, political theorists, sociologists and others have to deal with tribes, they turn to anthropologists for expert opinion on what tribes are and how they are constituted. In some countries what constitutes a tribe is of concern also to administrators and policy makers, and they too expect advice and guidance from anthropologists. Yet it cannot be said that anthropologists are themselves in agreement about the concept, and their disagreement is, if anything, even larger today than it was in the past.

A possible reason for the widening of disagreement is that anthropologists now study not only a wider range of topics but also a wider variety of societies. Until the 1930s or 1940s they confined their attention mainly to simple, pre-literate, small-scale and isolated societies in Australia, Melanesia, the Pacific Islands, North and South America, and sub-Saharan Africa. This was true as much of Boas, Lowie, Wissler and their pupils in the United States as of Rivers, Radcliffe-Brown, Malinowski and their pupils in the Commonwealth. The tribe was here the centre and focus of attention and, except where note had to be taken of recent changes introduced as a result of exposure to European culture, it was considered as a self-contained unit.

A major change of orientation came about in the 1940s when anthropologists began to claim that their discipline had a distinctive contribution to make to the understanding of not only tribes but also civilizations. This move was first made in the United States where the work of Robert Redfield[1] stands as a kind of watershed, although he had an illustrious predecessor in A.L. Kroeber.[2] Redfield popularized the study of the peasantry, especially in Latin America and Asia, and the view that peasants are 'part societies' and 'part cultures'.[3] The interest in studying large wholes gathered strength from other sources as well, and the study of civilizations in India, in the Arab world and in China, Japan and Indonesia has become as important as, if not more important than, the study of tribes.

The study of civilizations has given anthropologists a new awareness of the importance of history. The anthropologist who studies tribes in India today does not necessarily confine himself to the present or even the recent past, but might try to go back to medieval if not ancient times.[4] An important issue in the study of tribes today is how we understand the relationship between tribe and civilization. It is here that I would like to make a distinction between two approaches which I will describe as the 'evolutionary' and the 'historical'. The evolutionary approach takes a long-range view of the passage of time and stresses the *succession* of social formations. Evolutionists no doubt recognize the presence of survivals, but these are regarded as anachronisms, which they probably are on a sufficiently extended time scale. The historical approach limits itself to a particular framework of space and time and stresses the *co-existence* of different social formations within that framework. What is regarded an an anachronism in the evolutionary perspective may appear as a necessary component in the historical framework.

Morgan's conception of the tribe[5] and Durkheim's conception of the polysegmental society[6] were both rooted in the same evolutionary perspective. Their successors chose their examples not from India, China and the Islamic world, but from Australia, the Pacific Islands and North America where recent historical experience brought out the disjunction rather than the co-existence of tribe and civilization. Western civilization penetrated these areas in modern times, and tribe and civilization stood opposed there in every particular of race, language and culture. In many parts of the Old World the situation was different. There tribe and civilization had co-existed for centuries if not millenia, and were closely implicated in each other from ancient to modern times. In India the effort to disentangle tribe from caste began in a systematic way during British rule and led to unforeseen results.

Ethnographic material from India did not figure prominently in the general discussion regarding the definition of tribe. The problem in India was to identify rather than define tribes, and scientific or theoretical considerations were never allowed to displace administrative or political ones. This is not to say that those engaged in drawing up lists of Indian tribes did not have their own conceptions of tribe, but those conceptions were neither clearly formulated nor systematically applied.

Lists of Indian tribes were, in fact, drawn up, with or without benefit of clear and consistent definitions. These lists are not only in current use, but provide constitutional guarantee of tribal identity to those included in them. The present list shows more than 400 tribes with an aggregate population of over fifty million persons accounting for 7.76 per cent of the total population. Even a cursory look will show that it includes the widest variety of social formations, from small food-gathering bands to vast populations of settled agriculturists comprising three million persons and more.[7] Indian anthropologists have been conscious of a certain lack of fit between what their discipline defines as 'tribe' and what they are obliged to describe as 'tribes', but they have sought a way out of the muddle by calling them all 'tribes in transition'.[8] This does not settle the issue because in India tribes have always been in transition, at least since the beginning of recorded history.

Among recent attempts to provide a general definition of tribe, those by Ellman Service[9] and by Marshall Sahlins[10] have received some attention. What is interesting about their definitions is that they are part of a general classification of social formations set in an evolutionary framework. Underlying the classification is the dichotomy between 'State' and 'non-State' societies, but non-State societies are not viewed as being all of the same kind: they are divided into bands, tribes and chiefdoms.

The principal novelty in this scheme, it seems to me, is not the distinction between band and tribe or between tribe and chiefdom, but the definition of the tribe as a segmentary system. As Sahlins put it, 'A tribe is a segmental organization. It is composed of a number of equivalent, unspecialized multifamily groups, each the structural duplicate of the other: a tribe is a congeries of equal kin group blocs'.[11] Although the study of tribes had been the staple of Anglo-American anthropology from Morgan to Malinowski, the concept of segmentary system entered the scene relatively late, with the publication in 1940 of *The Nuer*[12] and of *African Political Systems*.[13] It is true that the idea of segmentary system had been used extensively in the 1890s by Durkheim, but it did not catch the imagination of students of tribal societies until the 1940s.[14]

The idea of segmentary system has had a very wide appeal among anthropologists working in different parts of the world. It has given a focus to the study of tribes in the Islamic world, particularly in the Maghreb.[15] It has enriched our understanding of the social system of the Pathans on what used to be the north-western frontier of India although there, as Barth has shown, tribe is already to some extent interwoven with caste.[16] There are, however, large parts of the world where the segmentary principle by itself does not greatly illuminate our understanding of what are commonly recognized as tribes. A tribe is best described as a segmentary system where it has a particular type of clan and lineage structure most fully developed among the Arabs but also found in parts of sub-Saharan Africa and elsewhere. There are various difficulties in making the segmentary principle as described by Evans-Pritchard in his studies of the Nuer and the Cyrenaicans the defining feature of tribes in all parts of the world. On the one hand, Sahlins himself argues for a very restricted use of the term 'segmentary system';[17] and, on the other, the contributors to *African Political Systems* give no indication of using 'tribe' and 'segmentary system' as interchangeable terms.

These or similar considerations must have weighed with Sahlins, for in 1968 he modified his original fourfold scheme of 1961 into a threefold scheme, comprising band, tribe and State. The category 'tribe' was expanded to include tribal chiefdoms in addition to the segmentary tribes which had earlier made up the whole category. It is not as if Sahlins saw no difference whatever between segmentary and chiefly tribes but he felt on reconsideration that the difference entailed no discontinuity, that they were 'permutations' of the 'same general model'.[18] But, as Godelier has rightly pointed out, if Sahlins went so far in one direction to include chiefdoms in the category of tribes, he might have gone a little in the other direction to include bands as well within the same category.[19]

The need to define tribe in an evolutionary perspective has been reiterated by Godelier in a recent critical essay. For Godelier the tribe is at one and the same time a type of society and a state of evolution. As he has put it, 'The link between the two uses of the term tribe, seen as a *type of society* and as a *stage of evolution*, is very clear since, each stage of evolution is characterised by a specific mode of social organisation'.[20] He attributes the failure of anthropologists to arrive at a clear conception of the tribe to their lack of a consistent theory of evolution.

For Godelier there is a fundamental difference between tribe and chiefdom because inequalities of class which are absent in the former become established in the latter. Work is organized differently in the two types of society and the primacy of kinship is undermined by the appearance of class in the evolution from tribe to chiefdom.[21] The assumption here is that wherever we find a chiefdom we will also find a division into classes. This, as the editors of *African Political Systems* had warned us, is far from the case. Even in the African chiefdom, 'Distinctions of rank, status or occupation operate independently of differences of wealth'.[22] Moreover, as recent students of the subject have realized, a segmentary system need not necessarily be acephalous.[23]

Godelier's essay exposes the limitations of the evolutionary point of view. The evidence is too thin to support his assumption of the uniform co-variation of mode of livelihood, kinship structure and political system within the range of societies with which we are concerned. Both segmentary tribes and tribal chiefdoms are supported by various modes of livelihood.

The Tallensi and the Bemba are both agriculturists, the Tallensi having fixed and the Bemba shifting cultivation, but they have very different political systems. The Nuer and Logoli of Group B and the Zulu and Ngwato of Group A alike practise mixed agriculture and cattle husbandry.[24]

There is, if anything, an even greater range of variation in the nature and function of kinship in each of the two types of society.

It would be a great convenience if some simple scheme could be devised for classifying the 400 odd communities designated as tribes in India. Various classifications have been proposed on the basis of ecological, racial, linguistic, religious and other criteria. Perhaps the most convenient is the one persistently recommended by N.K. Bose on the basis of mode of livelihood: hunters and gatherers, animal herders, shifting cultivators and settled agriculturists.[25] But very little is to be gained by trying to fit this kind of classification into any rigid evolutionary scheme. It is now being increasingly recognized that tribes with some of the simplest technologies have been more closely integrated with the wider society than others with a more advanced technology.[26] If isolation, self-sufficiency and autonomy are characteristics of the tribal condition, there is no simple correlation between these and the level of technology.

Not all anthropologists who write about tribes adopt an evolutionary perspective. Morton Fried has presented us with a rather different notion of tribe.[27] He has not only criticized existing definitions but argued that the very concept of tribe, so extensively used by anthropologists, is inherently ambiguous. His criticism is very far reaching, and we must examine briefly the factors behind the ambiguities it has exposed.

It was Morgan's argument, which Godelier repeats with approval, that the tribe is a '*completely* organised society'.[28] When we speak of the tribe as a 'completely organized society', we assume that there are boundaries separating tribes from each other and from other types of society. What is the nature of these boundaries? Can they be easily recognized? Do they really exist? No student of tribal life in India can afford to ignore these questions. But the boundary problem has its own peculiar features in India, for what is unclear there is not so much the boundary between one tribe and another as that between tribe and non-tribe. The boundaries between tribes are perhaps a little more clear than Fried would allow for, because in India tribes have since time immemorial lived in the shadow of a civilization which has been strict about maintaining the boundaries between castes.

Fried rejects the argument, apparently popular among some physical anthropologists, that the tribe is a breeding population whose boundaries circumscribe the range of sexual relations.[29] He marshals evidence to show that not only unsanctioned sexual unions but also socially approved marriages frequently take place across the boundaries of what are called tribes. But the point about outmarriages ought not to be taken too far. There are probably genuine differences here between, let us say, Amazonia and South Asia. In India tribes such as Khasi, Garo, Santal, Munda, Oraon and many others are known to have a marked preference for endogamy which is not surprising in view of the high value placed on endogamy everywhere in India.[30] As I shall point out later, there have been innumerable cases of tribes becoming castes – the Indian equivalent of 'passing' – and when this happened, the rule of endogamy was probably reinforced.

Fried also questions the test of language, or the view that each tribe has its own distinctive language which defines its boundaries. 'The idea,' he says, 'that tribes, whatever else they may be, are somehow minimal speech communities, turns out to be no sounder than the notion that they are basic breeding populations'.[31] There are well-known examples, even in small-scale societies, of people speaking the same language being divided into several endogamous groups as well as examples of people intermarrying though their native languages are different. Again, the significance of language in the definition of tribe will depend on the extent to which the tribe is implicated in the civilization in its vicinity.

In India the test of language has always been an important one in the identification of tribes. There are fifteen officially recognized languages listed in the Eighth Schedule of the

Constitution of which four belong to the Dravidian family and the rest to the Indo-Aryan family. Besides these, there is an assortment of several hundred languages, usually not counted as literary languages, and spoken by smaller populations, though in some cases these may comprise as many as a couple of million persons each. By and large, it is the communities associated with these languages that are recognized as tribes in India.

Two brief comments must be made here about the relationship between civilization, language and tribe. The Dravidian languages of India include not only Tamil, which is one of the oldest literary languages of the world, but also languages spoken by a number of tribes such as the Baiga and the Kond who lived by shifting cultivation until the other day. The Tamils are proud of their ancient and medieval civilization which created elaborate irrigation works on the one hand, magnificent temples on the other, but their cultural affinity with some of the simplest tribes of peninsular India would appear to be beyond dispute. In a recent impressive work, Trautman has shown how the Tamils share the same fundamental structure of kinship and affinity with the Baiga and the Kond.[32] Further, Dravidian kinship, in both its 'civilized' and 'tribal' forms, is markedly different from North Indian kinship.[33] Nothing could demonstrate more effectively the hazards of using kinship as a basis for discriminating between 'tribe' and 'civilization' or 'tribe' and 'State'.

The second point to note is that some of the tribes, including a few very large ones, have no separate language of their own but use the language prevalent in the region they inhabit. This is particularly common in the western part of India, in the states of Rajasthan and Gujarat. There obviously has been a loss of language in some cases but it is impossible to date this loss in most cases. When the loss of language is accompanied by a loss of other cultural traits, a sort of invisible threshold is crossed, and the tribe ceases to function as a tribe although it does not thereby lose its identity as a community.

Economic relations can of course be easily shown to overflow the boundaries of the tribe, no matter how we define 'tribe'. Fried would argue that the political boundaries of what are called tribes are usually far less clear than is assumed in the model of either the tribal chiefdom or the segmentary tribe.

It may be recalled that Evans-Pritchard's original model of the segmentary political system was presented as a kind of solution to the boundary problem among the Nuer who lack all constituted political authority.[34] If a conflict took the form of feud, it was within the tribe; if of war, it was between one tribe and another. This method of solving the boundary problem cannot be easily applied everywhere, for even if we admit that the segmentary principle is a kind of universal principle, its operation does not have everywhere the same consistency and constancy that Evans-Pritchard reported it to have among the Nuer. The model of the tribe as a segmentary system is a tempting one, but one faces many pitfalls in yielding to the temptation.

Fried's argument would therefore be that what are generally designated by anthropologists as tribes represent neither a definite type of society nor a definite stage of evolution. They are too amorphous and too assorted to qualify for either role. The tribe, according to Fried, is much better regarded as a kind of secondary phenomenon which in the typical case acquires its form and identity from some external source.

> While being bold, I shall go on to say that most tribes seem to be secondary phenomena in a very specific sense: they may well be the product of processes stimulated by the appearance of relatively highly organized societies amidst other societies which are organized much more simply.[35]

The formation of a tribe as a secondary phenomenon is familiar to anthropologists. Perhaps the best known example in the literature is that of the Makah Indians who, according to Elisabeth Colson, were given their present identity by the Indian Service of the American Government: 'The people regarded as Makah, by themselves and by those who are not of their group, are such by a political definition framed to organize a group of people with political rights as members of the Makah Tribe'.[36] Extending her observations to another continent, Colson argues that 'contemporary African tribes are either new forms of political organization created for administrative purposes by the modern states within which they exist or they represent the emergence of self-conscious nationalistic movements comparable to those of Europe and Asia'.[37]

It is true that in some parts of the world colonial rule has had cataclysmic effects, dissolving old identities and precipitating new ones. But to say that tribes as we now know them are all of recent origin or are all secondary phenomena would be to take a holiday from the lessons of history. Tribe and civilization have encountered each other for centuries in many parts of the world, and it is only in some areas and at certain periods that the encounter has been sudden and cataclysmic.

In the historical relations between State and tribe, the State has not by any means always had the upper hand. Not only has it often lacked the strength to resist encroachment by tribes, but the tribal way of life has appeared to many as superior to that represented by the State. Writing about the Pakhtuns in what used to be the north-western frontier of India, a recent observer notes, 'Indeed as far as they are concerned, it is "state" and not "tribe" which occupies the periphery of things, and it is to the state *all* the characteristics of the peripheral attach, most especially dissipation'.[38]

We should neither ignore the civilization in the background when we write about tribes, nor argue as if the relationship between tribe and civilization were the same everywhere. It is here that we see the flaws in both of the two schemes proposed by Sahlins. It is one thing to make a direct contrast between tribe and State. Sahlins does not stop there but proceeds to divide tribes into tribal chiefdoms and segmentary tribes, adding bands at the other end. Surely, this should oblige him to consider corresponding distinctions among what he calls states, for these differ among themselves as much as do stateless societies. To take two neighbouring countries, the Soviet State is very different from the State in Afghanistan in many respects, and certainly in relation to tribes. It may be preferable in a historical context to speak of civilization rather than State as the complement of tribe, for certainly in the Indian case, civilization has shown far greater unity and continuity than any state.

The co-existence of tribe and State has been discussed by students of the Islamic world from Ibn Khaldun down to the present.[39] Indeed, what has been stressed in their writings is not merely the co-existence of tribe and State but their complementarity. As a recent student of the Middle East has put it, 'The tribes have always been a part of, as well as being in varying degrees apart from, the Iranian state'.[40] Given the acknowledged significance of the tribal component in the origin and growth of the Islamic State, it would be misleading to refer to these tribes, whether in Ibn Khaldun's time or in our own, as secondary phenomena. Nor can we regard them and the states, which for centuries they regularly overran, as two separate stages of social evolution.

The Islamic tribes were external to the Islamic State in a way in which they were not external to Islamic civilization. Conversely, subscribing to the values of Islam did not require submission to the discipline of the State. One might even say that some of the most fundamental values of Islam – equality, community, brotherhood – found a more authentic expression in the 'tribal' than in the 'civilized' sector of Islam. The Islamic case teaches us to use the concept of civilization in two senses: in the first or unmarked sense civilization includes tribe and in the second or marked sense it is contrasted with tribe.

India has unfortunately had no Ibn Khaldun to record and reflect on the relationship between tribe and civilization in pre-modern times. The Indian intellectual tradition, which is both ancient and rich, is remarkable for its lack of historical sense, and hardly any history was written before the advent of Muslim rule.[41] We are therefore forced to rely on conjecture and reconstruction to a far greater extent than in the case of Europe, China or the Islamic world.

Both historians and anthropologists have noted that in traditional India tribes were not only recognized to exist but were given a definite designation: *jana* as against *jati*.[42] However, it is not easy to determine the exact connotation of the term *jana*, and the distinction between *jana* and *jati* must have been even less clear in ancient times than the corresponding distinction today between tribe and caste. Each category was heterogeneous and there was always some overlap between the two. The historian Niharranjan Ray has noted that:

in Indian historical tradition there were two sets of *janas*, one who are still recognised by anthropologists and sociologists as *tribes*... and another set who were at a relatively higher level of socio-economic and political organization and of aesthetic and religious culture.[43]

It would be rash to seek to identify these two sets of *jana* with segmentary tribes on the one hand and tribal chiefdoms on the other, but it is clear that some of them founded states and joined the mainstream while others either remained isolated or were pushed into marginal areas.

Historians of both ancient and medieval India have spoken repeatedly of the rise to power of tribal dynasties in various places and at various times. Some of these, like the Ahom in the thirteenth century, came as intruders from outside. Others, like the Chandela, allegedly of Gond origin, rose to power from within. It is obvious that the term 'tribe' has been used in a loose sense, meaning different things to different historians, but it is possible to reconstruct with a degree of accuracy the tribal origin of some at least of the ruling dynasties of the pre-British period.

The rise to eminence of a tribal dynasty did not lead necessarily or even generally to a radical change in the mode of life of the tribe as a whole. Only some sections of it would become Hinduized while others might survive more or less in their previous condition. What is characteristic of the relationship between tribe and civilization in India is that there was virtually no way in which a tribal dynasty could legitimize its rule without becoming Hinduized. This meant, among other things, bringing in Brahmin priests, Barbers, Washermen and the rest, and replicating in due course of time the hierarchical structure of caste. Although only the ruling families or lineages became fully Hinduized, some of this rubbed off on their poorer cousins who might continue in their previous tribal condition, sometimes in the remote hills and forests. This kind of survival cannot in any meaningful sense be described as a secondary phenomenon even where it was affected by influences from a newly established kingdom.

As the State became more powerful and society better

organized, the scope available to tribal lineages to establish new dynasties became more restricted. But the State was not the most durable product of Hindu civilization. The weakness and decay of states always left room for the emergence of tribal chiefs whose aim was to create not tribal chiefdoms so much as kingdoms after the Hindu model.

When a tribal lineage established a Hindu kingdom there occurred what may be described as integration at the top. Although the historical record is likely to furnish evidence of integration mainly at that level, what must have been far more common is integration at the bottom.[44] This kind of integration is by its nature difficult to document for the ancient and medieval periods. It took place whenever a tribe or a section of it, usually through force of economic circumstances, became involved in the larger division of labour by providing specialized products associated with their habit, such as lac, honey, ropes, baskets, mats, etc., or a regular supply of manual labour.

Despite changes in the fortunes of individual tribes and despite incursions into tribal territories by Hindu kings and Hindu ascetics, the tribal identity never became fully effaced in any of the major regions of the country. It is remarkable how close to such renowned ancient and medieval centres of civilization as Gaya, Ujjain and Madurai tribes could still be found living in their natural setting, so to say, well into the present century. The Hindu kingdom – and to a large extent its Muslim successor – did not seek to eliminate tribes but allowed or even encouraged them to live on its margins. This is not a setting in which one can proceed very far by viewing tribe and state as two distinct and successive stages of evolution.

Students of Indian society and history have been struck repeatedly by the presence of survivals at every level. As D.D. Kosambi, the historian of ancient India has put it, 'India is a country of long survivals'.[45] Kosambi tried to use these survivals for developing a method for reconstructing India's past. Our concern is not so much with that method, whose limitations are well known, as with the co-existence down to our times of diverse social formations, tribal as well as non-tribal.

Kosambi provides a fascinating thumbnail sketch of this co-existence in his own time – the 1950s – and around his own home in the city of Poona.[46] Nearest in location he found a group of tent-dwelling nomadic families belonging to the Ras Phase Pardhi tribe, divided into six exogamous clans bearing Brahmin and Rajput names; they led a precarious existence by snaring small animals, working as casual labourers and begging. Then there were Ramosis who were rapidly discarding their 'tribal' customs and becoming like the general Maratha peasantry in appearance, language and religious observance. In addition to these there were two Telugu speaking tribal groups, the Vaidu who were snake-charmers and medicine men and the Vaddar who worked as stone cutters.

It is now widely acknowledged that what were until recently regarded as hunting and gathering tribes were in many cases reduced within the last hundred years or so to an economic condition in which they are forced to survive by foraging, begging, thieving and other such activities.[47] These would appear to correspond to the kind of secondary phenomena to which Fried has so convincingly drawn attention. It is almost certain that such secondary phenomena have increased in scale and intensity from the middle of the nineteenth century to the present, and the idea of 'ex-criminal tribes', if not of 'criminal tribes', sounds definitely modern. But it would in my view be a mistake to believe that such secondary phenomena have no precedents in the past. Indeed, there is reason to believe that both detribalization and retribalization occurred in the distant as well as the recent past. But they did not alter everything, for collective identities often outlived changes in economic and political fortunes.

I have so far been comparing tribe with State – or tribe with civilization – in a very general way. I must now make a little more specific my comparison of the morphological features of tribal society with those of Hindu society. But what is the morphological analogue of tribe in Hindu society? Is it the whole of Hindu society, or is it the individual caste which is, as it were, the building block of that society?

As soon as we enter into a close comparison, we are struck by a paradox. When we place tribal society beside Hindu society as a whole with its elaborate arrangement of castes, we observe the sharpest possible contrast. Tribal society is homogeneous, undifferentiated and unstratified; Hindu society is heterogeneous, differentiated and stratified. The polarity of equality and hierarchy is much more clearly represented here than in any other comparable case. Muslim society would appear to stand at the other end of the scale, at least on the plane of values.

When, on the other hand, we compare individual castes, which are the constituent units of Hindu society, with individual tribes, we observe a certain homology. Caste and tribe emphasize and perpetuate collective identities in strikingly similar ways; a caste or tribe may change its name and, within limits, also its mode of livelihood and yet retain its collective identity. Other societies, whether Islamic or Christian, are not made up of segments that at least outwardly resemble tribes to such a large extent. Traditional Hindu society was at one and the same time both hierarchical and segmental. It is no accident that observers down the ages have so persistently mistaken castes for tribes, and tribes for castes.

From the end of the nineteenth century onwards, ethnographers, who were mainly British civil servants working in India, began to publish descriptive catalogues of the tribes and castes in the different parts of the country.[48] A perusal of these will show how unclear the line of division sometimes is between tribe and caste. There are, firstly, castes of tribal origin in areas in which the caste-based division of labour is well established, and these include both agricultural and artisan groups. But one encounters also the converse phenomenon, namely, the growth of occupational specialization and the emergence of caste-like groups in the interior of a tribal area. I am not saying that it is generally difficult to distinguish a tribe from a caste, only that the difficulty often arises at the margins of Hindu civilization.

A number of historians have argued that the Hindu social structure owes its uniqueness to the manner in which it was built up, block by block so to say, by the accretion of tribes. D.D. Kosambi has put it in the following words:

The entire course of Indian history shows tribal elements being fused into a general society. This phenomenon, which lies at the foundation of the most striking Indian feature, namely caste, is also the great basic fact of ancient Indian history.[49]

Kosambi was a pioneer among Indian historians in carefully observing the present as a way of understanding the past.

Professor Irfan Habib, our leading authority on Moghul India, has in a recent paper tried to follow Kosambi's lead in tracing the origin of caste.[50] Habib's argument is that the structure of Indian society was not fundamentally different from the structure of other societies, such as Safavid Iran, at comparable levels of material advancement. How then did India come to have a caste system of such great rigidity? Habib makes the interesting point, *contra* Dumont, that virtually all outside observers, from Megasthenes to Bernier were struck not by the "hierarchy" of the system, but its hereditary occupation'.[51] In addition to this, he stresses rigid endogamy which he regards as a 'tribal' characteristic. The caste system was in this view the outcome of the fusion into the general society of tribal communities which were from the start rigidly endogamous.

The argument about the caste-based social order in India being built up by the cumulative accretion of tribal communities answers some questions but raises many others. Tribal components have contributed to the origin and development of civilizations everywhere: why did the accretion of tribes lead to the formation of a caste system only in India? Why did the fusion of tribal elements into the general society not lead to the formation of a caste system in medieval Morocco or medieval Poland?

The argument that a strict rule of endogamy was carried over from tribe to caste is not wholly convincing. As Fried has ably demonstrated, endogamy is not a universal characteristic of tribes. If there is evidence of strict endogamy among Indian tribes, that may be an *Indian* rather than a *tribal* characteristic. Hindu society no doubt carries the marks of tribal culture, but tribal society also carries the marks of Hindu culture in India as it does of Muslim culture in Morocco. The Indian case reveals not only the co-existence of tribe and civilization but also their interpenetration.

What is important therefore is not that tribal elements fuse into the general society but that collective identities survive the conversion of tribe into caste. It is this process that N.K. Bose set out to analyse in his brilliant paper published forty years ago on 'The Hindu method of tribal absorption'.[52] The argument of that paper was elaborated in a book first published in Bengali and later translated into English as *The Structure of Hindu Society*.[53]

I must repeat before presenting Bose's argument that there are over 400 named tribes in India whose conditions vary so much that it would be naive to expect the argument to apply equally well in all cases. At one extreme are the indigenous tribes of the Andaman Islands – the Onge, Jarawa and others – who, until the nineteenth century, remained almost completely isolated from the mainland and therefore unaffected by the Hindu method of tribal absorption. Then there are the tribes in the north eastern hill areas – Konyak, Abor, Dafla and many others – who, because of their location on the frontier of more than one civilization, were better able to withstand the pressure to become castes, although the Ahom, now regarded as a caste, were once clearly a tribe, and the Khasi, still regarded as a tribe, were developing a state with unmistakably Hindu features.[54] Even in the north west, in what is now Pakistan, the Swat Pathan, though primarily a group of Muslim tribes, have divisions that are not wholly unlike Hindu castes.[55]

The tribes that have been affected the most by the Hindu method of tribal absorption are the ones in the interior hill and forest areas where influences from other civilizations, whether Islamic or Chinese, have been feeble or absent. These tribes comprise a large array – Bhil, Munda, Santal, Oraon, Saora, Juang and numerous others – and account for the bulk of the tribal population of the country. It was Bose's argument that there was a symbiotic, though unequal, relationship between these tribes and the larger society of castes which became apparent as soon as one viewed them on a sufficiently broad geographical canvas and a sufficiently long historical scale.

Bose took pains to describe the economic context of the symbiosis between tribes and the wider society, arguing that the absorption of the former by the latter was generally of some material advantage to both, though not in the same way or to the same extent. He believed that the caste-based economy and its division of labour enabled it to support populations of greater size and density than in a tribal economy whose material base was at a lower level. When that material base became precarious due to expansion of population or for some other reason, a tribe or a section of it sought economic security through closer attachment to the wider society. This attachment was generally granted by the wider society on the condition that the newly attached group took the lowest position in it. Bose combined fieldwork in the tribal areas with a study of the classical texts to establish his argument.

Bose believed that the whole order of Hindu society, since at least the time of the Mahabharata, had been structured in such a way that a tribe or a section of it was not only allowed but encouraged to maintain a hereditary monopoly over its occupation. Whole groups would thus function as basket makers, or rope makers, or collectors of lac, or dealers of some other product, usually of the forest. But, while specialized occupations were extremely important in maintaining boundaries between groups, such boundaries could be maintained even in their absence through the enforcement of strict rules of endogamy. Bose laid great emphasis on the economic ethic of the wider society which put a high value on hereditary occupations, protected the occupational monopolies of groups and discouraged competition between individuals in the occupational sphere.

The distinctiveness of what has been called the Hindu method of tribal absorption is seen when we examine the American approach to the assimilation of tribes till the time of the Indian Reorganization Act of 1934. Here I turn again to Colson's study of the Makah Indians. The goal of the Indian Service, she tells us, 'was the complete assimilation of the Indians, and therefore the Makah, into American society in as short a period as possible', and this goal would be frustrated 'in so far they emerged from the moulding process one jot different from the ideal average American'.[56] In the event, the goal was frustrated as it was bound to be: 'Today American Indian tribes continue to exist. They are deviant groups within American society'.[57] The Hindu method of tribal absorption did not seek to efface the tribal identity fully or in the shortest time, and the end product was a caste, usually of the lowest rank but not a deviant group.

Bose has been criticized for dwelling too much on the symbiotic nature of the relationship between the tribe and the wider society and not enough on its asymmetrical and exploitative character.[58] The precariousness of the tribal economy was not always its natural condition. It resulted sometimes from a tribe being pushed back by its more prosperous or better organized neighbours from a better to a worse location where it could survive only on the lowest economic plane. As a recent writer has tersely observed about a major area of tribal concentration in Bihar, 'it can be surmised that the people of Chota Nagpur remained primitive so that their neighbours could grow'.[59] But, whether these tribes were pushed out or pulled in, their lives were never wholly unaffected by the larger currents of Hindu civilization.

Our understanding of the transformation of tribe into caste or the fusion of tribal elements into the general society will remain incomplete without an appreciation of the role of the economic ethic of Hinduism. Evidence of oppression and exploitation cannot be used to discount its hold over the minds of people in the entire subcontinent down to our own times. The economic ethic was part of a wider system of beliefs and values which we describe broadly as Hinduism and which overflowed the boundaries of Hindu society in the narrow sense.

When a tribe stood on the threshold of closer economic interaction with Hindu society, it would normally not be a complete stranger to the beliefs and values of the society on whose threshold it stood. Hindu saints and ascetics have from time immemorial gone into the remotest hill and forest areas in the pursuit of their religious vocation. It would be a truism to describe the forest as a category of Hindu civilization. The forest and its people had as important a place in it as the desert and its inhabitants had in Islamic civilization. Just as the desert was the great source of political renewal in Islam, so was the forest the perennial source of religious renewal in Hinduism.

Sometimes the forest retreat of a saint or an ascetic became a famous centre of pilgrimage, ensuring a regular flow of traffic through the tribal area surrounding it. This traffic might influence the religious life of the tribal people even when they remained largely outside the organization of economic activities based on caste. There is evidence of deep-rooted and widespread Hindu beliefs and practices throughout the tribal areas in the interior of India.[60] Within the traditional order strict sanctions were developed for maintaining the boundaries between one community and another, but there were no comparable sanctions for maintaining the boundaries between Animism and Hinduism, or between tribe and Hindu society.

In the light of what I have said above, it will be easy to see why I prefer the historical to the evolutionary approach in the definition and identification of tribes. Where tribe and civilization co-exist, as in India and the Islamic world, being a tribe has been more a matter of remaining outside of State and civilization, whether by choice or necessity, than of attaining a definite stage in the evolutionary advance from the simple to the complex. We cannot therefore dismiss as anomalous the Indian practice of regarding as tribes a large assortment of communities, differing widely in size, mode of livelihood and social organization. They are all tribes because they all stood more or less outside of Hindu civilization and not because they were all at exactly the same stage of evolution. Similarly, a recent student of tribes in Iran and Afghanistan has noted that they range 'from fragmentary and independent communities somewhat resembling the bands of hunting and gathering peoples, to centralised chiefdoms involving hundreds of thousands of people, considerable differentiation of wealth and status, and many of the trappings of states'.[61]

I have sought to stress the permeability of the boundary between tribe and non-tribe, not to deny the presence of tribes in either the past or the present. The permeability of the boundary in India, in the Islamic world and perhaps also in China obliges us to adopt a flexible rather than a rigid attitude towards the definition of tribe. It makes the presence of borderline cases an inescapable feature of the system, but does not permit us to argue as if all cases were borderline cases. It may be difficult to decide whether the Bhumij in eastern India or the Dubla in western India are a tribe or a caste, but there should be no difficulty in deciding that the Vadama are a caste in Tanjore or the Juang a tribe in Mayurbhanj.

The traditional social order tolerated or even encouraged the proliferation of borderline cases, but the modern State cannot afford to do so. It demands clear categories in place of ambiguous ones. The Indian Constitution now recognizes the Scheduled Tribes as a separate category with specific claims and entitlements. The State has thus an obligation to list and label the tribes for whose benefit it has adopted special measures, and these tribes have in their turn acquired a new interest in being listed and labelled.

The process of designating or 'scheduling' tribes in India began during British rule and acquired a systematic character from the time of the 1931 census. It became involved in political controversy from almost the very beginning. On the one side were the official anthropologists, mostly British members of the Indian Civil Service, who argued that the aboriginal tribes had a distinct identity that marked them out from the rest of Indian society.[62] On the other were the nationalist anthropologists who argued that they were part and parcel of Hindu society.[63] These points of view, though apparently contradictory, have both been accommodated in the present Constitution which recognizes that tribes are different from castes, but treats tribals, with individual exceptions, as Hindus all the same.

The Government of India Act of 1935 had introduced special provisions for the tribal people and a list of Backward Tribes was promulgated in that connection in 1936.[64] After the new Constitution was adopted in 1950 the President promulgated in the same year a list of Scheduled Tribes which was based very substantially on the list of Backward Tribes promulgated in 1936 by the colonial government. The list was revised in 1976 and is due for another revision soon. A list of Scheduled Tribes is required in connection with a set of special provisions in the Constitution some of which, though not all, are for only a limited duration of time.

The Constitutional provisions have in certain respects sealed the boundaries between tribe and non-tribe, and given to the tribal identity a kind of definiteness it lacked in the past. Until recently a tribe was part of a regional system, and tribes from different regions had little to do with each other. Ao Naga, Munda, Dubla, Baiga and Toda lived their separate lives without a sense of their common identity. The new legal and political order has changed this to some extent. There is now not only a definite tribal identity enjoying a legal sanction but a political interest in maintaining and strengthening that identity.

Political forces released in the last few decades have not only arrested the absorption of tribes into the wider society but have to some extent reversed the process. The case of the Mahato of Chotanagpur illustrates the point. They had been counted as a tribe until 1921, but had themselves declassified in the census of 1931 when they made a bid to identify themselves with the large Kurmi-Mahato caste of Bihar. They are now trying once again to have themselves reclassified as a tribe.[65] Paradoxically, the number of communities deemed to be tribes has increased with the modernization of India between 1950 and 1976, and the tribal population as a proportion of the total population has risen steadily from 5.30 per cent in 1951 to 7.76 per cent in 1981.

It is doubtful that this assertion of tribal identity in the political domain can be described as retribalization in any meaningful sense. The categories involved are very different in scale and orientation from those of the past. It is true that collective identities have proved far more durable in the face of economic and political change than was earlier envisaged.[66] But the collectivities to which the label 'tribe' will remain attached will depart in both form and function further and further from what can reasonably be described as tribes.

4 Caste and politics in Tamilnadu

Before discussing the role of caste in Tamilnadu politics, I would like to examine in somewhat general terms the relationship between caste and the political system. Most recent studies by social anthropologists have emphasized the role of caste in local politics and political scientists, too, have become increasingly sensitive to the part it plays in wider political systems. Some kind of interrelationship between these two sets of factors is also often assumed by journalists both in this country and abroad.

It is a truism that the nature and content of politics undergo transformation from one territorial level to another. What is rather less obvious to the non-specialist is that the caste system itself evinces several levels of differentiation. These levels require to be specified before a proper understanding can be achieved of the transformations in the relationship between caste and politics from one level of organization to another. Enough material now exists for the formulation of a common strategy for the analytical study of the relationship between caste and politics in the different parts of the country.

While public discussion on the 'communal' pattern of politics does draw attention to a significant social reality, it also tends to obscure the true nature of the relations between caste and the political system. Obviously these relations are more immediate at certain levels than at others. A failure to recognize such differences is likely to lead to hasty and unsound generalizations. It is also likely to divert attention from the fact that the relations between caste and politics are not static but change continuously over time. Finally, there are many alignments other than those based on caste which play an important part in the political process. Their role has often been undervalued because many of them are more fluid and amorphous in nature and hence more difficult to identify than is caste. The preoccupation with caste in the present paper is not intended to convey the impression that other factors are unimportant or play a less important part in political life, whether in Tamilnadu or elsewhere.

Studies on factions, particularly by Nicholas[1] and Brass[2], have drawn attention to the need for a more differentiated and flexible approach to the study of the relations between caste and politics. These studies show how alliances are often made across caste for the pursuit of political objectives. Some of the implications of alliances of this kind will be examined at a later stage.

I shall begin with a consideration of the political system and the way in which it can be best viewed for analysing the part played in it by caste and similar modes of grouping. As I see it, there are two major problems in the study of political systems. These are, (1) problems of distribution, and (2) problems of process. I shall briefly consider each in turn.

Problems of distribution   Every society or social segment is characterized by a certain distribution of power. Among these a central position is occupied by groups which have a territorial basis, such as the village, the district or the State. Each such unit is characterized by the presence of individuals or groups of individuals who can take decisions which are binding on the unit as a whole. The first task of political analysis is to identify these positions of power and to examine their hierarchy and interrelations.

Structures of power are of diverse kinds. They may be regional or local; functionally diffuse or specific; formal or informal. One important feature of contemporary India lies in qualitative and quantitative changes in structures of power. New types of structures of power such as parties, *panchayats* and machines have proliferated since independence and penetrated into the rural areas. The two main factors behind this are the adoption of adult franchise and the institution of Panchayati Raj.

Not only have structures of power multiplied but they have also become more differentiated. In the past at the local level the dominant caste was often the principal locus of power. Today there are differentiated political structures of various kinds such as parties, *panchayats* and machines. Such differentiated structures of power are generally more easy to identify since they have often a formal organization. But it has to be remembered that particularly at the local level real power may be vested in an informal body such as a group of lineage elders rather than in a formal structure such as the statutory *panchayat*.

Each structure of power can be examined for its caste composition and comparisons can be made between structures at different levels of organization. This will tell us about the distributive aspect of the relationship between caste and politics. General statements are often made about the control by the dominant caste or a group or coalition of dominant castes of the political system of an area. Such statements can be tested empirically although this is rarely done. It should be possible to study the frequency distribution of castes in given structures of power and to compare these with their distribution in the population as a whole. Such comparisons can be made fairly accurately at the village level and in somewhat more broad and general terms at other levels.

It is often found that a particular caste is highly represented in the village *panchayat* or the *panchayat samiti* or the *zilla parishad*. This high representation may at times be due to the fact that the caste in question is numerically preponderant and highly represented in the population as a whole. Also it seems likely that over-representation of castes in structures of power is more characteristic of certain territorial levels than of others.

A second kind of distributive problem relates to changes in the caste composition of particular structures of power over a period of time. A study of this kind will not be handicapped by the absence of reliable material on the distribution of castes in the total population, because here one has only to compare the caste composition of relatively small units at different points of time.

Two kinds of change seem to be taking place in the relation between caste and politics in Tamilnadu as well as in other parts of the country. In the first kind, power shifts from one dominant caste to another. This happened when Kallas and a few other castes wrested control over village politics from Brahmins in Sripuram.[3] It happened on a wider scale in Tamilnadu as a whole when Brahmins were displaced by non-Brahmins in important political bodies.

The second kind of change is perhaps more radical than the first. Here the locus of power shifts from the caste system itself to differentiated structures of power. As I have indicated earlier, a vast body of new structures of power has emerged in India since independence. Today traditional bodies such as groups of caste elders (which are functionally diffuse) have to compete increasingly with functionally specific structures of power such as parties and statutory *panchayats*. Often there are mechanisms which bring about the interpenetration of the two sets of bodies.

Problems of process   Structures of power exist within a context of events and activities. This flow of events and activities creates continuous changes in personnel and, over longer periods of time, changes in the structures themselves. The electoral process provides a good example of the way in which changes are brought about in the personnel of political bodies. Changes in personnel may be of minor or major significance; it is difficult to say at which point a change in personnel becomes so significant as to constitute a change in structure.

It is necessary for incumbents of political office to maintain support in order both to acquire such office and to act effectively within it. In no society is support given automatically; it has to be sought and cultivated more or less actively. In societies having representative government, such as contemporary India, there are specific institutional arrangements through which support is given and withdrawn. But the manipulation of support is an important feature of all societies including those areas of Indian society which are still largely governed by 'traditional' principles.

Support may be given in return for material benefits. But material benefits cannot be granted directly or immediately in exchange for every kind of support. For this reason the mobilization of support requires appeals to loyalties of various kinds which do not always have a tangible material basis.

In Indian society, as in other 'traditional' societies, an important place is held by groups based on what have been called 'primordial loyalties'.[4] Castes constitute typical instances of groups of this kind. Loyalties to caste and kin, whose psychological roots we need not examine here, provide powerful bases for political support. Other things being equal, people are expected to support members of their own caste or kin group.

To the extent that traditional values persist, loyalty and obligation to caste and community are considered 'good'. Such loyalty and obligation are expected as a matter of course in a variety of social fields; it is natural that they should be carried over to the field of institutional politics. A slogan used by candidates of the Meena caste during the elections in Rajasthan illustrates the manner in which loyalties from one field are carried over into another: 'Do not give your daughter or your vote to anyone but a Meena'. Similar slogans have been widely used during elections in Tamilnadu: *vanniyar Vottu anniyirkku illai* (the Vanniya vote is not for anyone else).

Even in traditional Indian society there were other loyalties besides those based on caste. Such for instance are the loyalties of class and of patron-client relationships. The latter in particular often cut across caste and are in conflict with it. Thus, the Palla client of a Vellala patron has one set of loyalties to his fellow Pallas and another to his patron who is of a different caste. Such divided loyalties, which are an inherent feature of the system, give to it a certain indeterminacy and always leave room for some manipulation of support. This is one reason why political events are difficult to predict though it is possible to interpret them.

Caste may enter into the political process in a number of ways. Firstly, appeals may be made to caste loyalties in a general way as when Vanniyas are exhorted to vote for Vanniya candidates. The force of this kind of appeal is made evident in Tamilnadu where rival parties often match caste with caste in the selection of candidates for electoral office. Secondly, networks of interpersonal relations are activated both during elections and at other times for mobilizing support along caste lines. Since kinship, marriage and commensality often stop short at the boundaries of caste, intra-caste relations are very important. Finally caste associations such as the Vanniyakkula Kshatriya Sangam may seek to articulate caste interests in an organized manner.

I now turn to a brief consideration of the nature of caste. The caste system in Tamilnadu is both elaborate and deeply segmented. Segments of different orders assume importance at different levels of the political system. It seems that the political process itself plays some part in bringing about changes in the nature of segmentation in the caste system. Organized politics often necessitates the fusion of adjacent segments and this fusion in the political context is likely in the long run to affect other aspects of inter-caste relations, such as commensality or intermarriage.[5]

The caste system evinces some of the structural properties of segmentary systems.[6] There are several levels of differentiation; large units are divided into smaller ones and these further subdivided on the basis of cleavages which are fairly enduring in character. The divisions and subdivisions either merge with one another or are placed in opposition, depending upon context and situation. Although in a given context a unit of a lower order may lose its identity through merger with an adjacent unit, it tends to reappear as an independent entity in a different context. Thus the system as a whole retains a degree of continuity over time.

The segments themselves are differentiated according to styles of life. Each segment – whether sub-caste, caste or caste-group – is characterized on the one hand by certain *diacritical* distinctions and on the other by a set of *syncretic* values. The diacritical distinctions 'define the unity of the segment in terms of differentiation from other segments', whereas syncretic values 'define the unity of the segment in terms of internal solidarity'.[7] One caste differs from another in matters of dress, diet and other habits, while within the caste there is a consciousness of community. It is this which facilitates the mobilization of support on the basis of caste as contrasted with other social categories such as class.

Diacritical differences between segments have been greatly elaborated in the caste system in Tamilnadu. In the past they were reinforced by a variety of sanctions, some of which are still in existence. Food habits, types of habitation, styles of dress and many other customs varied from one caste to another. The higher castes jealously preserved their traditional styles of life, even to the extent of cooking or serving food in a particular manner. The lower castes could imitate these ways to some extent, but ritual and other sanctions prevented such imitation proceeding beyond a certain point. In Tamilnadu such sanctions were employed with considerable force even thirty years ago.[8]

The unity which a caste derives from its diacritical distinctions is more in evidence at higher than at lower levels of segmentation. Members of a broad division such as the Brahmins share only a few diacritical elements in common, whereas those of a subdivision of the Smartha Brahmins, for instance, share many. Similarly, internal solidarity is likely to be more intense within a sub-caste than within a group of related castes. The highest order of segmentation in the caste system is represented by a small endogamous unit whose members are the bearers of a homogeneous cultural tradition and are, in fact, related to each other by ties of kinship and affinity. At the other extreme are the primary segments (viz. Brahmins, non-Brahmins and Harijans) whose members share a few common customs and are bound together by a broad feeling of community.

We can present here only a very brief and summary account of the caste structure of Tamilnadu. The population of Tamilnadu can be broadly divided into three groups, the Brahmins, the non-Brahmins and the Harijans (or Adi-Dravidas). In the villages the three groups are generally segregated in different residential areas. The Brahmins live in brick-and-tile houses in a separate part of the village known as the *agraharam* and are marked off from the others by distinctive patterns of speech, dress and diet; within the *agraharam* there is a fairly intense community life from many areas of which non-Brahmins and Harijans are excluded. The Harijans in their turn live in their own streets known as *cheris* which have a unity no less distinctive than that of the *agraharam*. The non-Brahmins represent a broader spectrum of cultural variations and appear to be on the whole less cohesive than the two other primary segments.

Each primary segment, which appears as a unit in relation to the others, is internally subdivided. The Brahmins in Tamilnadu are subdivided into Smartha, Shri Vaishnava, etc. Each of these evinces a greater measure of unity (both diacritical and syncretic) than the Brahmins taken as a whole. The Smartha Brahmins in their turn are similarly subdivided into Vadama, Brihacharanam, Astasahashram and Vattiman. The Vadama are subdivided into

Vadadesha Vadama and Chozhadesha Vadama. Segmentation among the non-Brahmins follows a more complex and less clear-cut pattern and the Harijans as a unit appear to be less deeply segmented than the Brahmins. But everywhere the pattern is broadly similar.[9]

At which level of segmentation does caste enter into the political process? When we seek to analyse the role of caste in politics, which should be our unit of investigation, a broad grouping such as the Brahmins or a small subdivision such as the Vadadesha Vadama or the Pramalai Kalla?

Some have been inclined to argue that castes can successfully enter politics only when they combine into fairly large aggregates; too much segmentation, in their view, tends to reduce the viability of castes in the competition for power. There can be little doubt that organized politics at the State level has tended to bring about a certain aggregation of adjacent segments within the caste system. This phenomenon appears to have an all-India character and has been commented on by many. Srinivas for instance writes, 'In order to be able to take advantage of these opportunities, caste groups, as traditionally understood, entered into alliances with each other to form bigger entities'.[10] He gives the example of the Okkaligas in Mysore who now include, in the context of State politics, several related but distinct entities. The same can be said of the Vellalas or the Kallas in Tamilnadu.

The Non-Brahmin Movement provided a common platform not only for a wide variety of Hindu castes but also for Christians and Muslims. It also added a new dimension to the unity of the Brahmins which grew in response to the non-Brahmin challenge. However, it would be a mistake to view this unity as something absolute or as having significance in every context. It is well known how the unity of the non-Brahmins was loosened after they gained ascendancy in Tamilnadu because of competition between rival dominant castes among them for power and office. It is hardly surprising that cleavages which are ignored in the interest of a particular objective should reassert themselves once that objective has been achieved.

The unity one encounters in the caste system is in a very real sense relative. Although a minor segment of a caste may be too small to act as an independent unit in state politics, it may be a viable unit in the village. Unity in one political context does not preclude opposition in another. The fact that a group of sub-castes unites against a like group over a certain issue does not mean that they cannot be divided over a different issue. Conversely, the fact that two sub-castes contend for power in a particular arena does not mean that they cannot unite against a different caste in a wider arena. In fact, the complementary processes of fission and fusion are an important feature of caste politics in Tamilnadu. Further, since caste is a highly structured system, fission and fusion are inclined to follow clearly defined patterns.

Many have observed that the unity provided by caste has different degrees of inclusiveness.[11] Srinivas tries to account for this in a way which appears to be characteristic.

> The point which needs to be emphasized here is that for purposes of sociological analysis a distinction has to be made between caste at the political level and caste at the social and ritual level. The latter is a much smaller unit than the former.[12]

To my mind, Srinivas draws the distinction at the wrong place. What is important here is to distinguish not between political and social levels, but between different levels of organization in a 'merging series',[13] viz. State, district and village, or caste-group, caste and sub-caste.

Srinivas' conclusion that 'caste at the political level' is generally a large aggregate derives from his preoccupation with the role of caste in state politics. But caste may also play a part in village politics and there the effective unit of organization may be fairly small. Nor is it correct to maintain that larger aggregates have no social or ritual unity. Such broad groupings as the Brahmins and the Harijans (and to a much lesser extent the non-Brahmins) do have a measure of diacritical and syncretic unity and it is this fact which largely accounts for their persistence at every level of political organization.

Srinivas also appears to suggest that the larger aggregates not only are specifically political in function but are somehow new to the Indian scene. Even this position cannot be well sustained. Broader groupings such as Brahmins, Shudras and Panchamas were relevant to a wide variety of contexts even in traditional society.[14]

We conclude that caste may be significant to the political process at every level of segmentation, although organized politics at State and district levels has often led to a quasi-permanent aggregation of segments. Further, there seems to exist some broad relationship between the arena of politics and the level of segmentation at which caste enters into it. At the State (or even district) level, minor segments merge with one another so as to be able to operate as viable units. But this kind of merger easily comes about precisely because a basis for it already existed in the traditional structure. At the village level a major segment may subdivide and its component units be opposed to one another, again because the cleavage was present even in the past. Thus, while fusion may occasionally be 'structural', very often it is merely 'situational'.

The principle of segmentation operates even *within* the sub-caste, viewed as the smallest unit of endogamy. In such cases the units which stand in opposition to each other are generally lineages. (A sub-caste which is an *endogamous* unit is often subdivided into lineages which are *exogamous*. In certain parts of Tanjore district where the Kallas are decisively dominant, rival candidates for political office often belong to different lineages of the same sub-caste. (In other contexts the three related castes, Kalla, Marava and Ahamudiya, may together operate as a single unit). When a sub-caste is large, culturally homogeneous and decisively dominant, the cleavages within the lineage system often assume great importance. (A very good example of this is provided by the Jats of Northern India.) Thus for certain purposes lineage,[15] sub-caste, caste and caste-group may be viewed as constituting a single series.[16]

Although both the territorial system and the caste system show a similar pattern of division and subdivision, it would be wrong to assume a high degree of correspondence between levels of segmentation in the two. Even a broad grouping within the caste system such as the Brahmins may be relevant to village as well as state politics. Much depends upon the caste composition of the village or other territorial unit in question. A village which has only a few castes of which one is decisively dominant will show a different kind of alignment from one where there are many castes among which none enjoys decisive dominance. Everywhere, however, the caste system provides *one* set of cleavages along which units tend to merge or subdivide. Whether they do merge or subdivide will depend upon a variety of other factors, some of which are extraneous to the structure of caste. It cannot be too strongly emphasized that political alliances, at every level, often cut across caste and are frequently based upon affiliations which have little direct connection with caste.

The threefold division of society into Brahmin, non-Brahmin and Harijan provides perhaps the broadest basis for 'communal' politics in Tamilnadu. (In the present analysis I ignore altogether the Hindu-Muslim cleavage; on the whole it has been of less importance than the cleavage between Brahmins and non-Brahmins or between non-Brahmins and Harijans.) This division provides the basic framework for the analysis of problems of both distribution and process. It casts its shadow at every level of political organization from the village to the State. Its importance is given tacit recognition in the composition of a variety of political bodies. The Madras Municipal Corporation, for instance, has long followed the convention of rotating the Mayoralty between one Brahmin, two non-Brahmins, one Harijan and one Muslim.

To what extent are we justified in treating such broad divisions as castes? I have shown that a certain measure of unity is associated with each category, and Brahmins and Harijans at least are certainly viewed as castes in a variety of contexts by the Tamil-speaking people. The non-Brahmins admittedly are a very broad and heterogeneous division and sometimes (though not generally) they are so broadly defined as to include even the Harijans. Even so, the Non-Brahmin Movement gave them a certain coherence and unity, which seem to have outlived the Movement itself. For that reason it becomes necessary to analyse their role in Tamilnadu politics even though they constitute a kind of residual category. (The term 'non-Brahmin' has been criticized by many precisely on this account; however, it has become a part of the political history of Tamilnadu and it would be unreal to dispense with it, at least in this context.)

Perhaps the most important consequence of the Non-Brahmin Movement (of which more later) was the introduction of a 'communal' or caste idiom into South Indian politics. The composition of political bodies was changed by it, sometimes artificially, through reserved seats, and everywhere communal loyalties became important in giving or withdrawing support. It is doubtful whether the Movement even attempted to organize politically the entire body of non-Brahmins. But it certainly did succeed in creating a lasting impression that in virtually every political context it was important whether a person was a Brahmin or a Non-Brahmin. It is this which gives the politics of South India - including Maharashtra but probably excluding Kerala – its distinctive character when compared with the politics of the North. The special position of the Harijans in the political system is acknowledged everywhere in India and is, in fact, sanctioned by the Constitution.

The Brahmins constitute a convenient starting point for a discussion of the role of caste in Tamil politics for their position is in many ways unique. As a social stratum they were the first to be politicized and up to the 1920s they enjoyed a dominant position in the former Madras Presidency. Their representation in most of the political bodies which then existed was far in excess of their proportion in the population as a whole. The changes in their political fortunes over the last fifty years bring into focus not only the role of caste in politics but certain major shifts in the bases of power in Tamil society. Certainly, no section of Tamil society of comparable size[17] has for so long occupied the storm centre of political debate and controversy and it is doubtful whether any other section has undergone a more radical change in its relation to the distribution of power.

To what do the Brahmins owe their exceptional position in Tamil society? I have already commented on the diacritical differences between the Brahmins and the others. These are certainly sharper in Tamilnadu, and in South India as a whole, than in North India. Two of them may be considered to begin with: the real difference in linguistic usage and the imputed difference in racial origins. These distinctions, in part real and in part imaginary, have combined to create a popular and wide-spread belief that the Brahmins represent an 'Aryan' element superimposed on an indigenous 'Dravidian' sub-stratum. This belief has far-reaching consequences for the development of political attitudes in Tamilnadu.

The opposition to Brahmins has been posed in economic as well as ethnic terms. On the whole, Tamil Brahmins enjoyed a favourable position in the traditional economic system. A considerable section of them owned land, though they were not all landowners and there was a large class of landowners – both big and small – among the non-Brahmins. Even in Tanjore district, which has the highest concentration of Brahmin landowners, the three biggest landowners prior to the fixation of ceilings were non-Brahmins[18] but the *proportion* of landowners among the Brahmins was much higher in Tanjore district than among any non-Brahmins caste or caste-group of comparable size (with the possible exception of the Mudaliyars).

It seems probable that large or moderately large Brahmin landowners were concentrated primarily in the Tanjore-Trichhy area and that few were to be found elsewhere. But Brahmin landowners, whether large or small and whether in Tanjore district or outside, have been related to the productive organization in a significantly different way from the non-Brahmins since they are debarred by scriptural injunction from the actual work of tillage. Hence a Brahmin who owns even a small parcel of land has to depend for labour on non-Brahmins and Harijans, whereas a non-Brahmin landowner in a comparable situation may not only till his own land but will probably take some additional land on lease and perhaps also work as a part-time agricultural labourer. The majority of non-Brahmin landowners are peasant farmers, tenants or agricultural labourers or some combination of the three. Among Brahmin landowners, on the other hand, a large proportion consists of rentiers and many are absentee landlords. This contrast between Brahmin and non-Brahmin landowners, arising from differences not so much in size of holding as in styles of life, has played a most important part in the development of the Non-Brahmin Movement.

The initial consequence of British rule was probably to increase the structural distance between Brahmins and the rest of Tamil society. Brahmins were the first to take to Western education and Western educated Brahmins entered the professions and services in large numbers. Those who entered Government and other services used the ties of kinship and affinity to recruit more Brahmins. It is difficult to form an accurate estimate of their representation in professional, administrative and managerial positions, but there is little doubt that during the first quarter of the present century it was extremely high. This was projected as a major issue by the Justice Party, which emerged in 1917 as a champion of non-Brahmin interests and demanded more equitable representation for them in the educational system, in local bodies and in the services.

In this initial phase (which may arbitrarily be considered as ending with the formation of the Justice Party in 1917) the cleavage between Brahmins and non-Brahmins was widened in two important ways. As Brahmins entered the institutions of higher learning, the professions and the services, everywhere they formed cliques from which non-Brahmins were excluded. Between 1892 and 1904, out of sixteen successful candidates for the I.C.S., fifteen were Brahmins; in 1913, ninety-three out of 128 permanent district *munsifs* were Brahmins; in 1914, 452 out of the 650 registered graduates of the University were Brahmins.[19] In a system which was ostensibly competitive but in which the scales must have seemed heavily weighted against non-Brahmins, the latter inevitably developed deep feelings of resentment.

There was another important consequence of Westernization. As its pace mounted, Brahmins began increasingly to look outwards to the towns and cities. They left the *agraharams* in large numbers – at first temporarily but with an increasing measure of permanence – and joined schools, colleges and offices in the urban centres. They had at no time had the same intimate relations with the land as the non-Brahmins and Harijans, and Westernization loosened considerably such bonds as they did have with tenants and labourers in their ancestral villages. But although they began to turn outwards, they did not dispose of their land to any great extent, at least not in the initial period. Rather, they became rentiers and absentee landowners, returning to the village from time to time and even while there, keeping one eye on a job as a clerk or school teacher in a neighbouring town. It is evident that even within the village relations between Brahmin landowners and non-Brahmin tenants were weakened as a general consequence of the Brahmins' Westernization. This is certainly true of the Tanjore-Trichy area and appears to be broadly true of other districts as well, although the changes in some districts seem to have been far less marked.

This then is the social background out of which the Non-Brahmin Movement emerged. The Brahmins were politically isolated first because they constituted a separate ethnic entity and then because they occupied privileged positions in the economy, both as landowners and as professionals and administrators. In addition, they formed a very small minority, only about 3% of the total population of the old Madras Presidency. Their proportion in contemporary Tamilnadu cannot be very much higher.

Once non-Brahmin opposition was organized, it did not take long to dislodge the Brahmins from their privileged positions. In 1921 Madras Presidency came under the control of the Justice Party. Non-Brahmin representation in political bodies increased and they were favoured by a series of legislative and executive actions. The Brahmins suffered on two accounts: they were in a minority and they were largely behind the Congress Party which either boycotted the elections or refused to form ministries. However, their decline during this period was only relative, in terms of their dominance prior to the formation of the Justice Party in 1917. In 1937 when the Congress staged a come-back, C. Rajagopalachari, the veteran Brahmin leader, became Chief Minister of Madras and other Brahmins were appointed to the Ministry.

For all this, the Brahmins were never quite able to regain the dominant position which they had once occupied in the Presidency. After a brief revival between 1937 and 1939, their position again declined, this time perhaps irrevocably. The Congress itself came gradually to be dominated by non-Brahmins. The 1940s saw the emergence of the militant Dravida Kazhagam which preached and at times practised violence against the Brahmins. With the extension of the franchise after independence and the introduction of Panchayati Raj a keen awareness developed among the Brahmins of their weakness and political isolation. In 1916 the Non-Brahmin Manifesto had made angry protests against Brahmin domination. In 1962 Brahmin voters in Trichy had to be escorted to the polling booths for fear of violence from the Dravida Kazhagam. Brahmin representation in the Ministry, the Legislatures and the Congress Party had dwindled into insignificance.

There is little precise information regarding the representation of Brahmins in political bodies at different levels. That there has been a general decline is beyond question. But it is possible that even today Brahmins are over- rather than under-represented in at least certain types of political organs.

Political developments over the last fifty years have created among Tamil Brahmins a strong sense of identity as a minority. I have heard Brahmins with a flair for metaphor describe themselves as the Jews of South India. A strong feeling has taken root among them that they were made victims of every kind of discrimination. But they have not sought escape from organized politics. On the contrary, because of their feeling of political isolation and also because of the high rates of literacy and education among them, they are perhaps the most highly politicized section of Tamil society.

There is ample indication that the Brahmins are rapidly growing alive to the fact that if they are to survive politically they must come to terms with the non-Brahmins. In both 1962 and 1967 they supported the DMK in spite of its non-Brahmin background. Many among them see the need to forge new alliances, transcending caste identities. In fact, the most bitter critics of 'communal' or caste politics today are the Brahmins. The Non-Brahmin Movement in its turn seems to have spent itself, having achieved its principal objectives. The DMK renounced its anti-Brahmin bias several years ago and canvassed actively for Brahmin support in the last two General Elections. It seems very likely that in the near future conflicts between Brahmins and non-Brahmins will play a less important part than they have done in the past.

Before turning to an examination of the role of the non-Brahmins in state politics, it may be useful to take a close-up view of the Brahmins, first at the district level and then at the village level. I shall consider here only one district, Tanjore, and this for two reasons. Firstly, Tanjore is the cultural homeland of Tamil Brahmins and contains the highest proportion of Brahmins in Tamilnadu. Secondly, it has been studied more intensively by social anthropologists than any other district in the State. In what follows I shall draw on the field materials of Gough,[20] Sivertsen[21] and my own research in and around village Sripuram.[22] Since these studies were all made in the same culture area but at different points of time (Gough's during the first and mine during the third General Elections), they offer useful material for an assessment of change.

Tanjore district has been the classic stronghold of Brahmin *mirasdars*. Gough estimates that the Brahmins 'number about 200,000 in this district' and 'own land and have administrative rights in about 900 out of a total of 2,611 villages'.[23] The Tanjore Brahmins are also highly educated and show a high degree of political consciousness. For all this, they are not very highly represented either in the organs of local government or in the local organization of the ruling party.[24]

When Gough made her study in the early fifties the Tanjore Brahmins were under attack from two quarters, the Communist Party and the Dravida Kazhagam, both of which were then quite strong. Further, the two parties were united in their opposition against them, the first on the ground that they were *mirasdars* and the second because they were Brahmins. At about this time peasant riots were organized in Mannargudi *taluka*, a stronghold of Brahmin *mirasdars*. The alliance with the staunchly anti-Brahmin Dravida Kazhagam seems to have made the Communists a little wary of antagonizing the non-Brahmin landowners. And there can be little doubt that in Tanjore district the Communists drew much of their strength from the Dravida Kazhagam. In 1952, when the DK supported the Communists, the latter held six Assembly seats out of a total of nineteen from the district.[25] When in 1962 the DK supported the Congress, the Communists were not able to win a single seat.

Until the mid-1950s the Tanjore Brahmins appear to have been solidly behind the Congress. This support was based as much on their traditional association with the Congress as on their opposition to the Communists and the DK, then the two principal antagonists of the Congress. Things began to change rapidly after the mid-1950s. The veteran Brahmin leader, C. Rajagopalachari, was replaced by the non-Brahmin Kamaraj as Chief Minister and the Dravida Kazhagam, known and feared for its militant anti-Brahminism, switched its support to the Congress. The Congress enacted a series of laws curtailing the rights of landowners and many of the Brahmin *mirasdars* in Tanjore viewed these as being specifically directed against themselves. Finally in 1959 the Swatantra Party was formed under the leadership of Rajagopalachari and many of the Brahmins of Tanjore turned avidly towards the new party. In each of the half-a-dozen Brahmin villages I visited in 1961-2, the Swatantra Party had a solid core of supporters in the *agraharam*. In Tanjore district the Swatantra Party soon came to be known as the Brahmin party, although many of its members were, in fact, non-Brahmins.

The 1962 elections found the Brahmins largely opposed to the Congress and, if anything, the mood was intensified in 1967. Since the late 1950s their political attitudes appear to have been defined primarily in terms of opposition to the party then in power. In 1962 they supported DMK candidates where the Swatantra Party did not put up any and the electoral alliance between the two parties in 1967 appears to have made their choice even simpler. In 1962 the Brahmins generally supported the Congress in only those rare constituencies where the Congress itself put up Brahmin candidates.

As indicated earlier, the Brahmins in Tanjore have developed a strong sense of unity in response to their political decline. Formerly there was active rivalry between the Smartha Brahmins and the Shri Vaishnavas and between the two sections of the Shri Vaishnava Brahmins. These are now largely forgotten. There is a conscious effort on their part today to foster a sense of oneness. The Brahmins see themselves as belonging to a minority and define their identity in opposition to the non-Brahmins and not to a different section of the Brahmins. In this regard their position seems to be somewhat different from that of the non-Brahmins.

Although the Brahmins constitute a very small minority in the district as a whole, their position is somewhat different in each of the three villages studied in detail. This is because these are all *agraharam* villages, i.e. villages with large concentrations of Brahmins, unlike the majority of Tanjore villages where there are no *agraharams* and at best only a few families of priestly Brahmins. Both Gough and Sivertsen report a decline in the traditional authority of the Brahmins in the villages studied by them. In both cases political parties and associations have played a leading part in organizing support against the Brahmin *mirasdars*. In Thyagasamudram the Brahmins organized them-selves into a Landlords' Association while the non-Brahmins and the Harijans rallied round the Cultivators' Union. Some of the bigger non-Brahmin landlords at first supported the Brahmins, but they seem to have been pressured at a later stage into joining the Cultivators' Union.[26]

The case of Sripuram merits discussion at greater length because changes there seem to have been more decisive in character. At the beginning of the present century Sripuram was a flourishing *agraharam* village, well known throughout Tanjore district for its large and prosperous community of Brahmins. The *agraharam* at Sripuram is rather unusual in the sense that it contains Brahmins belonging to a number of different castes and sub-castes. Fifty years ago the Brahmins of Sripuram enjoyed decisive dominance. However, the internal cleavages between the Smarthas and the Shri Vaishnavas, and among the latter between the Thengalai and Vadagalai sections, were reflected in the competition for power relating to the control of the village temple and other local institutions. Today the power of the Brahmins has declined considerably, the old disputes between the Smarthas and the Shri Vaishnavas have been largely (though not entirely) forgotten and the Brahmins try to face the challenge of the emerging non-Brahmin leadership with a measure of unity.

Sripuram is, in Dahl's terminology, being transformed from a 'system of cumulative inequalities' to one of 'dispersed inequalities'. In the past the Brahmins enjoyed the highest positions in the hierarchies of status, class and power. Today they continue to enjoy ritual and economic dominance but political power has shifted to the non-Brahmins. The shift in political power has been hastened by the introduction of Panchayati Raj.

Until the mid-1940s the Brahmins dominated the village *panchayat*. The *panchayat* head was always a Brahmin and the *panchayat* room was situated in the *agraharam*. Non-Brahmin members of the *panchayat* had more or less the status of second-class citizens. Everything changed after independence. Now the *panchayat* is completely dominated by the non-Brahmins: there are six non-Brahmin members as against three Brahmins. Both the President and the Vice-President are non-Brahmins and have been non-Brahmins ever since independence. Symbolic of the transfer of power from the Brahmins to the non-Brahmins has been the shift in the location of the *panchayat* hall from the *agraharam* to the non-Brahmin streets. In fact, this shift is of more than symbolic significance. In an *agraharam* village Brahmins and non-Brahmins live more or less segregated in their different residential areas and Brahmins do not normally go to the non-Brahmin streets unless specifically invited. Now that the *panchayat* hall is the venue of important political gatherings in the village, many of the Brahmin residents find themselves automatically excluded from such gatherings. For instance, when the Minister for Co-operation came to the village in 1962, he was entertained in the *panchayat* hall; few of the Brahmins attended the gathering and many of them came to know of it only after the event.

Changes in the relative positions of Brahmins and non-Brahmins in the political system of Sripuram are of course reflections of changes in the bases of power in the wider system. In the traditional system power was derived largely from landownership and high ritual status. The institution of adult franchise, the introduction of Panchayati Raj and the development of specialized political organs have created new bases of power. In Sripuram the Brahmin landowners have been edged out of the *panchayat* by popular non-Brahmin leaders who command the support of numerically preponderant groups and have access to leaders and party bosses outside the village.

In the 1957–62 period the Brahmins' isolation from structures of power in Sripuram (and to some extent in Tanjore district as a whole) was partly a consequence of their alienation from the ruling Congress Party. In 1962 the Brahmins in Sripuram supported the DMK candidate for the Assembly seat. The influential non-Brahmins, including the *panchayat* President, had then supported the Congress. This time the DMK has been returned to power, partly on Brahmin support. This may have some effect on the political situation of the Brahmins although it is difficult to say how permanent or far reaching this effect will be. In any event it seems more than likely that the levers of power will for some time to come be wielded largely by non-Brahmins whether at village, district or State level.

The non-Brahmin ascendancy in Sripuram can be made fully intelligible only in relation to wider structures of power and changes in the distribution of power over the last half-century. The Non-Brahmin Movement was formally launched with the issue of the Non-Brahmin Manifesto in December 1916. The Manifesto presented detailed figures showing an extremely high concentration of Brahmins in the public services, in public bodies and in the educational system and contrasting this with the 3% they formed of the total population of the Presidency.[28]

The Movement gathered strength within a very short time. The Manifesto 'was followed by the starting of three daily papers, in English, Telugu and Tamil, the English paper being called the *Justice* which became the mouthpiece of the movement, and supplied the name also to the party itself'.[29] The Party held its first Conference at Coimbatore in August 1917. Thereafter a series of Conferences was held in the Tamil and Telugu districts of the Presidency. The Conferences were evidently organized with expense and care and attended by a large number of notabilities.[30]

The Justice Party sent a powerful delegation to England in 1919 to present the non-Brahmin case before the Joint Parliamentary Committee set up in connection with the Government of India Bill. The Memorandum presented by K.V. Reddi Naidu on behalf of the non-Brahmins was one of the longest and was once again armed with facts and figures showing the domination of the Brahmins in every field. It argued that the interests of Brahmins and non-Brahmins were incompatible, that they claimed different racial origins and that if power were transferred without communal representation:

that power will be utilised for the aggrandisement of the Brahmins and to the detriment of the Non-Brahmins; that a Brahmin oligarchy will be substituted for a British bureaucracy; . . . . and that the Brahmin oligarchy will never be responsible to the masses and the middle classes, the poor and the proletariat.[31]

In retrospect, the Non-Brahmin Movement appears to have achieved singular success within a remarkably short period of time. Although the full demands for communal representation were not met, twenty-eight out of the ninety-eight elected seats in the newly constituted Madras Council were reserved for non-Brahmins.[32] The Justice Party captured the polls in the elections of 1920, no doubt partly because of the withdrawal of the Congress. The three Indian Ministers placed in charge of 'transferred subjects' were all non-Brahmins and Justicites. The same pattern was repeated in the succeeding Legislature constituted in 1923. In 1926 the Justice Party was defeated by the Swarajists, but the latter refused to form a Ministry and an Independent Ministry was formed under the non-Brahmin leader, P. Subbaroyan. The Justice Party rode into power again in 1930 and, though defeated in the elections of 1934, was not finally dislodged until 1937 when the Congress formed a Ministry under the leadership of C. Rajagopalachari.

After their success in the 1920 elections the leaders of the Justice Party settled down to the task of improving the position of Non-Brahmins through legislative and executive action. The debates in the newly constituted Council were replete with questions and counter-questions regarding the representation of Brahmins and non-Brahmins in the services and public bodies.

Forming a vast majority, the (Justice) party concerned itself with little more than communal questions, including the problem of communal representation in various areas of government service, and within one year the Council had become a forum of anti-Brahmin propaganda.[33]

One of the first moves of the Council was to recommend the appointment in every district of a Protector of Non-Brahmin Subordinates in Public Services (GO No. 114, dated 3.3.1921). Reservations for non-Brahmins were introduced in increasing proportion in the services, in local bodies and in the institutions of higher learning. With the Justice Party acting as the watchdog of non-Brahmin interests, changes began to come about in the distribution of power between castes.

Why did the non-Brahmins need a separate party and how far did the Justice Party represent their interests? The need for a separate party was made clear in the Non-Brahmin Manifesto. The Brahmins had virtually monopolized some of the crucial advantages offered by British rule and the threat of a 'Brahmin oligarchy' must have appeared very real to many non-Brahmins. The latter, in spite of their enormous strength of numbers and their wealth (for most big *zamindars* were non-Brahmins), lacked organization. The only existing party, the Congress, was virtually controlled by Brahmins. As the Manifesto pointed out, 'of the fifteen gentlemen elected from this Presidency to represent it on the All-India Congress Committee, with the exception of one solitary Non-Brahmin Indian, all are practically Brahmins'.[34] It is small wonder then that the Justice Party met with such immediate response when it was formed.

However, although the Justice Party did define its position in opposition to the Brahmins and although it did claim to speak on behalf of the forty million non-Brahmins of Madras Presidency, it would be a mistake to identify it with the interests of the non-Brahmins as a whole. First of all, the forty million non-Brahmins on whose behalf the Party claimed to speak included Muslims as well as Harijans, and people belonging to three language groups, Tamil, Telugu and Malayalam. While it is true that in its broadest definition the non-Brahmins included all who were *not* Brahmins, in practice the Depressed Classes and the Muslims were generally considered separately. Even after the exclusion of Muslims and Harijans the non-Brahmins would constitute a far more heterogeneous category than the Brahmins. And those who participated in the Non-Brahmin Movement in its first phase, supplying its leadership and controlling its organization, were, in fact, drawn from a very narrow social base. For the Justice Party was in a very real sense an élite party dominated by urban, Western educated, landowning and professional people. It contained a formidable array of Rajas, *zamindars*, industrialists, lawyers and doctors. It was by no means a mass party and it is doubtful whether any serious effort was made to draw peasants and workers into its organization.

I cannot do better here than to quote K.B. Krishna, himself a non-Brahmin:

> This movement represents the emergence of the educated middle classes who are not Brahmins. . . . The Non-Brahmin professional classes are no more champions of social justice than the Brahmin professional classes. . . . The Non-Brahmin movement of Madras Presidency is no other than the movement of the later educated middle classes who happen to be Non-Brahmins against the earlier educated middle classes who happened to be Brahmins.[35]

A more recent student has made a similar point:

> The leadership, financially well endowed, was drawn almost exclusively from a socially stable element of the urban population. While Chetty, Nair, Mudaliar and the early leaders of the movement spoke of the illiterate Non-Brahmin masses of Madras, they in no way represented them. . . . With the franchise limited to but a few hundred thousand, the party made little attempt to aggregate support at any wider level. Its demands were formulated, not so much to attract a following, as to influence the official policy of the British in Madras Presidency.[36]

Though markedly elitist in character, the leadership of the Justice Party was heterogeneous in terms of both class and caste. It would be a mistake to characterize it as a 'middle-class' party for besides professional people there were in it landed and capitalist elements. There was also a fairly wide range of castes although most of the prominent people belonged to the upper crust of non-Brahmin castes such as Mudaliyars, Chettiyars and Vellalas among the Tamils, Rajus, Reddis and Naidus among the Telugus and Nairs among the Malayalis. In the Tamil districts some large non-Brahmin castes such as the Padayachis and the Kallas and particularly the artisan and servicing castes do not seem to have been very strongly represented.

A word requires to be said about the territorial framework of the Justice Party and the Non-Brahmin Movement in South India. Boundaries between states have changed considerably over the last half-century and the Tamilnadu of today is very different from the Madras Presidency of the 1920s and 1930s.

The older unit was not only larger but culturally much more heterogeneous. It is difficult now to isolate the exact contribution of the Tamil speaking people to the Non-Brahmin Movement. But one must remember that a large number of the leaders of this Movement were Telugu-speaking people who combined with their Tamil- and Malayalam-speaking counterparts against the Brahmin élite which appears to have been predominantly, though by no means wholly, Tamilian.

Two broad conclusions emerge from a consideration of the Non-Brahmin Movement. Firstly, it created alliances which cut right across linguistic and cultural divisions: the significance of this in a society in which 'linguism' and 'regionalism' played such an important part only a short while later can hardly be over-emphasized. The second point which emerges is that the entire political arena in which Brahmins and non-Brahmins stood poised against each other was a very restricted one: the participants were drawn almost wholly from the urban, Western educated, landowning, business and professional classes.

It seems that little change took place in the distribution of power in the districts except in the towns. Non-Brahmin dominance in the organs of state and municipal Government began with the success of the Justice Party in the elections of 1920. Yet in the villages things appear to have remained very much as they had been in the past for many more years. Villages in which Brahmins had been the dominant caste did not witness a transformation comparable to that taking place in the Provincial Legislature or the Municipal bodies. In Sripuram, and presumably also in Kumbapettai and Thyagasamudram, the Brahmins continued to enjoy decisive dominance and to control the *panchayat* well into the 1940s. It was only after the introduction of adult franchise and particularly of Panchayati Raj that the tables were turned on the Brahmins. By this time the Justice Party had been almost forgotten and the Non-Brahmin Movement had acquired an entirely different character.

Yet it would be a mistake to minimize the role of the Justice Party and the Non-Brahmin Movement of the 1920s. The Justice Party not only prepared the ground for the induction of new social strata into the political system but also created a distinctive idiom for South Indian politics. This idiom remained as a crucial element in the political process long after the Justice Party itself disintegrated. It permeated every kind of political organization including the Congress Party.

The Justice Party was routed in the elections of 1936 and thereafter it was almost completely eclipsed. But its defeat did not lead to a complete reversal of the Non-Brahmin ascendancy. It is true that the helm of Madras politics was taken over for some time by the two Brahmin Congressmen, C. Rajagopalachari and S. Satyamurti. But the non-Brahmins began increasingly to infiltrate the Congress and to acquire key positions within it. Several prominent Justicites joined the Congress after the defeat of their party. But the non-Brahmins had to wait for independence and the first General Elections in independent India for their control over the Congress to become complete and decisive.

Efforts to rouse the non-Brahmin conscience were not confined to the sphere of politics in the narrow sense of the term. From the late 1920s onwards the Self respect Movement began to make concerted efforts to undermine the supremacy of the Brahmins in the ritual and social spheres. The Movement was welcomed by the Justice Party although its immediate objectives were not political. It sought rather to create for Non-Brahmins a climate of self-confidence and to liberate them from the ritual tyranny of the Brahmins. In the late 1920s and early 1930s it gained a measure of popular appeal under the leadership of the non-Brahmin ex-Congressman, E.V. Ramaswami Naicker. In 1944 Naicker created the Dravida Kazhagam and this association became the spearhead of militant anti-Brahminism in the South. Idols were desecrated, sacred books were burnt and some violence was practised against Brahmins. We have seen how during the mid-fifties the DK switched its support to the Congress which had by then come largely under non-Brahmin control.

The non-Brahmin ascendancy reached its peak some time in the mid-1950s. In recent years, with the consolidation of non-Brahmin power, internal cleavages have increasingly tended to manifest themselves. These cleavages, which had existed as an inherent feature of the caste structure, were to some extent subsumed under a wider unity during the initial phase of the

Non-Brahmin Movement. With the introduction of Panchayati Raj, rifts between subdivisions of the same caste are likely to widen, particularly at the village and Block levels.

Today the category non-Brahmin has become too broad to provide an adequate understanding of the role of caste in politics. In order to achieve such an understanding it is necessary to introduce the concept of dominant caste. This concept was first used systematically by Srinivas.[37] He has defined it in the following way:

> A caste may be said to be 'dominant' when it preponderates numerically over other castes, and when it also wields preponderant economic and political power. A large and powerful caste group can be more easily dominant if its position in the local caste hierarchy is not too low.[38]

Dominant castes have come to play an important part in every sphere of politics and in Tamilnadu today every dominant caste of any significance is a non-Brahmin caste.

It has been said earlier that the non-Brahmins in Tamilnadu constitute a congeries of castes. They include landowning and cultivating castes such as Vellala, Gaunda and Padayachi; trading castes such as Chetti; artisan castes such as Tachchan (Carpenter), Kollan (Blacksmith) and Tattan (Goldsmith); servicing castes such as Ambattan (Barber) and Vannan (Washerman); and a whole host of other specialist castes. Each of these castes enjoys a greater measure of unity than the non-Brahmins as a whole, although most of the major ones are themselves subdivided.

The major Peasant castes are not evenly distributed throughout the State but have areas of concentration within it. Although there is no exact correspondence between these areas of concentration and the division of the State into districts, certain castes can be said to be dominant in certain districts. A caste which is dominant in one district may not be dominant in another. There are certain districts in which more than one caste is dominant and certain castes which are dominant in more than one district. Thus the Mudaliyars are dominant in Chingleput district, the Padayachis in North and South Arcot districts, the Thevars in Ramnad district, the Gaundas in Coimbatore district, the

Vellalas in Tinnevelli district and the Nadars in parts of Madura district. In Tanjore district dominance is shared between the Kallas and the Vellalas.

Srinivas has enumerated a number of criteria on which dominance is said to be based.[39] In addition to the ones enumerated, geographical concentration may itself be seen as a criterion of dominance. Artisan castes are almost never dominant because they are territorially dispersed. A peasant caste may be dominant, although small in size, provided it is concentrated within a limited area. A caste tends to enjoy a higher position in a village within the area of its dominance than outside. Thus the Kallas of Sripuram, although out-numbered by the Vellalas, enjoy great power in the village which is in a Kalla-dominated area.

It is probable that every State has its pattern of dominant castes. Tamilnadu has a number of dominant castes, each concentrated in a particular area. In this it appears to be different from Maharashtra where a single caste, the Maratha, enjoys dominance, or Mysore where dominance is shared between two castes, the Lingayat and the Okkaliga.

The relationship between non-Brahmin dominant castes is important at every level of contemporary Tamil politics but in a special sense at the local level, particularly the village. Where the non-Brahmins operate as a single unit, they do so generally in opposition to the Brahmins (and today, increasingly, to the Harijans). In the vast majority of Tamil villages there are either no Brahmins or only a few families of priestly Brahmins who are politically insignificant.[40] In non-*agraharam* villages, which constitute the overwhelming majority of villages in Tamilnadu, the primary cleavages are often between two non-Brahmin castes or between two sub-castes of a single non-Brahmin caste. (The relationship between non-Brahmins and Harijans in such villages will be considered later.)

Fairly powerful associations began to emerge among certain non-Brahmin castes from the end of the last century. These associations addressed themselves to social reform within the caste and sought to secure a better position for the caste in the wider society. A good example is the Nadar Sangam in the southern districts which agitated successfully for the rights of temple entry for the Nadars. Such associations have occasionally provided useful bases for the mobilization of political support. How this could be done was demonstrated effectively by the Vanniyakkula Kshatriya Sangam (a caste association), whose two principal branches transformed themselves into political parties (Tamilnadu Toilers' Party and Commonweal Party), fought the 1952 elections and bargained with the Congress for positions in the State Cabinet.[41]

The Vanniyakkula Kshatriya Sangam appears to have remained politically inactive for a long time but was again revived on the eve of the 1967 elections. The southern district of Ramnad has been a stronghold of the Forward Block which is dominated by the Thevar caste and is generally referred to as the Thevar Party. This kind of association between a particular caste and a political party appears, however, to be exceptional rather than general. Caste interests – whatever their nature – are articulated more commonly through informal networks of interpersonal relations than through formally organized caste associations. A caste which is dominant in a particular district or *taluka* is likely to find strong representation in local bodies as well as in local units of the major political parties. This is so for two reasons. The dominant caste in a district or *taluka* is almost always a caste which enjoys numerical preponderance. Hence even if recruitment were made on a purely random basis, its representation would be high. But political recruitment is not made on a random basis. Ties of kinship and affinity and other personal ties play a very important part in this process at the local level where the syncretic unity of a caste or sub-caste is fairly strong. This unity tends to give additional weight to the representation of the dominant caste in local politics.

Thus *panchayats*, Panchayat Union Councils and local units of the Congress and DMK parties are likely to be dominated in South Arcot district by Padayachis, in Coimbatore district by Gaundas and in large areas of Tanjore district by Kallas.

The dominant caste operates in the political process not only through networks of interpersonal relations but also by virtue of an idiom which has come to be accepted by almost every section of Tamil society. A feeling has grown among people that members of non-dominant castes cannot compete successfully with those of the dominant caste. Political parties act on the basis of this feeling and are often unprepared to take the risk of setting up candidates from the non-dominant castes. Out of this has emerged the familiar electoral pattern of matching caste with caste. I am not able to provide figures to show exactly how far this is true but there is little doubt that the feature is a very general one. Later I shall discuss in some detail the manner in which it has worked in a particular Assembly constituency.

In what way is caste utilized for the mobilzation of political support? At the village level leaders of the dominant caste have direct ties of kinship and affinity with their caste-fellows. Such ties may also play an important part at the level of the Assembly constituency. But electioneering at that level also involves a more general appeal to caste sentiments. A typical example is the election slogan quoted earlier: the Vanniya vote is for Vanniyas alone.

The Vanniyas provide only an extreme example of what was a very general pattern in the 1962 (and other) elections. Every-where people discuss the chances of candidates in terms of their caste affiliation. To take the example of the key constituency of Sattur where two dominant castes, the Nadars and the Thevars, rallied round the two principal candidates:

> The intensity of communal feelings is evident from the fact that people irrespective of political affiliation are openly discussing the polling of votes on a communal basis. In Sattur, an enthusiastic Nadar worker confessed that he was a D.M.K. follower, but because he belonged to the Nadar community he would vote for Mr. Kamraj (a Nadar). Not a single Nadar vote, he added, would go to a non-Nadar.[42]

I now come to the Thiruvaiyar Assembly constituency in Tanjore district where I was able to watch developments during the 1962 General Elections. This is a Kalla area, the Kallas accounting for about 30% of the total population. They have a strong feeling of identity in relation to outsiders and Kalla leaders in the area have close contacts with influential Kallas in every village. In the 1962 elections three parties put up candidates for the Assembly seat, the Congress, the DMK and the PSP. All three candidates were Kallas. Since 1952, when the

First General Elections were held, only Kalla candidates have been successful at the polls. In 1952 the Congress put up an influential Muslim candidate but he was defeated by a Kalla. In 1957 the Congress changed its tactics, put up a Kalla candidate and won the seat. In 1962 the Congress again won the seat but with a different Kalla candidate. In 1967 the sitting member was defeated by a Kalla candidate put up by the DMK.

My first insight into Kalla politics was gained from a Kalla lawyer who had earlier contested the Thiruvaiyar seat. He began by saying that the much publicized unity of the Kallas was largely an illusion. This unity manifested itself only on certain occasions: in fact, in relation to other non-Brahmins, the three closely related castes, Kalla, Marava and Ahamudiya, often acted as if they were one. But in the heart of the Kalla area there were deep rivalries between villages in which different groups of Kallas were dominant. Even a single village, he said, may be sharply divided between different lineages of the same Kalla sub-caste. Thus here again we see the operation of the segmentary principle. In certain contexts all non-Brahmins might act as a unit; in other contexts the three castes, Kalla, Marava and Ahamudiya, act as a unit in opposition to other non-Brahmin castes; in still other contexts Kallas may be ranged against Ahamudiyas, or segments of the Kalla caste against one another.

So far I have not considered the Harijans as a distinct entity in relation to the non-Brahmins. As indicated earlier, a good deal of ambiguity attaches to the term 'Non-Brahmin' which by definition constitutes a residual category. A more precise term would no doubt be preferable to it but for its historical association with political movements and parties which have played a most important part in South India.

The Manifesto of 1916 used the term non-Brahmin in its most inclusive sense, to cover not only Muslims and Christians but also the Depressed Classes. In his address to the non-Brahmin Conference in July 1921, K.V. Reddi Naidu said, 'The great Non-Brahmin movement transcends over caste, over religion and over the language . . . . It really transcended caste and religion, and there were assembled Mohammedans, Christians,

Hindus and Panchamas'.[43] Other non-Brahmin leaders also made occasional references to the Depressed Classes and the need for ameliorating their conditions of life.

For all this, the separateness of the Depressed Classes remained a persistent feature of social and political life in Madras. They had hardly any representation in the leadership of the Justice Party; this is not surprising in view of the limited social base of the Party to which attention was earlier drawn. In the Memorandum presented to the Joint Parliamentary Committee in 1919 by the non-Brahmin delegation, the Depressed Classes were listed separately from the non-Brahmins in the Table showing the population analysis of Madras Presidency. Further, the separateness of the Depressed Classes was given implicit recognition in the Constitution of 1919 in which five seats were reserved for them, to be filled through nomination by the Governor.

It is difficult to say how far the policy of separate representation for the Depressed Classes adopted by the British fostered a spirit of alienation among them as Gandhi had feared it would. But it seems clear that, given the inherent cleavages of Tamil social structure and the general atmosphere of 'communal' politics, the Harijans could hardly fail to emphasize the special character of their social and political needs. But their political demands were to remain unorganized for a long time. During the first three decades of the present century organized politics was largely the prerogative of the Western educated urban middle class and the representation of the Harijans in this class was negligible.

It is to some extent an accident of history that in Maharashtra the Harijans found a leader of the stature of Dr Ambedkar who succeeded within a fairly short time in investing them with a degree of political consciousness on the whole absent elsewhere. In the meantime the British themselves gave some measure of protection to Harijan interests for a variety of reasons. In Madras there were also a few Western educated Harijan leaders, notably M.C. Raja and Dewan Bahadur Srinivasan; the latter was chosen to represent his community at the Round Table Conference in 1930-2 along with Dr Ambedkar. For all this, the Harijans had to await the extension of the franchise after independence before making their impact felt as a significant force in the politics of Tamilnadu.

The issue of civic rights has played a major part in the politicization of the Harijans in Tamilnadu. Among the non-Brahmins politicization was spearheaded by a Western educated urban middle class. Such a class did not exist among the Harijans in Tamilnadu. In their case it was more the ferment caused by the introduction (largely from outside) of liberal social values and the confrontation of these values with the traditional interests of the dominant castes which created the basis for organized political action. In the traditional system the Harijans had accepted their disabilities as a matter of course. As these disabilities came to be removed by law and as the Harijans sought to translate the new laws into practice, they came increasingly into conflict with the organized opposition of the dominant castes.

The disabilities from which the Depressed Classes suffered with regard to the use of amenities such as wells, roads and temples, or status symbols such as dress and ornaments, were generally more severe in Madras Presidency than elsewhere. Under the liberating influences of British rule and Gandhism the Harijans made attempts to do away with some of these disabilities. These attempts often met with reprisal from the dominant castes. In Tamilnadu, Ramnad district has been a major arena of conflict, although such conflict has been a pervasive feature of the relations between non-Brahmins and Harijans throughout the State during the last three decades.

For all the stubborn opposition of some dominant non-Brahmin castes, the Harijans have forged rapidly ahead in their bid for civic equality. But their journey has been by no means smooth or easy; the price of every significant advance has been a measure of violence. Today one can perceive everywhere a change of mood among them, particularly among those of the younger generation. In Tanjore district and elsewhere young Harijans acquired a taste of organized politics in the 1950s when their support was mobilized by the Communists and the DK against the Brahmin landowners. Independence, and subsequently four General Elections, have made the Harijans sensitive to their political rights and today they are no longer in a mood to have their houses burnt or their property destroyed without retaliation.

The introduction of adult franchise changed their political situation more radically than was the case with any comparable section of Tamil society. Although fewer in number than the non-Brahmins, they account for no less than 18% of the population of Tamilnadu. Their situation in relation to the non-Brahmins is, therefore, rather different from that of the Brahmins who constitute only about 3% of the total population. There are *talukas* in Tamilnadu where Harijans are matched fairly evenly with non-Brahmins and now a few villages in which they out-number them.

Along with their strength of numbers, the Harijans also evince a high degree of unity. There are still many diacritical differences between them and the non-Brahmins and their internal solidarity in relation to the latter is often very strong. This internal solidarity derives from many factors of which I shall here consider only one. In the Tanjore-Trichy area (and elsewhere too, though perhaps less noticeably) their unique position in rural society is made clearly visible in the settlement pattern of the village. They live in separate streets, known by a separate term, *cheri*, which are generally at some distance from the main village; frequently they are situated in the midst of paddy fields at a distance of three to four furlongs from the village centre. Further, the layout of these *cheris* differs significantly from that of the main village, so that two *cheris* which are physically contiguous and form a single social unit may be attached to two revenue villages which are quite distinct from each other. These *cheris* are linked by social and political ties which often cut across the boundaries of the 'village' as this is perceived by non-Brahmins or Brahmins.[44]

Perhaps because of the physical isolation of the Harijans, traditional caste organizations seem to have survived to a greater extent among them than among other castes. At least in those areas of Tanjore district which I came to know directly, the traditional *kuttam* of the Pallas and their leaders, the *nattanmaikkarans*, still exercise a measure of authority, whereas similar institutions which once existed among some of the non-Brahmins are now no longer to be found. The existence of these traditional institutions often facilitates the mobilization of support by Harijan leaders on a caste basis.

Along with numerical strength and organization, the Harijans are also able to carry a certain measure of violence into political life. The role of organized violence in politics, particularly local politics, has not been sufficiently stressed in studies made in India so far. Yet the support of people with a reputation for violence is an important factor in village politics in contemporary India. In Tamilnadu the Brahmins find the odds heavily against them in this regard. Nothing is more repugnant to the Western educated Brahmin than to be engaged in a village brawl with members of the lower castes. Such consideration of self-esteem do not deter the Harijan from confronting the non-Brahmins.

However, although the Harijans constitute important reservoirs of political power, there are many factors which stand in the way of this power being actualized. Their economic position is in general very weak and this weakness is frequently used against them by the non-Brahmins. A long tradition of servility often prevents them from asserting their rights, although young Harijans are rapidly developing a spirit of challenge. Finally, lack of education and contact with the outside world stands in the way of their developing some of the skills which are essential for organized politics.

In Tanjore district the Communist Party and the Dravida Kazhagam have both played a part in the politicization of the Harijans. An active *kisan* Movement was launched in the early 1950s and Mannargudi *taluka* became for a brief period the venue of bitter political strife. Young Harijan agricultural labourers were widely mobilized by the Communists who at that time collaborated with the DK. The *kisan* Movement subsided after a short while and the Harijans soon realized that they were up against something far more powerful than a few Brahmin *mirasdars*: when they tried to challenge the landed interests of the dominant non-Brahmin castes, they were put down with a heavy hand. None the less, the experience of the early 1950s has had some effect in kindling a spirit of challenge among them.

When this spirit of challenge confronts the entrenched interests of the dominant castes, the result is often a measure of violence. In the area around Sripuram where I did fieldwork, the Kallas constitute the dominant caste and they are feared throughout Tamilnadu for their violent ways. Relations between the Kallas and the Harijans have been strained for some time. In the village *panchayat* of Sripuram, the Harijans have five members against six non-Brahmins and they generally have a submissive attitude towards the Kalla President of the *panchayat*. In fact, meetings of the *panchayat* are often held without the Harijan members being informed, and the latter are too weak to protest against this kind of irregularity. In the adjacent village of Ponavasal, however, things are very different: the Harijans are in a majority in the *panchayat* and the *panchayat* President is himself a Harijan.

In another neighbouring village also the *panchayat* President is a Harijan. In this village, known as Maharajapuram, hostilities between Harijans and Kallas led to the murder of a Kalla landowner, allegedly by or through the collusion of the Harijan President of the *panchayat*. Some of the Harijan residents of the village were arrested and the Kallas tried to storm the court room at Tanjore in order to do violence to them.[45]

Certain sections of the non-Brahmins are becoming deeply resentful of the militant attitudes of the Harijans which, in their view, are fostered by the ruling party and the Government. For the poor and the landless non-Brahmins, the concessions to which the Harijans are entitled by law are a thorn in the flesh. For the landowners of the dominant caste, the rising demands of Harijan tenants and labourers appear as threats to their social and economic position. It is clear that the dominant castes in the villages are by no means reconciled to the high ideals of equality and social justice which seem to motivate legislatures at the State and the Centre. These conflicts are likely to persist irrespective of changes in the party in power. And the party leaders in their turn cannot afford to ignore the demands of the Harijans who constitute such an important reservoir of votes.

Old conflicts between the Harijans and the non-Brahmins are sometimes expressed in the new idiom of party politics. Ramnad district became the centre of turmoil in 1957 when riots broke out between the Harijans and the Thevars (who are closely related to the Kallas discussed above). This time the issue was a by-election in which the Harijans supported the

Congress candidate against a Forward Block candidate set up by the Thevars. A young Harijan leader called Immanuel was murdered because he is said to have insulted the much-respected Thevar Forward Block leader, U. Muthuramalinga Thevar. The Thevars were put down with a heavy hand by the Government, allegedly because they had consistently opposed the Congress party then in power.[46]

The politicization of the Harijans has, in a sense, helped to sharpen their identity in relation to the upper castes. But it has also drawn them into new networks of relationships which repeatedly cut across the barriers of caste. Harijan and non-Brahmin leaders have learnt to depend upon each other for support and patronage. New forms of association such as parties and *panchayats* are developing which are based on other loyalties than those of caste. It is true that such associations often mirror the cleavages of the wider society but there are clear indications that this is by no means always the case.

In the foregoing I have given an account of the part played by social entities of a certain kind in the political life of Tamilnadu. These entities are variously referred to as sub-castes, castes or caste-groups. Although there are enormous differences between a sub-caste such as the Vadama Smarthas and a broad aggregate such as the non-Brahmins, they are similar in one important respect: they are both based on particularistic criteria and as such are to be distinguished from universalistic groupings of the kind which democratic parties and governments are in principle supposed to be. In India, where particularistic groupings occupied such an important position in the traditional system, it would be unreal to expect the democratic process to operate without taking any account of them. But are such particularistic identities the only ones which are relevant to politics in India today? And does not the political process itself create new identities which cut across those of sub-caste, caste or caste-group?

Although most scholars would agree that caste and politics are closely related in certain parts of contemporary India, their assessment of the significance of this is likely to vary. There are some, like Srinivas, who would be inclined to argue that the political process tends to strengthen the loyalties of caste at least in the short run: 'One of the short-term effects of universal adult franchise is to strengthen caste'.[47] There are others like Gough who would argue that politics in the modern sense tends to be disruptive of caste.[48]

Before turning to these questions, it is well to remember that there are everywhere in India today forces external to the political system which tend to erode the loyalties of caste. I shall consider briefly some of the factors which, on the one hand, weaken the diacritical and syncretic unity of caste and, on the other, create interests based on income, occupation, education, etc., which tend increasingly to become dissociated from the structure of caste.

Castes can best be viewed as status groups and as such they should be distinguished from classes. As status groups, castes are differentiated from one another through the pursuit by tradition of distinctive styles of life. Over the last hundred years new criteria of social differentiation have been introduced – Western education, occupation in non-traditional sectors and so on. To the extent that the new forms of differentiation run along traditional grooves, caste loyalties tend to be reinforced. We saw how the introduction of Western education at first served to increase the social differentiation between Brahmins and non-Brahmins, leading to political conflict between them. However, when the new forms of differentiation cut across traditional ones, the loyalties of caste may be weakened. And there is little doubt that castes are becoming more and more heterogeneous in terms of income, occupation and education and that new status groups based on these criteria are likely to compete with caste for people's loyalties.

It appears that caste is less crucial to one's status identification in urban as compared with rural areas. In the cities, Brahmins frequently work with non-Brahmins in the same professions, live in the same neighbourhoods and send their children to the same schools. Such people are likely in their styles of life to have more in common with one another than with their caste fellows in the rural areas, although it must at once be pointed out that traditional patterns of behaviour tend to show remarkable persistence in Tamilnadu. Even though urban,

Western educated professional Brahmins and non-Brahmins do share many common patterns of behaviour, they are mutually differentiated with regard to many others.

It is probable that caste plays a less important part in urban than in rural politics. A recent study of trade union politics in Coimbatore tends to confirm the view that caste enters into the political process there in only a marginal way.[50] Among textile workers in Coimbatore, income, occupation and personal loyalties tend to play a far more important part in the determination of political attitude than caste. The factory system tends to break down the homogeneity of caste and to replace its unity by unities of a different kind.

The political process seems to have a dual effect on the caste system. To the extent that the loyalties of caste or sub-caste are consistently exploited, the traditional structure tends to become frozen. Thus there can be little doubt that the Non-Brahmin Movement arrested to some extent the attenuation of caste identities by driving a wedge between Brahmins and non-Brahmins. But the political process – whether in Tamilnadu or elsewhere – does not operate by mobilizing only the loyalties of caste. To the extent that it leads to new forms of association and new alliances cutting across caste, it tends to loosen the traditional structure.

There are some who have gone even further and argued that the political process destroys irrevocably the very nature of caste. Leach raises the question, 'If a caste group turns itself into a political faction does it then cease to be a caste?'[51] He answers the question with a clear affirmative, but his answer is based on a peculiarly personal view of caste: 'People of different castes are, as it were, of different species – as cat and dog . . . . But with members of different grades of the same caste, the exact opposite is the case'.[52] Enough has been said earlier about the manner in which castes are divided and subdivided to expose the futility of trying to impose a radical opposition between 'different castes' and 'different grades of the same caste'.

In Leach's view, competition for power is antithetical to the very nature of caste and consequently wherever castes act 'in competition against like groups of different castes . . . they are acting in defiance of caste principles'.[53] In a democratic system virtually any kind of social identity may be used as a basis for mobilizing political support and it is difficult to deny that caste continues to play a major part in this regard in Tamilnadu today. It is equally difficult to see how a particular mode of social grouping becomes its very antithesis by the sole fact of engaging in competition with groupings of a like order. To quote an earlier statement:

> The continuity of the politically organized castes of today with their forebears is not simply one of habits and tradition, but also one of personnel. Shall we say that as soon as people start talking about the "Padayachi vote", the Padayachis cease to be a caste, and become its antithesis? What shall we call them then?[54]

While some have emphasized the role of caste in Indian politics there are others who have drawn attention to the part played in it by factions. Brass has characterized Indian politics as a politics of factional bargains.[55] In many ways factional politics may be contrasted with caste politics. A faction is generally mixed in its caste composition and factional loyalties cut across caste. It happens very rarely that groups which contend for power are homogeneous in their caste composition. A political unit, if it is to be viable, has generally to draw its support from a number of castes and not just one. Conversely, a caste whose members enjoy social prominence is likely to be divided by rival contenders for power. But even when a caste is divided by factions, support within the faction may still be partially drawn on the basis of caste. Faction leaders often choose their inner circle from among persons who enjoy some support in their respective castes. When two rival groups are similar in their caste composition it does not follow that their leaders cease to appeal to caste in their efforts to undercut each other's support.

There are various ways in which participation in organized politics tends to alter the structure of caste, although the processes by which this comes about are only now beginning to be investigated. Rudolph and Rudolph have drawn attention to an important change which accompanies the emergence of caste associations. A caste association is no longer a birth status group in which membership is automatically ascribed at birth; membership in a caste association has to be acquired, although the base of recruitment may be restricted to a single caste or a group of castes.[56]

Party programmes can have significant consequences for the unity of caste. They may, and increasingly do, lead to splits within a caste and to alliances across castes. It is thus important to investigate not only how caste acts upon the political system but also how the latter acts upon caste.

Political alliances between castes and between castes and political parties tend to be rather unstable. Sub-castes, castes or caste-groups which are in the same camp today may find themselves in opposite camps tomorrow. It is perhaps becoming less and less common for the same caste or sub-caste to identify itself persistently with a particular political party or movement over any significant length of time. And to the extent that a caste does not identify itself persistently with any particular party but tends to divide and sub-divide and to enter into multifarious alliances across its boundaries, its very contours ultimately become blurred.

Politicians of every kind in Tamilnadu have learnt to manipulate caste in the furtherance of their interests. But politics is a dynamic phenomenon and the politician whose only skill is caste politics is likely to become obsolete. In this context what Dahl says of ethnic politics in the USA is particularly relevant: 'In order to retain their positions, politicians are forced to search for new issues, new strategies, new coalitions'.[57] This is in many ways as true of caste politics in India as of ethnic politics in the USA.

The disruptive effects on caste of flexible and changing political arrangements must not be exaggerated. It is true that political parties tend to cut across caste but so do factions and, as Brass has rightly pointed out, factions are a feature of the traditional order.[58] Caste loyalties have persisted in spite of decades of factional politics and it is unlikely that party politics by itself will lead to their immediate dissolution. This is not to deny the significance of parties and other differentiated structures which now operate in addition to factions, but only to draw attention to certain persistent elements in the cultural idiom of Indian society in general and Tamil society in particular.

Parties, to the extent that they are responsible for the aggregation of interests, tend increasingly to cut through the organization of caste, uniting people belonging to different castes and dividing those belonging to the same caste. Everywhere leaders of the dominant caste try to capture the major political parties and this is rarely if ever done on a basis of planned, mutual understanding. Parties in their turn try to create an appeal for every major group and not merely a single group. As Lipset has argued, 'A stable democracy requires a situation in which all the major political parties include supporters from many segments of the population'.[59]

The relevance of Lipset's argument to Tamilnadu politics can be illustrated with a brief consideration of the changing relations between the Brahmins and the DMK. When the DMK started its career as a separate political party in 1949, its leaders were closely associated in the popular mind with anti-Brahminism. The party decided to start with a clean slate, declared itself against discrimination and even offered to accept Brahmins as members. The Brahmins remained for a long time suspicious of the new party and were not in any case much in sympathy with either its style or its policies. However, in 1962 the DMK emerged as one of the strongest Opposition parties in any state, and this it did only *after* it had come to terms with the Brahmins and shown itself prepared to treat them with consideration. In fact, in more than one constituency the DMK owed its success to Brahmin support. In 1967 Brahmin support for the DMK was, if anything, even more enthusiastic. Today the Brahmins' attitude towards the DMK is very different from what it was in 1957 although even now not all of them are its ardent supporters. Even the Congress, which has in recent years alienated itself so much from the Brahmins, set up Brahmin candidates in certain constituencies and gathered Brahmin votes.

Today the political system is becoming increasingly differentiated. This does not, of course, mean that it is unrelated to caste and class or that it will be so in the near future. But as the political system becomes more and more differentiated, new loci of power develop and these tend to acquire a weight of their own. In the past – at least at the local level – dominant caste and faction were probably the only significant loci of power,

and the faction itself was largely structured by caste. With
the development of Panchayati Raj and political parties and
machines of various kinds, this is no longer the case. Today
it is possible for a man to acquire a certain measure of power
by virtue of his position in the party hierarchy, irrespective of
his caste or class. No doubt membership of the dominant caste
helps a great deal, but other factors are also becoming important.
A fuller understanding of politics in Tamilnadu can be achieved
only by considering the changing relations between caste, class
and party in addition to other major sources of power.

5 The politics of 'non-antagonistic' strata

In recent years social anthropologists have developed a certain conception or 'model' of traditional Indian society based primarily on a set of ideas elaborated in the classical Hindu texts. This conception has come to play an important part in the interpretation of social life in India in both historical and contemporary times. I propose to examine the basic ideas underlying it and its usefulness as a scheme of analysis, particularly in regard to what can broadly be described as political activity.

I shall begin by describing some of the main features of the model. (1) It is based primarily on the ideas held or expressed by certain sections of society and not on the observed or recorded behaviour of people. (2) It attaches a kind of primary and universal significance to caste as this has been conceived in the classical texts. (3) The entire system is viewed as being governed by certain more or less explicitly formulated principles or 'rules of the game'. (4) The different castes which are the basic units in the system are conceived as fulfilling complementary functions and their mutual relations as being 'non-antagonistic'.

There is no question that this model brings into focus some of the most important features of traditional India society. Its utility has been amply demonstrated in the works of Louis Dumont, particularly in his recent impressive analysis of the values of traditional Indian society (see Dumont, 1966). However, there are two dangers in the use of a model of this kind. When it is made too general it can be applied to almost every society and therefore does not tell us very much about the specific properties of any society: I shall illustrate this point later with a brief comparison of traditional Indian society with contemporary socialist societies. When, on the other hand, the model is made too specific it fails to take into account certain crucial features of economic and political life.

The strength and the weakness of this model, which has been most systematically elaborated by Dumont, is that it is concerned essentially with ideas and values. As such it has been most successful in the interpretation of systems of religious belief. It has failed, however, to give its proper place to material interests in social life. For this reason its application to the analysis of political and economic problems leads to major distortions of social reality.

The purpose of this paper is not to deny the validity of a sociology of values and ideas. It is rather to draw attention to another realm of social reality, that of material interests, which has been somewhat neglected, particularly in studies of traditional society and culture in India. Interests not only exist as much as values and ideas but can also be represented as structures. A comprehensive sociology of India must give their proper place to both values and interests for it is the dialectical relation between these two which gives to human societies their distinctive qualities.

As I have mentioned, two major sources of distortion in our understanding of Indian society are the overriding importance given in it to caste, and the conception of caste itself as a system of non-antagonistic groups having complementary functions and each enjoying its own set of privileges. When the basic groups in the social system are defined as being non-antagonistic very little room is left for the analysis of either conflict or change. In fact, this conception of Indian society is only one step short of the popular nineteenth century view of it as integrated, harmonious and unchanging.

Social anthropologists have done much to popularize the view of Indian society as a 'caste society'. This emphasis is partly dictated by the preoccupation with native categories of thought rather than the dynamics of real life. The classical Hindu texts give a much fuller elaboration of fundamental religious values than of the interplay of material interests in the relations between individuals and groups. Field studies by social anthropologists have also attached overwhelming importance to caste. Caste groups being both visible and mutually exclusive are relatively easy to describe and it is natural that they have attracted the attention of European and American scholars seeking new insights from an alien society.

It is in some contexts unavoidable to characterize total societies in terms of a unique structural principle. Thus, one speaks of medieval Europe as an 'estate society', of the modern West as a 'class society' and correspondingly of traditional India as a 'caste society'. For certain purposes such characterizations are useful but they can also be misleading. They tend to focus attention on one particular aspect of a society and to divert attention from the others. The view that traditional Indian society was a caste society together with the definition of caste in terms of a set of ideal principles has led to the construction of models from which economic and political conflict have been virtually excluded. One has either to adopt a broader conception of caste or to take into account other principles of organization in addition to those of caste. In doing this one will have to devise conceptual categories which will apply to both traditional and modern India.

It is hardly necessary to repeat that even in traditional India control over property was not always dependent on caste (see, for instance, Metcalfe, 1969, pp. 133-41). As such, the relations of production had a certain autonomy although they were often subsumed by caste. The distribution of power was likewise partially independent of caste particularly at higher levels of territorial organization than the village. It would thus be a mistake to try to understand traditional Indian society solely in terms of the rules of intercaste relations. Conversely, in 'class societies' such as modern America, religious and ethnic divisions are not only partly independent of class but also govern social and political life in important ways. A scheme which seeks to reduce every aspect of social reality to a single principle of organization cannot account either for the diversity of facts or for changes in patterns of organization and can present only a flat, monotonous and one-dimensional picture of social life. In short, it is misleading to represent India as a 'caste society' in the same way and for the same reason as it is misleading to characterize the United States as a 'class society'.

I now turn to the view that caste is a system in which the relations

between groups are non-competitive and from which antagonism and conflict are in principle excluded. This view has been
tersely put forward by Leach who maintains that 'wherever caste
groups are seen to be acting as corporations in competition
against like groups of *different castes*, then they are acting in
defiance of caste principles'(1960, p. 7). There is further
the suggestion that in such cases these groups are acting
in accordance with class principles. This way of contrasting
caste with class seems to me to be based on a rather uncritical
acceptance of the classical Hindu view of Indian society (in
which all is harmony) and the Western radical view of capitalist
society (in which all is contradiction).

Much the same view has been put forward by Bailey who
speaks of castes as groups 'which co-operate and do not
compete'(1963, p. 121).[1] It is, of course, possible in theory
to define the systematic properties of caste in such a way as
to exclude both competition and conflict and indeed this would
correspond very well with the representation of it in classical
Hindu texts. But the question is, how far one can proceed in
the understanding of economic and political life in India on
the basis of such a definition. Very few anthropologists would
seriously contend that competition, conflict or even politics was
absent from real life in the traditional set-up. How, then, was
competition organized in the past? What were the social bases
of conflict? Did caste play no part whatever in the organization
of mutually opposed factions or political groups? Such questions
can be fully answered only by empirical research but it should be
possible to clarify certain issues deductively.

Both Leach and Bailey have sought to accommodate competition and conflict in their models of the caste system. Leach has
done this by means of a radical opposition between castes and
what he calls 'grades within a single caste'. Between different
castes there can be no competition, whereas the exact opposite
is the case between different grades of the same caste. 'In this
respect grades within a single caste have the nature of social
classes rather than of castes' (Leach, 1960, p. 7).

Leach's attempt to invest the caste system with a semblance
of vitality by contrasting caste grade with caste is bold but
not convincing. Having found the ideal conception of caste

insufficient for explaining politics, he invents the notion of caste grade but the classical texts themselves do not make any distinction between the two, and both Dumont (1966, pp. 85-90) and I (Béteille, 1964, pp. 130-4) have suggested why this distinction is inappropriate. Leach rejects Yalman's treatment of 'distinctions in grade within a single named caste as different only in degree from distinctions between separate named castes' (1960, p. 7) but gives no convincing reason for doing so. Those who have done field research in India would surely support Yalman and not Leach.

Bailey's attempt to accommodate politics in his model of caste resembles that of Leach up to a point but it has wider theoretical implications. In his scheme the basic distinction is between the dominant caste and subordinate castes. 'Only the dominant caste has an autonomous political existence, not as a corporate political group, but as [a] field for political competition. Certainly no subordinate caste is a corporate political group' (1963, p. 118). We might add that a social entity need not be a corporate group in order to be politically significant. Lineages in tribal societies, classes in modern society or racial groups where they co-exist often play a significant part in ordering political relations without always being corporate groups.

Bailey argues that 'political cleavages (i.e. competitive relationships) are between vertical groups, not social strata: cooperative relationships run up and down between families in the dominant caste and families in the service castes' (1963, p. 118). This seems to suggest a classification of societies into two broad kinds, those in which conflict takes place between strata and those in which it is contained within the dominant stratum. Marxian sociologists in the East European countries sometimes use a similar scheme for differentiating 'class societies' from societies of other kinds. I do not believe that such a distinction is always useful and I shall try to justify my misgivings by examining certain assumptions implicit in Bailey's formulation.

When Bailey argues that 'only the dominant caste has an autonomous existence' as a 'field for political competition', he assumes that every area has always a single dominant caste. How are we to define the terms of competition when a village has more than one dominant caste? This is only partly a question of terminology. Suppose in a single village Smartha and Shri Vaishnava Brahmins are evenly matched in terms of numbers and control over land: are we to regard them as two separate castes or as 'two grades of the same caste'? Suppose, instead, they are Jats and Ahirs: can we reasonably extend the meaning of 'caste' far enough to regard them as two sections of the same unit?

However broadly we may define the term 'caste', there is no reason to assume that every village has a single dominant caste or that the presence of more than one dominant caste in a village is of recent origin. It is well known, for instance, that in Tanjore district *agraharams* were set up in villages which had pre-established communities of landowning non-Brahmins; later, Maratha Kshatriyas were granted land and occasionally settled in villages where *agraharams* were already in existence. Thus the balance of power between castes in a village might be altered from above. It might also change due to internal causes such as differential birth and death rates or differential rates of migration. Adrian Mayer (1955, p. 1147) gives the example of a village where Rajputs are now dominant but where formerly they shared dominance with Dhakars. I am not sure whether Leach would consider Dhakars and Rajputs as grades within a single caste or whether Bailey would regard them as belonging to the same stratum.

Once we leave the village and enter into wider territorial fields it becomes increasingly clear that we have to deal with not one but a number of dominant castes. Even in a small chiefdom the dominant castes might range from Brahmins and Rajputs to fairly low peasant castes. Srinivas has recently brought together a body of evidence to show how the fluidity of political boundaries in the past enabled different groups to compete for power (see Srinivas, 1966). It is unlikely that rival groups when of different castes did not draw upon the loyalties of caste in competitions of this kind.

A recent case study by Frykenberg shows effectively that the allocation of power between castes was much more differentiated and fluid than is allowed for in the schemes discussed above (see Frykenberg, 1965). This analysis of Guntur district between 1788 and 1848 reveals the existence of several loci of power:

landownership, the official bureaucracy, and so on. It also shows that these were controlled and used by members of a succession of different castes such as Nyogi Brahmins, Desastha Brahmins, Velamas and Kammas. Frykenberg centres his study around the administrative bureaucracy and shows how the Desastha Brahmins used the ties of caste to keep it within their control. But he also tells us that in the earlier phase the Desasthas had to contend for power with the *zamindars* many of whom were not Brahmins at all but Kammas, Velamas and Rajus. This structure of competition was evidently not created *ex nihilo* by British rule, since an official bureaucracy (controlled generally by Brahmins) had been in existence during the Maratha period and earlier.

One may, of course, argue that in Guntur district Desastha officials and Kamma or Velama *zamindars* contended for power not as castes but in accordance with the rules of a different system. That, as we have seen, is one way of defining caste and it is impossible to argue against a definition except by showing where it limits or obstructs analysis. What is important is that officials and landowners both used the ties of caste (as well as other ties) in gathering support to further their respective material interests.

To make a radical distinction between the dominant caste (as constituting the field for political competition) and subordinate castes is to prejudge the basic issue, i.e. that of the distribution of power between different castes. It is to assume that a caste, once dominant, remains in that position for all time. What the sociologist and more particularly the social historian has to study is how one caste is displaced by another from its position of dominance. My argument against this approach to the problem is that it is static and assumes a fixed and immutable distribution of power between castes. It leaves no room for changes in the power positions of castes which are an important feature of both traditional and contemporary Indian society.

The analysis of political life is concerned to a large extent with material interests whose demands are often at variance with the ideal values of a society. The initial conception of caste as a system in which groups 'cooperate and do not compete' can hardly do justice to this type of analysis. The attempt to save the conception by introducing artificial distinctions between castes and caste grades (or between dominant and subordinate castes) leads to ambiguities and inconsistencies of the kind I have indicated above.

I have said already that some scholars make a distinction between two kinds of society. In the first, the basic political cleavage is between vertical groups each of which is composed of a similar set of strata; in the second, the principal cleavage is between the strata themselves. Caste and estate societies are viewed as examples of the former and class societies of the latter. I now propose to examine briefly the validity of this dichotomy.

The dichotomy rests on the assumption that in estate and caste societies the arena of politics is narrow whereas in class societies it is greatly extended. This is a valid distinction and it is particularly relevant in the comparison of formal political institutions. It is true that in traditional societies support was to a great extent determined by pre-existing relations of patronage so that the principal contenders for power were either rival barons or rival leaders of the dominant caste (or castes) each with his respective set of followers. Traditional societies of either kind provided limited scope for people to switch their support from one leader (or faction) to another.

It has been argued that the distinctive feature of politics in modern Western societies is that there the government is "put in a kind of market situation" (Macpherson, 1966, p. 8). Individuals and groups are able to exercise choice in giving power to some and withholding it from others. The exercise of this choice is formalized through the institutions of representative government, plurality of parties and freedom of association. While undoubtedly these institutions give a distinctive character to modern democratic systems they do not by themselves define the nature of politics. In any event one must not exaggerate either the freedom of political choice in the modern West or its absence in traditional societies. Social anthropologists working in Africa have been led to give a more comprehensive meaning to the term 'politics', one which is better suited to an understanding of the working of traditional societies including pre-British India.

Each society is characterized at a given moment by a certain distribution of power. In one sense politics is the expression of tensions between those who seek to maintain this distribution (in order to use it for various ends) and those who seek to change it. Admittedly, the limits within which changes are sought to be made are highly variable. At one end are attempts to replace one set of incumbents by another; at the other, to transform the very nature of the roles themselves. I am not sure that it is always possible to draw a clear line between the two sets of phenomena, between what Gluckman calls 'rebellion' and 'revolution' or what Duverger calls 'lutte dans le régime' and 'lutte sur le régime'. Conflict over a régime is perhaps exceptional and occurs only at certain moments in history; conflict within a régime is an inherent feature of all political systems, traditional as well as modern.

In order to maintain themselves in power individuals and groups require support. This support they obtain by drawing upon the ties of kinship, caste, religion, race and class, or by appealing to some more universal loyalty. Comparative studies of political systems have clearly established that support does not flow automatically in any society. Even where people appear to be rigidly bound by custom, it has to be actively sought and cultivated. This is as true of the Zulu under Shaka as of present regimes in the West. There is little reason to believe that in traditional India leaders of the dominant caste could always count on the automatic support of members of subordinate castes; or that the latter never transferred support from leaders of one dominant caste to another, altering thereby the distribution of power between castes.

Any conception of politics presupposes a certain indeterminacy both in the composition of groups wielding power and in the support they are able to command. Politics in this sense is a universal feature of all human societies; one cannot picture a society in which choice and uncertainty in the pursuit of material interest are totally absent. Such a conception of politics leads to questions regarding shifts in patterns of support and consequent changes in the distribution of power. Given the nature of traditional Indian society and the importance of caste in it, it is difficult to visualize rival groups competing for support without making use of the loyalties of caste. Nor can one assume that caste was the only basis on which power was allocated and support gathered. In fact, the task of the political sociologist is to investigate the specific ways in which caste combined with other factors to create and maintain particular constellations of power.

It would clearly be an over-statement to contend that in traditional India ruling groups found themselves 'in a sort of market situation'. For the limits within which choices were made were fairly narrow, subordinate groups were less free to exercise choice *overtly* and radical changes in the character of the ruling group were perhaps few and far between. Such politics as did exist was clearly not party politics in the modern sense of the term but a politics of factional bargains. Some social anthropologists believe that factions in India are expressions of cleavages *within* the dominant caste rather than *between* rival dominant castes. Actually, our knowledge of the anatomy of factions is too limited to enable us to say anything categorical in this regard. But given a certain instability of economic and political power, there is no reason to assign greater importance to intracaste as opposed to intercaste factions in either the present or the past.[2]

To carry the analysis a little further, one may argue that the market in which groups contend for power in modern societies is fully free in only the formal sense of the term. The arena of effective political participation, though greatly extended, never becomes coterminous with the whole society. Even in modern democratic systems the distribution of power is never entirely dissociated from race, religion or region. To say this is not to deny that considerable differences exist between politics in traditional and modern societies. It is merely to insist that both can and should be studied within a common theoretical framework.

The need to accommodate both material interests and ideal values in this framework becomes evident when we examine available explanations of the divergence between principle and practice. Most authors seem prepared to concede that castes may, in fact, engage in politics but that one has to make a distinction between principle and practice or between what Bailey calls 'the rules of the game' and 'the way it is played'.

One may ask whether this divergence is a recent deviation in Indian society (as Leach would imply) or inherent in the tension between values and interests which is characteristic of all human societies.

The confusion seems to lie in this, that in talking about the properties of the system Dumont, Leach and Bailey are concerned essentially with the structure of values and not with the structure of interests. The analysis of political processes requires that we identify structures of interests and not explain them away as deviations from the structure of values. To extend the metaphor a little, the rules of the game are complex because it is not always the same game that people are playing.

The pitfalls of ignoring certain practices because they do not conform to particular 'rules of the game' can be illustrated from Bailey's own analysis. It is perhaps true that the rules of the game do not – or did not – permit conflicts between castes. But did they, for that matter, permit conflicts *within* the dominant caste? Political cleavages between vertical groups divide the dominant caste into opposed lineages, opposed branches of the same lineage and opposed families within the same branch. Is it correct to assume that such conflicts – which no doubt existed – were more in conformity with 'the rules of the game' than conflicts between castes? Those who invoke the rules of the game are obliged to be consistent: conflict between agnates is as much contrary to the rules of their game as conflict between castes.

I have argued so far that a conception of traditional Indian society as a system in which groups 'cooperate and do not compete', based as it is on the people's own representations, tends to obscure some of the most important features of political life. I shall now try to show that representations of a very similar kind have existed in all or most societies and by themselves tell us very little about certain aspects of social reality. Societies throughout the ages have created images of their being in terms of harmony, order and unity. The details of these have varied but the broad outlines show almost everywhere a remarkable quality of sameness.

It would be all too easy to explain away these images or conceptions as 'myths', 'ideologies' or 'false consciousness' and it is far from my intention to do this. Their influence on social action is important enough to assure them a place in any scheme of analysis irrespective of one's views about their ultimate reality. But this is not to say that they tell us the whole truth about human societies or even provide the best point of departure for every type of sociological enquiry.

It is unfortunate that those who have started with ideal representations of Indian society in their analysis of it have ignored similar conceptual schemes which exist in other societies. Such representations are not a unique feature of Indian society or even of traditional societies but are present everywhere in the socialist countries today.

A very fruitful comparison can be made in terms of the stated principles of organization between the regime of caste in traditional India and the socialist regimes of today. I am aware that there are enormous cultural differences between the two kinds of societies and between their actual patterns of stratification. But I am not now concerned with these; my objective is to show certain correspondences between representations which people create of the societies in which they live.

I do not wish to give the impression that there is complete unanimity in the views expressed by East European scholars about the nature of their own society. But such differences as do exist are slight or insignificant when compared with the diversity of views about capitalist society expounded by Western scholars. At any rate, if it is possible to speak about the stated principles of organization of traditional Hindu society, one should be able to do the same for contemporary socialist society.

Soviet scholars recognize the existence of divisions in their own society: what they deny is the presence of antagonism between these divisions. According to them also the divisions (which they usually call strata) are in relations of co-operation and not conflict with each other. Their views of their own society are thus essentially similar to what Dumont, Leach and Bailey believe to have been the views of the Hindus of the past about traditional Indian society.

Contemporary Marxists in East European countries make a radical distinction between stratification in capitalist and socialist societies. This distinction centres around the presence or absence of what is variously described as 'antagonism' or 'antagonistic contradiction'. The distinction between 'antagonistic' and 'non-antagonistic' contradiction was elaborated by Stalin who argued that the relations between strata in socialist society were non-antagonistic whereas under capitalism the corresponding relations were antagonistic.[3]

Soviet scholars generally represent their society as being divided into two major classes, namely, workers and peasants. In addition to these, there is a third category, the 'intelligentsia', to which the term stratum and not class is applied (see Nemchinov, 1957, pp. 179-84). The recognition of the separate identity of the intelligentsia and the reluctance to characterize them as a class reflects a basic ambiguity in Soviet Marxism to which both Marcuse (1961, pp.91-3) and Aron (1964, p. 127) have drawn attention.

The persistence of classes in socialist society (over and above the division into workers and peasants) is an anachronism from the viewpoint of Marxist theory. At the same time, the existing divisions between workers and the 'intelligentsia' or between various groups within the bureaucracy are too obvious to be denied recognition. Their presence is taken into account in a model elaborated by the Polish economist, Oskar Lange. Lange (1962, pp. 1-15) makes a clear distinction between classes and strata, denying the existence of the former in socialist society while recognizing that of the latter. Relations between classes are, in his view, antagonistic, being based on property; relations between strata, which arise from the division of labour, are, on the other hand, complementary and non-antagonistic.

The same contrast between 'classes' and 'strata' has been made on the same basis in a recent paper by the Polish sociologist Wlodzimierz Wesolowski. Wesolowski (1967, pp. 145-64) maintains that there are 'workers' in both capitalist and socialist society and in both cases they are involved in a certain type of production (industrial production) and they perform a certain type of work (manual work). But their relations with other groups are radically different in the two kinds of society. Therefore, he argues that workers in socialist society should be described as a 'stratum' and not as a 'class'.

My purpose in drawing attention to Lange's model of socialist society is twofold. It is to argue, first of all, that formulations of ideal patterns of relationship have certain basic things in common irrespective of the societies in which they emerge. It is to argue further that an uncritical acceptance of statements regarding the rules of the game may hinder rather than help the analysis of effective social relations. Even Marxist sociologists view with scepticism the distinction between 'antagonistic' and 'non-antagonistic' contradiction and few sociologists outside Eastern Europe would deny the existence there of conflicts within and between strata. Not only do such conflicts exist but they constitute the very core of what the political sociologist has to study, rules of the game notwithstanding.

East European ideologues are not alone among publicists of the modern world in representing their own society as basically harmonious, as one in which the different strata fulfil complementary functions. The view that Western society is torn by class conflict is as often as not an outsider's view of it. It is not true that those who have written about capitalist society from within have all taken the Marxist view that relations between classes are in their essence relations of conflict. On the contrary, the nineteenth century produced a considerable number of writers whose mission was to show that the different classes were complementary to each other and that basically the social order was in a state of equilibrium.

The idea of the complementarity of classes can be amply illustrated from the writings of classical economists, liberal political philosophers, and sociologists of the 'organismic' school. The persistence of this conception of society has been nicely summed up by Ossowski and I cannot do better than to quote him:

> From legendary Agrippa, from Aristotle to Herbert Spencer and Durkheim, from St. Clement of Alexandria to modern papal encyclicals, to Oxford Movement declarations and fascist manifestos, the defenders of the existing order endeavoured to represent it as based on mutual dependence resulting from the division of tasks equally useful for the whole society (1956, p. 21).

It is true, as Ossowski points out, that there were other representations of society in Western culture but are we certain that these did not also exist in India? At any rate, the classical religious texts are not the best place to look for them.

Some Western sociologists have constructed conceptual schemes of their own society which are not in their essentials different from those of classical Hinduism or of contemporary socialist doctrine. The argument of Durkheim is characteristic: organized society is based on *complementary* differences and class conflict is an *abnormal* form of the division of labour.

It was a common argument among nineteenth-century Conservatives and Liberals in the West that not only were social classes complementary but that each had certain rights and society had an obligation to protect the weak from being exploited by the strong. This was the theory of it, not very different from the one that *every* caste, not merely the upper élite has its 'privileges'. It is perhaps true that *legally* every caste had its privileges just as capitalists and workers have been since the nineteenth century 'equal before the law'. Equality before the law does not exclude the political domination of one set of people by another; privileges conferred by traditional usage can be set aside by the will of the strong and the powerful.

One may say, following Mannheim (1960, pp. 97-104), that the province of politics begins where that of law ends. It is difficult to study the realities of politics in capitalist society if one remains confined to the maxim that all men are equal before the law. It should be equally difficult to study politics in traditional India unless one is prepared to see beyond the principle that each caste is entitled to its special privileges. The proper subject matter of politics is the ambiguity in practice of privileges which are clearly defined in principle. In some societies the law defines a certain fundamental equality of every citizen; in others, it grants special privileges to various categories of people. But in all societies there is an area of indeterminacy beyond what is formally defined by law; the sociologist has to analyse how choices are made within this area.

To justify or even to explain the continued existence of a society, it is perhaps simplest to present it as a unity in which the different components fulfil necessary and complementary functions. Thus, castes are represented as complementary to each other in traditional India; likewise classes in nineteenth-century

Europe and strata in the socialist countries today. To represent such divisions as complementary is perhaps the easiest way of explaining why people accept them and why they persist over time. The Marxist theory of capitalist society was exceptional in that it sought to explain and justify not the existence of a particular order but its dissolution.

The kind of questions that I have raised would perhaps gain in clarity by being related to a debate of a more general scope in contemporary sociology. This debate centres around the priorities to be assigned to values and to interests in the understanding of social life. Dumont has clearly chosen to assign primary significance to values and in this he seems to be followed by Leach and apparently in some measure also by Bailey. Anthropological studies of Indian society are clearly dominated by a concern for values and show a corresponding neglect of the systematic analysis of interests.

On this point Dumont makes his position quite explicit: 'A ce niveau, le système des castes, c'est avant tout un systeme d'idées et de valeurs, un système formel, compréhensible, rationnel, un système au sens intellectuel du terme' (1966, p. 53).[4] And he soon goes on to say 'Notre première tâche consiste à saisir ce système intellectuel, cette idéologie' (1966, p. 53).[5] Leach appears to follow Dumont quite closely but Bailey's general position is not as simple. He was not only one of the first to make detailed monographic studies of economic and political life but also challenged Dumont's and Pocock's excessive preoccupation with ideas and values (see Bailey, 1959, pp. 88-101).

It is, therefore, by no means true that students of Indian society have ignored altogether either economic and political life or material interests in general. What is lacking, however, is a comprehensive framework for the study of interests of the kind which Dumont has developed in relation to his study of values. The construction of such a framework will be a major step in the direction of a more balanced appraisal of social reality in India.

The main points of difference in the broader field of sociological theory between approaches based on values and on interests have been summarized by Dahrendorf (1959). He describes the adherents of the two principal approaches as

Utopians and Rationalists, a choice of terminology which no doubt reflects his own preference. Alternatively, Dahrendorf speaks of two theories or metatheories which he describes as the 'integration theory of society' and the 'coercion theory of society'.

It is not necessary to follow Dahrendorf in every detail of his analysis but one of the points which he makes is of particular interest here. This is the general preoccupation of those concerned with the study of values with order, harmony, integration and a static view of society and the corresponding neglect by them of differences of interest, coercion, conflict and change. The argument that the emphasis on values at the expense of interests leads to certain basic distortions of social reality had been earlier put forward by Lockwood (1956, pp. 134-46).

It might appear a little harsh to label as Utopians those who have contributed so richly to the understanding of Indian society. But it would be hard to deny that there is a certain Utopian element in Dumont's insistence on the universal significance of *dharma*, in Leach's contention that '*every* caste not merely the upper élite has its "privileges"' and in Bailey's definition of castes as groups 'which co-operate and do not compete'.

The preoccupations with values on the one hand and with interests on the other derive respectively from the sociologies of Durkheim and Marx. The influence of Durkheim has greatly outweighed that of Marx among social anthropologists engaged in the study of primitive or pre-industrial societies. It is interesting that Leach was one of the first British anthropologists to lament the preoccupation among his colleagues with '"functional integration," "social solidarity," "cultural uniformity," "structural equilibrium"' (1954, p. 7). In his own studies of caste, however, he does not seem to have gone far enough to redress the balance towards a more dynamic conception of society.

Recently, both Lockwood and Dahrendorf have emphasized the importance of interests in the study of human society. Dahrendorf's argument is that while it is useful to study both values and interests, which particular framework one chooses ought to depend on the problem one wishes to study. He has in his own work shown that systematic studies of interests are as much within the proper domain of sociology as systematic studies of values. It is important now to turn our attention to the former kind of study in India because the role of values themselves can never be fully assessed unless we study them in their continuing interaction with interests.

6 Networks in Indian social structure

With M.N. Srinivas

Much has been written on the concept of social structure since Radcliffe-Brown first started making systematic use of it more than thirty years ago. Apart from writing about it in abstract and general terms, most British anthropologists have used it as a central concept in presenting their field material.

Evans-Pritchard's use of the concept in *The Nuer*[1] remains as a model of its kind. There the concept was used to mean 'relations between groups of persons within a system of groups', such groups, further, having 'a high degree of consistency and constancy'.[2] This way of viewing social structure has enabled the fieldworker to present his data in an economical manner. The concept is also relatively easy to handle. One begins by locating the enduring groups in a society, then proceeds to define their boundaries, and finally one specifies their mutual positions, or their inter-relations in terms of a series of rights, duties and obligations.[3]

The approach outlined above has been widely used by social anthropologists (particularly British anthropologists or those trained in Britain) in the study of Indian village communities. The papers by Srinivas and Kathleen Gough in Marriott's collection[4] may be taken as illustrations. The village is viewed there principally in terms of a set of enduring groups and categories such as castes, sub-castes and economic classes.

A model of society which is conceived in terms of enduring groups and categories has also to deal with the problem of interpersonal relations. It has, in addition, to devise ways of depicting the relations between groups and categories which form parts of different systems, e.g. between lineages, territorial segments and age sets, or between castes, classes and power blocks.

The distinction between a system of groups and a system of interpersonal relations has been nicely posed by Evans-Pritchard. This distinction, it appears, is a part of Nuer kinship terminology. The Nuer used the word *buth* to refer to relations between lineages viewed as groups. The word *mar* is, by contrast, used to refer to kinship relations between persons belonging either to the same agnatic lineage or to different ones.[5]

It should be recognized in this connection that, when one talks of the 'relations between groups in a system of groups', one is representing things at a certain level of abstraction. Representation of the relations between castes in a system of castes involves one level of abstraction. On the other hand, a representation of the relations between the system of castes and the system of classes involves an abstraction at a higher level. Evans-Pritchard shows a clear awareness of the problem which this raises, and its difficulties.

> Not only can we speak of the relations between territorial groups as a political system, the relations between lineages as a lineage system, the relations between age-sets as an age-set system and so forth, but also in a society there is always some relationship between these systems in the whole social structure, *though it is not easy to determine what this relationship is* [6]

It may be pointed out that the abstract relations between groups and systems of groups can be better understood by mapping out the concrete relations between individuals in their diverse roles. This may be achieved by making a shift from a study of groups within a system of groups to a study of social networks. What are the concrete relations which an individual has in his capacity as Brahmin, landowner and *panchayat* member with other individuals? The concept of social network paves the way to an understanding of the linkage existing between different institutional spheres and between different systems of groups and categories.

It is necessary to point out that the model of social structure which bases itself on enduring groups and categories, and their interrelations, has been developed largely by social anthropologists engaged in the study of primitive societies. Such a model does, indeed, take one a long way in the description and analysis of societies which are small, homogeneous and relatively static. In the study of large, complex and changing societies, however, this approach is faced with certain limitations.

In a complex society such as India the number of enduring groups, classes and categories is very large, and they present a bewildering variety of types. It may be difficult within the compass of a single study even to enumerate such units, not to speak of providing a coherent account of their complex interrelations. Evans-Pritchard has been able to provide a fairly comprehensive account of Nuer social structure while confining himself almost wholly to three systems of groups. Clearly, it is impossible to analyse in such an economical manner the social structure of even a single district in India.

There is another factor which imposes limitations on the approach which confines itself to the study of enduring groups and systems of groups. In traditional India groups such as village communities, sub-castes and lineages had sharply defined outlines. It was relatively easy to delimit their boundaries. Today the situation is somewhat different. Boundaries between groups tend to be blurred or broken down, there is greater circulation of personnel, and an increasing degree of interpenetration between different systems of groups, classes and categories.[7] This process makes it increasingly difficult to locate and define the boundaries of groups, and hence to talk meaningfully of groups of persons within a system of groups.

In India this partial dissolution of a rigid, segmental and hierarchical social structure is associated with increasing social mobility, both horizontal and vertical. It is also associated with the transition from a status-bound ascriptive social order to one which gives greater scope to contractual relations based on personal choice. The allegiance of the individual to his village, his sub-caste and his lineage has, to some extent, loosened. Along with this, the individual is being progressively drawn into networks of interpersonal relations which cut right across the boundaries of village, sub-caste and lineage.[8]

The process outlined above may be illustrated with a concrete example. Let us consider the case of Sripuram, a multi-caste village in Tanjore district which has been exposed to the forces of change since the end of the nineteenth century. Sixty years ago one's social position in Sripuram was defined largely in terms of one's membership of the village, of a particular territorial segment[9] of it, of a sub-caste, a lineage and a household. Much of the social life of the villagers could be understood in terms of the relations between these diverse groups, each of which had fairly easily determinable boundaries. Today the social contours of the village are becoming blurred, its population has acquired a shifting character, and lineages and families have become greatly dispersed.

Many of the former residents of Sripuram have left the village and gone to Tanjore, Madras, Delhi, Bombay and Calcutta. In each of these centres they have developed new relations, while retaining many old ones with people who still live in the village. Many of those who have left the village continue to influence its social life in a number of ways. Often they return at harvest time to receive rents, and renew leases with their tenants. Several of them send remittances to relatives in the village every month. On occasions of birth, marriage and death they revisit the village.

The concept of social network makes for an effective representation of the links radiating from the village to the outside world. These links sometimes stretch across wide territorial gaps, and often they are made up of strands of diverse kinds. One of the Brahmin landowners of Sripuram wanted to get a seat for his son in an engineering college at Madras. He approached an influential non-Brahmin friend at Tanjore who was also his father's client, the father of the Brahmin landowner being a lawyer in a nearby town. The non-Brahmin friend, who is chairman of a transport undertaking at Tanjore, had influential business associates at Madras. Some of these persons were able to put the landowner from Sripuram into touch with a member of the committee of the college to which he was seeking admission for his son. In the contemporary world of Sripuram the individual finds it increasingly necessary to become a part of the kind of network described above. Sixty years ago, when the social horizons were narrower, this necessity was far less keen.

Having sketched the conditions under which networks emerge and become increasingly important in social life, let us consider the distinctive features of networks as opposed to groups, classes and categories. The distinction between groups and networks is primarily one of boundaries. A group is a bounded unit. A network, on the other hand, ramifies in every direction, and, for all practical purposes, stretches out indefinitely. Further, a group such as a lineage or a sub-caste has an 'objective' existence: its boundaries are the same for the 'insider' as well as the 'outsider'. The character of a network, on the other hand, varies from one individual to another.[10]

This distinction between groups and networks, which was first elaborated by Barnes,[11] should not, however, be pressed too far. Networks can be either close-knit or loose-knit. In other words, the chain of relations emanating from a person may either lead back to him, or it may not. In traditional India, particularly in the South, the network of kinship and affinal relations was a close-knit one. In fact, this network had, inevitably, to stop short at the boundary of the sub-caste, and therefore to form a closed circuit. Mrs Karve[12] has shown how, in many cases, an entire sub-caste can be placed on a single genealogy. Here we have an instance where the kinship network is, in reality, coterminous with a bounded group, namely, the sub-caste. Thus, in the limiting case, a close-knit network becomes a group (or a category).

A social network can be viewed as a set of concrete interpersonal relations linking the individual to other individuals who are members of diverse systems of enduring groups and categories. Here we represent the network from the viewpoint of the actor, and there are as many networks as there are actors in a social system. Before we pass on to a consideration of the network from the viewpoint of the 'observer' (i.e. the anthropologist), let us examine a little further the implications of the subjective definition of a network.

The anthropologist as fieldworker begins to learn about the way in which a society works precisely by following concrete networks of interpersonal relations with the individual actor as his point of departure. He sees how individuals cut through the boundaries of household, lineage, sub-caste, village, district, party and class so as to form interpersonal relations in the pursuit of interests of diverse kinds. He learns to differentiate one individual from another in terms of the range and variety of interpersonal relations, and tries to relate these differences to factors such as generation, education, occupation and so on.

A network, even when viewed from the standpoint of a single individual, has a dynamic character. New relations are forged, and old ones are discarded or modified. This is particularly true of rapidly changing societies in which individual choice plays an important role. However, extensions of the individual's social network may also be studied in relatively static societies. Thus, in the field of kinship we may observe how the individual's network of effective interpersonal relations is extended as he passes from birth through initiation and marriage to death.

Although the anthropologist may begin by mapping out the concrete networks of interpersonal relations of individual actors, this mapping, in itself, does not fully meet the needs of his analysis. At best it can provide him with a broad idea of the linkage between the groups and systems of groups in a society. For a deeper understanding it is necessary not only to chart the concrete networks of different individuals, but to relate these different networks to one another, to draw up, so to say, a master chart, in a coherent and systematic manner. This involves abstraction and synthesis.

It is easy to see what one means by an individual's network of interpersonal relations, for this has a concrete character. But can one speak, for instance, of the social network of a village? What would such a statement mean? The village comprises a diversity of individuals, each with his own network of concrete interpersonal relations. These partly overlap, and partly cut across, and are, in fact, related to one another in very complex ways. In some spheres, the separation of one individual's network from that of another is quite clear. Thus, the network of kinship and affinal relations of a Brahmin will not at any point meet that of a non-Brahmin, even though they be of the same village. In the economic sphere, on the other hand, these networks are likely to meet at a number of points. Can one distinguish in a systematic way between different institutional areas in which networks are relatively close-knit or loose-knit?

It seems evident that the kinship network in India is relatively close-knit as compared, let us say, to the economic or political network. It may be that the same forces which lead to the extension and loosening of the economic and political networks also lead to the shrinkage and tightening of kinship networks in contemporary India. Territorial dispersal and mobility lead to the extension of economic and political ties; they often also lead to a shrinkage of the network of *effective* kinship relations based upon reciprocal obligations.[13]

We have now been led to a point at which it is necessary to talk in somewhat more abstract terms. From viewing the concrete networks of interpersonal relations of a number of individual actors we have been led to talk about networks pertaining to different institutional areas. We can now speak about economic networks, political networks, ritual networks, and so on. It is evident that when we speak, say, of an economic network, we are making an abstraction. A concrete network of interpersonal relations cannot be wholly economic in its constitution, except in the limiting case. Generally such relations have economic components which have to be abstracted from their concrete matrix, and then put together.

The economic system may be viewed as a network of relations regulating the flow of goods and services. The political system may, likewise, be viewed as a network of relations regulating the flow of command and decision. It must be pointed out that the links in networks of this kind are unitary in character, as opposed to concrete networks of interpersonal relations where the links are usually composite or multi-bonded.

Economic, political and ritual networks of the kind described above would correspond to what Marion Levy[14] characterizes as 'analytic', as opposed to 'concrete' structures. Thus, a network of economic relations provides an understanding of the organization of production in a society, and a network of political relations provides an understanding of the distribution of power. Such networks in a complex society cut across the boundaries of communities and corporate groups and, in fact, serve to articulate them to wider social systems. And, once we shift from the individual actor and his network of concrete interpersonal relations to the productive system and its corresponding network, we move from the 'subjective' network of the actor to the 'objective' one of the observer.

We have seen earlier that a crucial distinction in the study of networks is that between close-knit and loose-knit networks. It may be urged that one way of understanding social change in India would be to analyse the manner in which close-knit networks are being transformed into loose-knit ones. Traditionally the villager lived in a narrow world where the ties of locality, caste, kinship and hereditary service led back and forth between the same sets of persons. Relations were multiplex in character, and the circuit of relations had a tendency to become closed.

The situation is changing in contemporary India. New interests tend to create relationships which cut right across the boundaries of the old established groups. Increased mobility has led to the physical dispersal of castes, lineages and families. The individual cannot any longer afford to confine his relations within a village, a caste or a kin group. He has to develop relations with people who are spread far and wide and who have diverse social, economic and political positions and interests. The network of social relations emanating from the individual does not as easily lead back to him. The closed circuit tends to become more and more open.

The phenomenon sketched above can perhaps be best illustrated from the field of politics. To take once again the instance of Sripuram, one can get only an imperfect understanding of its political life by confining oneself to groups such as the *panchayat*, the party or the sub-caste. What appear to be of greater importance are the networks which link the village leaders to politicians and influential people outside, and which cut right across the boundaries of parties, *panchayats* and sub-castes. Bailey[15] has spoken of 'brokerage networks' in the context of Orissa. Such networks are of great importance to the working of the political process throughout the country. In and around Sripuram they link the village leader with the district leader, the patron with the client, the MLA with the 'vote-bank', the party boss with the financier, and the *panchayat* president with the contractor.

It is evident that some of the most radical changes taking place in Indian society today are in the field of politics. A rigidly hierarchical and segmental social structure is being transformed into one which seeks to bring about political articulation between people at all levels of society. The peasant in a Tanjore village is linked directly with the Member of Parliament at Delhi. To what extent can such a linkage be effective or successful? It is in this context that the problem of communication acquires central importance to both the politician and the political sociologist in India. How does the system of political communication actually operate? How does it affect the existing systems of groups and categories in Indian society, and how is it, in turn, affected by them? A study of the concrete links between villagers, local leaders, party bosses, MLAs, and MPs is indispensable to an understanding of the channels along which communications flow, and the barriers at which they are blocked.

In a recent paper Ithiel Pool[16] has emphasized the importance of informal social channels of communication in providing necessary support to the mass media in traditional societies. Political events in the state capital are interpreted and transmitted along social networks of various kinds whose nature requires to be investigated. There is little doubt that such networks today link individuals not simply on the basis of caste or occupation or locality, but on the basis of a complex combination of these and numerous other factors.

India has embarked on a course of planned social change and economic development. This involves, among other things, the transmission of certain key ideas, principles and values from the highest to the lowest levels of society. What are the social networks along which such ideas are transmitted? What kind of refraction do they undergo as they pass from one level to another? How is this refraction conditioned by the nature of the social network along which the ideas flow?

The entire process of political mobilization in a country such as India highlights the importance of networks of interpersonal relations. How does the politician reach down to the voter, and how does the latter, in turn, articulate with the former? In a country where literacy is low and where the mass media are new and limited in scope, networks of interpersonal relations are of primary importance to the mobilization process.

The process of political modernization has many immediate and far-reaching consequences for the structure of traditional society. It breaks down the barriers between groups which had crystallized over centuries. It gives a new amplitude to individual choice in severing old relations and forging new ones. All this leads to the development of networks on the basis of new interests which criss-cross the entire social fabric.

In conclusion, we have to consider briefly the existence of social networks and the part played by them in traditional Indian society. It would, of course, be far from correct to say that networks had no existence in traditional society, or that the social life of the individual was completely contained within systems of enduring groups. Even in the past the village was never entirely a closed or self-sufficient unit. Links of various kinds radiated from it, connecting its individual members to other individuals outside. Such links, however, played a far less important part in the past than they do today. Even the extra-village ties of the individual often articulated him with other groups such as lineages or sub-castes which were themselves closed in character.

A village community which forms part of a wider civilization can never be entirely a closed unit. In fact, articulation of a particular kind is a basic characteristic of a civilization as distinguished from a primitive society. The manner in which little and great traditions are articulated through social networks in a primary civilization has been discussed by Redfield, Singer and others.[17] But it cannot be denied that the nature of articulation in a relatively static and compartmentalized social order is different from one which is fluid and changing in character.

7 The future of the Backward Classes:the competing demands of status and power

The Backward Classes[1] constitute an important section of Indian society. In all they account for more than 30% of the total population of the country. Their condition is intimately linked with many of the basic features of Indian social structure and, as such, is likely to be affected by any significant change in these. Clearly, an assessment of the future of the Backward Classes cannot be made in isolation from social and political forces which operate through the entire range of Indian society.

Studies in social and political projection are faced with problems of a special nature. Predictions in the social sciences cannot be made with the same certainty or the same degree of probability as in the natural sciences. This is so even when the social scientist has at his disposal the entire body of data considered necessary for his analysis. For here the validity of the analysis depends not only on the quality of data but also on the values which direct one's research.

Sociologists such as Mannheim[2] and Myrdal[3] have shown how different persons may arrive at different (though not necessarily contradictory) conclusions even when they analyse the same body of facts. The values and interests of the sociologist give a direction to this research and no method has as yet been devised which can eliminate their influence altogether. Values play a part not only in the formulation of the problems to be investigated but also in the selection and arrangement of data.

The problem of the Backward Classes may be posed in a variety of ways. Is it essentially a political problem or is the problem basically educational and cultural? Should the Backward Classes be treated as a homogeneous, undifferentiated unit or should one view separately the problems of the Scheduled Tribes, the

Scheduled Castes and the Other Backward Classes? Finally, does one accept the prevalent basis of classifying the Indian population into 'backward' and 'forward' as a rational one?

One is likely to have specific views on all these questions, not only as a sociologist but also as a member of Indian society. There are special problems inherent in the study of one's own society, particularly when such a study deals with issues which are of general and fundamental importance. The outsider has a certain advantage. He is able to approach the problem with a more open mind, relatively free of preconceptions. This, of course, is not to deny that an inside view of social problems has advantages of its own.

If value preferences tend to distort interpretations of the past, their role in projections is likely to be even more decisive. An effort at projection faces a bigger challenge in the matter of valuation. For here one has to evaluate the significance not only of elements and forces which have established themselves but also of those which are in a process of emergence. One has to uncover potentialities inherent in factors whose contemporary significance may not appear very great. Here the judgement of the social scientist is put to a kind of test which he is normally inclined to avoid.

It cannot be too strongly emphasized that objectivity in social research is not merely a question of good intention or even of professional competence. It is also a function of the social position of the person who conducts the research. As such, a full and objective picture of social reality can hardly be drawn with a single stroke of the brush. Rather, the area of objectivity can be expanded only by slow degrees as different people, occupying different social positions and representing divergent interests, examine the same problem from a variety of angles. It would be well to bear these limitations in mind while making an assessment of the analysis which follows.

Who are the Backward Classes? In India, the Backward Classes constitute a category of people who are for the most part officially listed and given special recognition in a variety of contexts. In every complex society, of course, there are individuals who may be considered as economically or educationally backward; generally, such people have also a low social status. However, backwardness as understood in the Indian context has a number of distinctive features. Firstly, it is viewed as an attribute not of individuals but of certain clearly defined social segments in which membership is generally acquired by birth; thus, the Backward Classes may in theory include individuals who are highly advanced both educationally and economically. Secondly, membership of the Backward Classes entitles one to certain advantages and concessions specifically conferred by the Government.

There is a good deal of overlap in reality between the Backward Classes and certain economic categories such as the agricultural labourers. But it would be a mistake to view the problems of the two as identical. The Backward Classes have as a set of communities certain distinctive problems which derive from the status ascribed to them in traditional Indian society. It is these distinctive problems which will engage our attention in the analysis which follows. The very nature of the Backward Classes and most of their special problems can be understood only in terms of the basic character of Indian society, namely, its division into a multitude of closed status groups of unequal rank, each associated with a variety of privileges and disabilities supported by traditional sanctions.

It may on a first examination appear tempting to restructure the definition of the Backward Classes and to view their problems principally in economic terms. This would, however, divert attention from the specific nature of backwardness in Indian society. In the first place, the Backward Classes are by no means homogeneous economically. Secondly, the Backward Classes as officially viewed are a part and parcel of modern Indian social and political reality. They are a product of forces which are in many ways unique and distinctive of Indian history. Their identity does not derive solely, or even primarily, from a common economic experience but from the very nature of the traditional system of stratification to which economic, political and ritual factors have contributed in various ways.

The term 'Backward Classes', which has been given currency through official publications, is not altogether a happy one. The word 'class' suggests not only an economic category but also one which is relatively open. In reality the Backward Classes are not classes at all but an aggregate of closed status groups. One's economic position is not a determining factor in one's membership of the Backward Classes; rather, membership is determined generally by birth.

The Backward Classes together account for more than 30 per cent of the total population of India. They are not a homogeneous category but consist of three broad divisions, each having its own distinctive background and, to some extent, its own problems of transformation. The three broad divisions are the Scheduled Tribes, the Scheduled Castes and the Other Backward Classes. The Other Backward Classes are the least homogeneous and the most loosely defined of the three subdivisions. Their problems also are in many ways different from those of the first two and it may be misleading to consider the three together beyond a certain point.

An element of confusion pervades the discussion on Backward Classes due to a certain misapplication of terms. In this essay the term 'Backward Classes' will be used to refer to the most inclusive category and the term 'Other Backward Classes' will be reserved for that section of the broader category which remains by exclusion of the Scheduled Tribes and Scheduled Castes. It seems to be a common practice, not only among scholars but also among politicians to use the term Backward Classes as being synonymous sometimes with the Scheduled Tribes and Scheduled Castes and at other times with a somewhat broader category. This ambiguity in terminology leads to certain important issues and problems being obscured.[4]

The position of the Scheduled Tribes and Scheduled Castes is defined in a more or less specific manner in the Indian Constitution. Lists of these communities are drawn up by the Central Government and can be revised only by Presidential authority. There is, in addition, a Commissioner for Scheduled Castes and Scheduled Tribes to look into the affairs of these communities on a continuing basis.

The Other Backward Classes, by contrast, are a more nebulous category. They are mentioned in the Constitution in only the most general terms. There is no all-India list for the Other Backward Classes. They are not separately enumerated in the

Census and, in fact, one has to work with only a rough estimate of their population. Their position was sought to be defined in more specific terms by the Backward Classes Commission set up in 1953 under the chairmanship of Kaka Kalelkar. The Commission, which was not a standing body, could not in fact come to any tangible or agreed conclusions.

The Scheduled Tribes or Adivasis numbered 29.9 million in 1961 out of a total population of 439.1 million. They are popularly believed to constitute the aboriginal element in Indian society. They are generally concentrated in the hill and forest areas and until recently the political system of the different tribes enjoyed a certain measure of autonomy. Today, however, it is difficult to define the tribal peoples of India in terms of any single set of formal criteria although attempts have been made at such a definition.[5] Elements which would have to be taken into account in such a definition are the ecological isolation of the tribal people, the relative autonomy of their political and cultural systems and the antiquity of association with their present habitat.

The difficulty of applying a set of formal criteria in defining the Adivasis arises from the fact that tribes in India are (and have been for some time) tribes in transition. The political boundaries of most tribal systems had collapsed well before the beginning of the present century. A certain amount of cultural interchange between the tribal people and the outside world has existed for centuries. Sections of the tribal population tend to get absorbed into Hindu society by a process which has been fairly widespread. In fact, it is often very difficult to say of a particular social unit whether it is a tribe or a caste. The complexity of the phenomenon defeats any attempt to solve such problems by means of precisely formulated definitions. Each case has to be examined on its own merits and in relation to the specific social and historical factors prevalent in an area before one can decide whether or not a particular unit qualifies as a tribe. Lists of the Scheduled Tribes have, in fact, been drawn up after careful consideration of a variety of individual cases.

The tribal population is concentrated in certain geographical areas.

Speaking very broadly, they may be divided into three groups according to their distribution, namely, the tribes living in the Northern and North-Eastern zone in the mountain valleys and Eastern Frontiers of India. There is a second group which occupies the Central belt of the older hills and plateaus along the dividing line between Peninsular India and the Indo-Gangetic Plains. In addition, there are tribes scattered over the extreme corners of South-Western India, in the hills and the converging lines of the Ghats.[6]

These tribes speak a large variety of dialects and there are enormous variations in their habits, customs and arts. Historically one of the principal features of the tribal population has been its ecological and social isolation. For centuries the tribal people have been confined to hills and forests and this isolation has left a definite impress on their social systems. It has also given them, in spite of wide cultural variations, a common destiny in Indian society. For, one of the crucial problems faced by all tribal communities in India is the problem of integration into the wider social, economic and political system.

The Scheduled Castes or Harijans have not had a history of isolation comparable to that of the Scheduled Tribes. They have been segregated rather than isolated. Thus, whereas the tribal people are concentrated in blocks, the Harijans are scattered through every state and practically every district. The different distributional characteristics of the Scheduled Tribes and the Scheduled Castes lead to certain differences in their problems of transformation. It is easier to implement special programmes of development for the Scheduled Tribes who live in compact blocks than for the Scheduled Castes who are geographically scattered. On the other hand, the concentration of the tribal population in particular areas provides better scope for the development of separatist political movements among them.

The Scheduled Castes numbered 64.5 million at the 1961 Census, thus giving a figure which is more than twice that of the Scheduled Tribes. They are concentrated in rural areas and are found commonly in multi-caste villages. Although they live in close interdependence with the higher castes, many areas of social life have been (and continue to be) inaccessible to them. They generally live segregated in their own settlements which are often a little distance away from the residential quarters of the upper castes. They have been debarred by tradition from full participation in many of the collective activities of the village and some of these restrictions are still operative. Their economic, social and ritual status continues to be depressed although there are certain indications of change which will be discussed later.

The Scheduled Castes have been known in popular parlance as the untouchables. Their social condition has been governed in important ways by the Hindu concept of pollution. Although the practice of untouchability has been made an offence, the stigma of pollution has not by any means been entirely removed.

The Other Backward Classes constitute a congeries of communities of rather uncertain status. Lists had earlier been prepared by the Ministry of Education and by the State Governments. The Backward Classes Commission under Kaka Kalelkar reported a good deal of ambiguity in these lists. 'But there was no authoritative list of Other Backward Classes. The Census had assumed one list; the Ministry of Education had prepared another; and it was left to the present Commission to recommend an authoritative list.'[7] The recommendations of the Commission were not, in fact, accepted as authoritative. The State Governments have in general been allowed to use their own criteria in drawing up lists of the Other Backward Classes. These, in turn, are not always held to be binding by the Supreme Court which, in the case of M.R. Balaji and Others versus the State of Mysore, decided against the recommendation of the Nagana Gowda Commission.

The Central Government have particularly since 1961, been pressing for the adoption of economic criteria in defining the Other Backward Classes but there has been resistance to this from a number of State Governments. Some of the castes included in the earlier lists of the Other Backward Classes are fairly powerful in state politics and have therefore been in a position to exert pressure on the State Governments to have the old criteria retained. The Lingayats of Mysore and the Ezhavas of Kerala provide good instances of powerful dominant castes which have exerted pressure on their respective State Governments for the retention of caste as the basis for defining backwardness.

Although the Central Government has not insisted on the old lists being abandoned altogether, economic and other pressures have been exerted on the State Governments for the adoption of economic criteria. Since 1963 they have made the use of Central Government funds for the award of scholarships to members of the Other Backward Classes conditional upon the use of economic criteria for defining such classes. By now the majority of the states have adopted this criterion for defining backwardness for the award of scholarships to‍ the Backward Classes other than the Scheduled Castes and Scheduled Tribes. The Central Government have also since 1962 decided to use the term Backward Classes to refer only to the Scheduled Tribes and the Scheduled Castes.[7] However, the broader usage is retained in this paper since the Other Backward Classes continue to retain a certain amount of significance at the level of the State Government.

It is difficult to give exact figures for the Other Backward Classes because they are not enumerated separately in the Census and because such lists as do exist are subject to revision from time to time. Some estimate can, however, be made of their strength by projection of the caste returns in the 1931 Census. Speaking in very broad terms, then, the Other Backward Classes constitute about one-seventh of the total population of the country, being thus approximately equal in numerical strength to the Scheduled Castes.

The core of the Other Backward Classes consists of peasant castes of various descriptions. The position occupied by these castes in the wider society is rather different from that of the Harijans. Frequently they occupy a low position in the *varna* hierarchy and they have in general been devoid of traditions of literacy. Further, since they have also lagged behind in the pursuit of Western education, they are often poorly represented in Government jobs and white-collar occupations in general. In spite of this, such castes sometimes occupy a dominant position in the economic and political systems of the village. Not infrequently they are small landowners. When they are also numerically preponderant, their control over a village, a group of villages or even a district may be decisive.

Dominant castes of this kind have developed a vested interest in remaining backward. It enables them to enjoy a number of benefits in education and employment. What is more, they sometimes have enough political power to exert pressure on the State Government to have their names included or retained in the list of Backward Classes. The case of the powerful Lingayat caste of Mysore, which had first been excluded from the list recommended by the Nagana Gowda Commission and had later to be accommodated, has by now become well known.

This, then, is the broad social background against which we have to consider the issues which confront the Backward Classes in their efforts at transformation. The issues, it will be evident, are many and diverse. In many ways they are different for the three broad divisions, the Scheduled Tribes, the Scheduled Castes and the Other Backward Classes.

The tribal people have had a history of isolation which gives in many ways a unique character to their problems. They are faced with the task of achieving integration without doing violence to their rich cultural and artistic heritage. In the case of the Scheduled Castes an important problem is to break through the barrier of untouchability, not simply in its formal legal sense but in its widest social application. Both have to face the challenges of poverty, illiteracy and social prejudice, and this is true to some extent of certain sections of the Other Backward Classes too. But the latter also include a number of dominant castes who have 'arrived' so to say, at least politically, and have now to think of consolidating their power against politically weaker sections of society which may appear to threaten their dominance.

In the discussion which follows we shall try as far as poss- ible to consider separately some of the distinctive features of each of the three sections of the Backward Classes keeping in mind the more general problem of backwardness. This should not, however, be taken to mean that each section constitutes a homogeneous or undifferentiated unit. In fact, there are numerous social and economic differences within each but a detailed consideration of these would require a far more exhaustive study than the present one. Here we can provide only a few illustrations of these differences. The condition of tribal people in non tribal areas, for instance, is likely to differ greatly from their condition in an area which has a predominantly tribal population. The Scheduled Castes in South India occupy a somewhat different position from their counterparts in North India; an understanding of these differences would require analysis of the differences between the social systems of North and South India, including the differential importance of the idea of pollution in the two systems. Finally, everywhere there are great disparities of wealth and power within the all-too-loosely defined category of the Other Backward Classes.

That Indian society is passing through a phase of active social change will not be disputed by many. In a sense the impact of change appears more striking among the lower strata of society partly because these strata had remained relatively immobile in the past. Changes in the status of the Backward Classes, which may appear limited in absolute terms, tend to acquire a different significance when viewed against the background of traditional society.

It is well to remember that the currents of change do not all run in the same direction. Sometimes they run counter to one another. There are on the one hand certain factors which tend to blur the outlines of the traditional structure and to bridge the gaps between the Backward Classes and the advanced sections of society. The modern educational system may be viewed as one such factor. On the other hand, the frequent use made in politics of the loyalties of caste and tribe tends in some measure to freeze the traditional structure.

In spite of the apparent confusion of currents and counter-currents, the scales seem to be decisively weighted in favour of a lowering of many of the barriers of traditional society. In the traditional system, society was divided and subdivided into a large number of segments which were kept rigidly separated from one another. New networks of interpersonal relations are now being created in every field and these tend increasingly to cut across the boundaries of the old, established groups. New areas of social life are being opened up in which individuals from widely different backgrounds are able to come together on the basis of achievement, interest and personal choice. The change from a segmental and particularistic social order to a more fluid and universalistic one is bound in the long run to change the very character of the Backward Classes. But paradoxically enough, it seems that this change cannot be effected without widespread use being made of the particularistic loyalties of tribe, caste and community.

Of the many changes which are taking place among the Backward Classes, we shall consider two in particular: changes in their style of life and in their relation to the distribution of power.

When members of a lower caste change their style of life and move up in the hierarchy of prestige and social esteem, we speak of this as mobility along the axis of status. When on the other hand, they advance themselves by securing material benefits through office in an organ of government or a party or a pressure group, we speak of this as mobility along the axis of power. Our analysis of the future of the Backward Classes will centre around the chances of their movement along these two axes.

British rule provided the Backward Classes with increasing opportunities to imitate with effect the styles of life of the upper castes. These opportunities were extensively used by the Other Backward Classes and also the Scheduled Castes and Scheduled Tribes who set about 'Sanskritizing' themselves with varying degrees of success. Since independence, however, the emphasis seems to be shifting from Sanskritization to competition for positions of office and power. It appears that at many points the demands of prestige and power came into conflict and this conflict is likely to make itself felt more acutely among the Scheduled Tribes and Scheduled Castes. Present indications seem to suggest that in the years to come the latter will turn increasingly to politics as an avenue of social mobility.

We shall first consider the changes which the different sections of the Backward Classes have been undergoing in their styles of life. It may be useful to fix our point of departure in the past in order to be able to see the future from a proper point of vantage. It must not be thought, however, that changes in the styles of life of the Backward Classes are likely to follow a regular path. In fact, one of the points of the present argument is that political forces of a certain kind tend to arrest some of the changes which had been taking place more or less continuously over the last several decades.

Traditional Indian society had a structure which was highly segmental and hierarchical in character. The segments within it were separated from one another by clear-cut boundaries and marriage, commensality and many other forms of social interaction generally stopped short at these boundaries. The social separation of the different segments was bolstered by the fact that Hinduism allowed within its fold the practice of a wide variety of styles of life. Each group of castes, each caste and sometimes even each sub-caste was allowed to cultivate its distinctive styles of life in the matter of diet, dress, worship, marriage, etc. Hinduism tolerated a plurality of cultures but the price of this was the maintenance of a certain structural distance between people traditionally associated with divergent styles of life, e.g., between vegetarians and non-vegetarians, or between people practising different crafts or worshipping different gods.

Social separation between different segments, each pursuing its own style of life, could be kept intact so long as the world was fairly static or the pace of change not very rapid. In the traditional system, mobility – whether vertical or horizontal – was slow and limited. The expansion of transport and communication, the spread of education and new economic opportunities, and an increasing degree of political articulation are bringing about fundamental changes in the traditional structure. The system now tends to become relatively more open, allowing for greater mobility and greater variety in the combination of class, status and power positions.

Culturally the distance was greatest between the Adivasis and the Harijans on the one hand, and the advanced sections of society on the other. The tribal people, who were ecologically isolated, had developed their own traditions, habits and ways of life. The Harijans also lived in a cultural world of their own, shut out in many ways from the world of the 'twice born'. In the case of the Harijans there were often specific sanctions against the adoption of the styles of life of the upper castes. Even until recently the 'exterior' castes in South India were disallowed the use of sandals, umbrellas and silken cloth; they were not allowed to live in brick and tile houses; and their women could not wear upper garments. These disabilities were often enforced by powerful traditional sanctions.

Thus, the Adivasis because of their physical isolation and the Harijans for other reasons were unable to fully identify themselves with the higher strata of society or to use many of their distinctive symbols of status. For all this, social forces have been at work, leading to a transmission of cultural elements from the more advanced sections of society to the more backward. Two of the most important of such forces are Sanskritization and Westernization.[9]

Sanskritization was an important feature of traditional Indian society where it appears to have been the principal idiom of social mobility. Its role in contemporary Indian society was first analysed in detail by Srinivas in his study of the Coorgs of South India.[10] Sanskritization can be defined as a process by which a caste or a group of people moves up the social hierarchy by adopting styles of life associated by tradition with the upper castes. The Sanskritic model should not be viewed as an undifferentiated one; in addition to the Brahminical model, people seem at various places or various times to have made use of a Kshatriya model and perhaps even a Vaishya model.[11] But what is of particular importance in this context is that the idiom of Sanskritization is essentially traditional in nature.

In the past, the process of Sanskritization was slow and gradual and it offered very limited possibilities to the lowest sections of society. Social horizons were narrow, the economy was relatively static and population movements were limited. This made it difficult for a lower caste to acquire quickly economic and political power or, having once acquired it, to shed its traditional marks of inferiority. There were, in addition, legal and ritual sanctions which acted against a too radical change in life-styles. These sanctions operated with particular force upon the Harijans who were able to cross the barrier of untouchability rarely, if at all.

British rule released the Backward Classes (including the Harijans) from the grip of many of the traditional sanctions. The new courts of law refused to recognize the rights of the upper castes to the exclusive use of particular symbols of status. The avenues of Sanskritization were thrown open to ever-increasing sections of society. The first to seize the new opportunities were those whose social position had been low in traditional society but above the line of untouchability. These included many of the castes hitherto classified under the Other Backward Classes.

Castes which had been fairly low in the traditional hierarchy changed their diet, their social customs and sometimes even their gods in favour of those of the upper castes. The decennial Census provided them with opportunities to replace their traditional names with new and more high-sounding ones. Caste associations were formed throughout the country and these not only put forward claims to higher social status but also urged their members to abandon many of the practices considered degrading by the upper castes. Thus, Sanskritization served to lower the barriers between sections of society which had at one time been clearly separated. It is paradoxical that this process, which in a way represents the distinctive idiom of traditional society, had to await the coming of the modern age before it could acquire its full momentum.

The increased pace of Sanskritization has been dependent upon a number of forces, some of which are likely to extend their influence in the years to come. These include improvements in transport and communication, greater mobility in non-traditional sectors of the economy, the spread of literacy and education among the lower strata and (paradoxically) the institution of a secular legal order. Each of these forces, however, has other consequences which are likely to alter the very meaning of Sanskritization and in the long run to undermine its significance.

The revolution in transport and communication has thrown open pilgrim centres to people from far and near. Every year more people visit such important centres as Mathura, Kashi, Gaya, Tirupathi and Rameshwaram. In the past a visit to a distant centre of pilgrimage was not only replete with hazards but also a costly affair. Now even the moderately poor find it within their means to undertake journeys by bus or train to places which in the past would have appeared remote. It seems that these facilities will be used to greatest advantage by the better-off sections of the Other Backward Classes in the years to come.

The mass media have been harnessed for the diffusion of Sanskritic values and ideas. Mythological films and radio broadcasts of devotional programmes are becoming increasingly popular in the villages. This trend in the direction of Sanskritization is likely to persist in the rural areas, particularly among castes which are above the line of untouchability. Among the top castes there seems to be a trend away from popular Sanskritic culture and towards new values and symbols of status. The Other Backward Classes are still too much within the grip of the traditional system to be able to follow the top castes in this regard. The Harijans and the Adivasis are, in turn, different from the Other Backward Classes; their commitment to the traditional system was never so intense as to prevent them altogether from seeking alternative avenues of mobility.

The Other Backward Classes include a number of castes which enjoy a certain measure of economic and political dominance. A good example of these is provided by the Okkaligas of Mysore who have been studied by Srinivas.[12] Such castes or sections of them are often the ones to benefit most from the new economic opportunities. And they are also the ones most likely to Sanskritize their style of life in order to set the seal of social acceptance on their material success.

Sanskritization affects the culture of castes in the lower and middle regions of the hierarchy in a variety of ways. To begin with an example which may appear trivial, but is nevertheless of considerable significance, one may consider changes in personal names among them. These changes appear particularly striking in South India where sharp linguistic differences exist between typically Brahmin names and names common among the non-Brahmin peasantry. Among the latter the most common personal names have been typically non-Sanskritic, such as Pazhani, Thangavelu, Nadugowda or Puttappa. Today one encounters in increasing number such typically Sanskritic names as Narasimhan, Parthasarathy, and Srinivas. This change, trivial in itself, is symbolic of the penetration among the Backward Classes of a culture and a style of life which had virtually been a monopoly of a few upper castes.

Other, more fundamental changes are also taking place.

There are changes in occupation, diet and social practices of various kinds. Occupations considered degrading in the Sanskritic scale of values, such as distilling or oil-pressing or tanning, are often forsaken and there is a tendency even to deny any past association with them. Items of food such as pork and the drinking of alcoholic beverages are often given up. There is a pervasive tendency to abandon widow remarriage and to replace bride-price by dowry. Finally, castes which had done without Brahmin priests in the past now try to secure their services on occasions of birth, marriage and death. The pace of Sanskritization has been heightened not only by the activities of caste associations but also of such organizations as the Arya Samaj and the Sanatan Dharma Samaj. The latter act as important agencies for the diffusion of Sanskritic styles of life among large sections of people including the Backward Classes and especially in the rural areas. The Arya Samaj in particular combines Sanskritization with certain universalistic principles which create a special appeal among the hitherto underprivileged strata of society.

Sanskritization, which was the principal idiom of social mobility in the past, appears to have special significance today for castes in the middle and the lower-middle regions of the hierarchy. This is partly because the top castes are reaching forward to new social values and to new symbols of status. Thus, in Sanskritizing their life-styles, the Backward Classes are emulating models which certain sections of the traditional élite are already trying to put behind. And, some of the forces which impel the emerging élite to attach themselves to new models operate also among the Backward Classes. One of the most important of these is what Srinivas refers to as Westernization.[13]

Sanskritization can be seen not only as an idiom of mobility but also as an important source of continuity with the past. Its symbols and values are essentially those of the traditional order. At a time when a modernist élite is trying to push the country towards a secular and Westernized social order, it is not unlikely that those who had in the past occupied a fairly low social position may set themselves up as the bastions of traditional values. Unable to cope with the process of Westernization or the pace of rapid social change, such people may well throw in their lot with traditionalist or even revivalist movements and parties. It may appear ironical that the defence of the traditional order should become the burden of the people who had in the past been denied a position of honour within it.

The Sanskritization of the Backward Classes provides a stabilizing influence in Indian society. The Western educated élite in India is often impatient with the slow rate of change in the country. But in order to bring about change effectively it will have to make many compromises with some of the hitherto backward communities which are beginning to develop a new sense of commitment to the values of traditional society.

It would, of course, be unreal to suggest that every section of the Backward Classes is developing a stake in the traditional order. What has been said above applies principally to the upper strata among them and in particular to dominant peasant castes such as the Okkaligas or the Ahirs. The lowest sections of the Backward Classes are often under the influence of forces of a very different kind. It is well to remember that there are sharp cleavages within the Backward Classes, some of which may have greater significance than the ones which separate the dominant castes among them from the advanced sections of society.

Sanskritization has never meant the same thing for the Harijans as it has for castes above the line of pollution. Everywhere the effective adoption of the Sanskritic style of life has depended upon a number of preconditions. These include a minimum of economic and political power and a not too inferior ritual status. A caste may adopt a new name and claim a high social status but such a claim is not likely to be very effective where most of its members are landless labourers and are refused the services of the village barber or the village washerman. Dominant castes such as the Okkaligas develop a commitment to the Sanskritic style of life because their economic and political position enables them to adopt such a style with some effect.

In the past the Scheduled Castes were prevented from Sanskritizing their styles of life by a variety of sanctions.

They were excluded from temples, bathing *ghats*, wells and other public places. A large number of civic rights, necessary preconditions to Sanskritization or upward mobility of any kind, were denied to them by legal and ritual sanctions. The new courts established by the British introduced the principle of equality before the law and by doing so removed one set of restrictions to changes in the social life of the Harijans.

However, the removal of legal disabilities did not automatically enable the Harijans to exercise their civic rights. Various kinds of sanctions were applied to keep them in their inferior position. They were (and still are) economically dependent on the upper castes whom they dare not offend by pressing too far their legal claims to equality. A Harijan tenant or agricultural labourer who dares to behave as the equal of his master on social or ceremonial occasions may find himself deprived of his source of livelihood. And here it should be pointed out that dominant castes among the Other Backward Classes rarely look with favour upon the Harijans' claim to equality of status.

Apart from moral and economic pressures, physical violence or the threat of it is a very effective deterrent, particularly in a village. It is not unknown even now for Harijans to be beaten by caste Hindus for attempting to exercise their civic rights. The dominant caste of an area is rarely (perhaps never) a Harijan caste. It often has the strength of organized numbers and this can be used against Harijans who are too eager to appropriate the traditional symbols of honour. In the past the Scheduled Castes had accepted their civic deprivations as a matter of course. Now that a spirit of challenge has been kindled among them, it is likely that conflicts between the Harijans and dominant peasant castes will become more pervasive.

In order to gain an understanding of the issues involved in the conflicts between Harijans and caste Hindus it may be useful to go back a little in time. The growing emancipation of the Adi-Dravida untouchables from traditional disabilities had aroused the wrath of the Kallas as early as the 1930s. The Kallas are a dominant peasant caste in Tamilnadu, classified among the Other Backward Classes. Hutton reports that:

In December 1930 the Kallar in Ramnad propounded eight prohibitions, the disregard of which led to the use of violence by the Kallar against the exterior castes, whose huts were fired, whose granaries and property were destroyed, and whose livestock was looted.[14]

The 'eight prohibitions' related, among other things, to the use of ornaments of gold and silver, the use of upper garments by women, and the use of umbrellas and sandals. Hutton further writes:

In June 1931, the eight prohibitions not having been satisfactorily observed by the exterior castes in question, the Kallar met together and framed eleven prohibitions, which went still further than the original eight, and an attempt to enforce these led to more violence.[15]

It may be mentioned that one of the eleven prohibitions was that, 'Their children should not read and get themselves literate or educated'.[16]

The attempt of the Harijans to change their social customs does not proceed by way of Sanskritization alone. There are many non-traditional elements in the life-styles of the upper strata which the Harijans also seek to imitate. Whatever may be the idiom adopted, the very fact of upward mobility requires the rejection of many of the civic disabilities imposed by the former upon the latter. The upper castes are likely to see in this a threat not only to their social status but also to their political and economic power. This being the case, conflicts between Harijans and caste Hindus are likely to continue for some time. Anthropologists who have done field work in village India in recent years report the existence and sometimes the intensification of such conflicts. But one important point has to be borne in mind: the nature of these conflicts and in particular the issues over which they arise tend to change.

Even in South India the issue of wearing upper garments or constructing brick and tile houses is no longer a living one. In these matters the Harijans seem clearly to have won their battle. But other issues remain, and new ones tend to emerge as the hitherto untouchable castes press forward in their campaign to gain full social equality with the caste Hindus. Before taking up some of the issues which are likely to figure in the immediate future, it may be useful to take stock of the gains which the Harijans have accumulated over the last few decades.

Diacritical distinctions in the matter of dress, ornament and habitation are now rarely enforced by caste Hindus upon the Scheduled Castes. When the latter continue to retain their former style of life, it is more because they lack the economic resources to acquire the symbols of upper caste society and less because they are coerced by the latter to retain their traditional marks of inferiority. While doing field work in Tanjore district, I was struck by the difference in dress between Palla women of the younger and older generations. The younger women, particularly on festive occasions, now commonly wear blouses and saris of synthetic fibre. This does not any longer evoke violence from the upper castes; all that remains is a faint attitude of mockery among the Brahmins at the extravagance and vulgarity of the new generation of Harijans.

The adoption by Harijans of some of the upper caste symbols of status is likely to become increasingly common. These symbols, however, are by no means all a part of the Sanskritic model. The Tanjore experience referred to above seems to be of widespread occurrence. Bailey reports a comparable situation from Bisipara, a hill village in Orissa. In describing the participation of Pan untouchables in an annual festival in 1959, he says:

> Many of the men wore shirts and long trousers and shoes, certainly as a mark of status and emancipation because the normal dress of the villagers is a *dhoti*, and even sandals are worn only when the ground gets unbearably hot in April and May. The Pan women wore blouses and mill woven *saris*, and several of the younger ones had put on lipstick and face-powder.[17]

There are even now certain pockets where the old disabilities continue to be enforced. The *Report of the Commissioner for Schedules Castes and Scheduled Tribes for 1961- 65* states:

> The Scheduled Castes are not allowed to wear *dhotis* below the knees, and a Scheduled Caste bridegroom cannot put on a turban with a *turra* in some of the villages of Madhaya Pradesh. In some areas of this State band music is not allowed to be played at the

time of marriage among the Scheduled Castes, their women folk cannot wear bangles and other ornaments made of silver and the Scheduled Caste people are not allowed to ride a horse or use a bullock cart as means of transport.[18]

There can be little doubt, however, that the areas in which such restrictions are enforced are shrinking at a rapid rate.

There is a certain measure of ambivalence in the attitude of the Harijans towards the traditional status symbols of the upper castes. There is, on the one hand, an urge to adopt many of these symbols and, on the other, an undercurrent of resentment against the entire traditional order. The rejection of the traditional symbols of status is helped by the existence of alternative styles of life towards which the Harijans are likely to turn in increasing degree. Before discussing the significance of some of these it may be useful to consider briefly the part played by Sanskritization in tribal society.

It is clear that the tribal people have been isolated to a far greater extent from the broad stream of Sanskritization than have the Scheduled Castes or the Other Backward Classes. In spite of this they have felt the impact of Sanskritic ideas and values and this impact has gathered momentum over the last several decades. This has no doubt been largely due to the opening of the tribal area to traffic from outside. One of the most general effects of Sanskritization in this case is that it leads to the integration of segments of tribal society into the wider caste structure. Historically there have been numerous examples of this kind of integration. The Bhumij in Eastern India, the Raj Gond in Central India and the Patelia in Western India provide instances of tribes which have been integrated into the caste structure.

The Sanskritization of tribal communities and their integration into the caste structure cannot be understood simply as a change in rituals or life-styles. Rather this change in life-styles usually symbolizes a more fundamental transformation in their productive organization. Generally, it is only as tribal people get integrated more fully into the wider economic system that Sanskritization begins to act in a significant way.

As a typical example of Sanskritization of tribal communities one may, among other things, consider the Bhagat Movement among the Oraons of Chhota Nagpur. Over the last several decades certain sections of the Oraons have sought to mark themselves out from the main body of their tribe by adherence to a style of life in which vegetarianism, teetotalism and ritual abstentions of various kinds are given a prominent position. The connection of these codes of conduct with Sanskritic Hinduism has been noted by many anthropologists. That such movements are often defined in opposition to the wider Hindu society should not be allowed to obscure the fact of their absorption of many of the values of that society.

The Meenas of Peepulkhunt in Banswara district in Rajasthan offer another striking example.[19] Until recently classified as a section of the Bhils, they are now taking in a big way to the adoption of Rajput names and other elements of the Rajput style of life. This leads in some cases to the repudiation of their tribal ancestry, followed by claims to Rajput status. In concrete terms, the consequences of this kind of 'passing' can be seen in changes in dress, worship, rules of marriage, etc. In this area also one encounters the development of Bhagat Movements comparable to the ones of Chhota Nagpur.

The efforts of Harijans and Adivasis to Sanskritize their life-styles are not always met with success. The structural distance between these communities and the upper castes is still too great for the former to pass successfully into the ranks of the latter. In Indian society the rules of caste endogamy ensure the maintenance of structural distance between groups which are of widely different background. Even when intermarriages do take place across castes, the barrier of untouchability is rarely crossed. Indeed, it continues to restrict intermarriage even after conversion to Christianity. Nor is the Adivasi, even when he is highly educated, in a better position when he seeks intermarriage with a caste Hindu.

Where attempts at Sanskritization fail, the consequence is often a feeling of deep resentment among Harijans and Adivasis against the upper castes. This resentment is born out of an attitude which is different from what prevailed in the past. In traditional society inequality between communities was accepted as a fundamental value. This value has been formally rejected by the new legal and political order and where it still exists it is challenged at every point.

The attitude of resentment against the traditional order is most easily perceptible among the younger generation of Harijans who have been exposed to the ideas of secularism and democracy. In some places it has been nourished by social movements of a fairly organized nature. In Tamilnadu the Self-respect Movement challenged the traditional social and ritual order and sought to emancipate the lower castes from the domination of the Brahmins. It played an important part in the creation of a new climate among the Backward Classes, including the Harijans.

In Maharashtra over 2,000,000 Harijans became converts to Buddhism. The Neo-Buddhist Movement was spearheaded by the late Dr B.R. Ambedkar, a Harijan leader who enjoyed an all-India reputation. Dr Ambedkar was an indomitable critic of the traditional Hindu social order with its emphasis on inequality, segregation and ritual pollution. The conversion to Buddhism can be seen as an assertion of self-respect on the part of Harijans who refused to accept the degraded position assigned to them in Hindu society. The neo-Buddhists have dispensed with some of the traditional rituals of Hinduism although in other regards their style of life has not altered very significantly.

Buddhism is not the only religion which has attracted the alienated sections of Hindu society. Islam, Sikhism and Christianity have also attracted converts from the lower strata. Christianity plays a very active part today among many tribal communities. Throughout tribal India a variety of Christian Missions and, in particular, the Roman Catholic Church operate as active agents of social change. Besides providing an alternative system of religious values, the Missions have introduced many new features into tribal society such as education and modern medical facilities. It is no accident that many of the leaders of tribal India are Christians or at least have been educated in Mission schools. The Harijans also have been converted in large numbers to Christianity particularly in South India.

The Harijans and the Adivasis – particularly the younger generations among them – seem to be groping for new symbols to which they might attach themselves. The symbols of traditional Hindu society are no longer adequate and it is for this reason that the Adivasis (and sometimes also the Harijans) endeavour to recreate a largely imaginary past in which their life was more pure and had not been corrupted by the priest, the moneylender and the other evils of upper caste Hindu society. It should again be emphasized that the kinds of symbols to which these sections of the Harijans and the Adivasis are reaching forward are likely to be very different from the ones which the upper layers of the Other Backward Classes tend to adopt.

But the Harijans and the Adivasis are not entirely tied to an imaginary past in their search for new symbols. The modern secular social order provides alternative symbols and values which are likely to become increasingly important in the future. In order to understand how this is likely to come about we have to consider the process of Westernization in contemporary India.

We shall not attempt here to give a precise definition of Westernization.[20] Broadly speaking, the process refers to the adoption by a community of Western elements in dress, habits, manners and customs. An important agency of Westernization in this sense is the modern educational system which is associated with new norms and values, and new symbols of prestige. The English language, which occupies a central position in the new educational system, is an important symbol of status in every sector of Indian society.

Fifty years ago Western education was virtually a monopoly of the Brahmins and a few upper castes. The Backward Classes made a belated start in the adoption of Western elements into their style of life. However, since the end of the First World War demands began to be made by the leaders of these communities for the benefits of Western education. In fact, the demand for educational concessions was a major plank in the Backward Classes Movement. These demands were put forward in a particularly organized manner in South India, especially in Madras and Mysore and also in Maharashtra.

The Backward Classes in general and particularly the Other Backward Classes have been trying consistently to narrow the gaps in Western education between themselves and the 'forward' classes. Mysore State offers a striking example where rapid strides have been taken in this direction by the two dominant backward castes, the Lingayats and the Okkaligas. Such gains which may appear rather limited in absolute terms have, of course, to be measured against the past, and the rather low *average* rate of literacy and education in the country. Further, whatever may be the results achieved so far, there is every indication of a continuous rise in the demand for education by all sections of the Backward Classes.

There is no gainsaying the fact that literacy and education among the Scheduled Tribes and the Scheduled Castes are still very low. But once again what has been achieved must be measured against the background of traditional society which denied almost wholly the benefits of education to these sections of society. Viewed in the light of the past, the progress of some of these communities (e.g. the Lushais of Assam or the Mahars of Maharashtra) appears remarkable. The benefits of education are most likely to spread with increasing speed among the Scheduled Tribes and Castes. For, not only are demands being generated from within but the Government is investing increasingly larger sums of money to meet these demands.

It is difficult to provide accurate figures for Harijan and Adivasi intake into schools and colleges. Isaacs gives certain estimates which present a general picture of changes that have come about since Independence.

> In the past fifteen years, while the total school population has more than doubled, the figures for ex-Untouchables has swelled eightfold or tenfold, to almost six million, and now, as already indicated, there are more than four million ex-Untouchable children in primary schools (which are now largely free to all), and something close to a million and a half in middle and high schools (in which the Scheduled Castes are exempt from fees and in many places receive stipends for support), and about fifty-six thousand in institutions of higher learning.[21]

Over the last two decades there has been a phenomenal rise in the number of scholarships awarded by the Government of India to members of these communities. In 1944-5 only 114 post-matric scholarships were awarded to members of the Scheduled Castes. The figure had risen to 10,034 by 1954-5 and to 60,165 by 1963-4. Corresponding figures for the Scheduled Tribes are, 84 for 1948-9, 2,356 for 1954-5 and 11,670 for 1963-4.[22] There can be little doubt that these figures will continue to rise (though certainly not at the same rates) over the next ten years.

There are indications that the Harijans and the Adivasis are making increasingly effective use of the facilities provided by the Government to better their economic and social positions. Formerly many of the posts in the higher services reserved for members of these communities could not be filled for want of suitable qualified candidates. This is no longer the case today and is not likely to be so in the future. To take a crucial example, whereas only five of the sixteen posts reserved for the Scheduled Castes in the IAS were actually filled in 1957, since 1962 all the posts reserved for them have been actually filled.[23] The position with regard to the Scheduled Tribes is similar.

Modern education acts in a very special way as a solvent of the barriers between different communities. The modern school is an effective area of desegregation and this is of particular importance from the viewpoint of the Scheduled Castes. The school brings together in increasing numbers children from castes which are widely separated from one another. Even in the orthodox South, Brahmin, non-Brahmin and Harijan children come together in the school. In the villages of Tanjore district, for instance, it is a new experience for Harijan children to sit with the children of their Brahmin masters in the same room and study and play together. This early experience, even when it is short-lived, creates a new sense of confidence among the Harijans which is almost entirely absent in the older generation.

The differences in attitude between the generations and the future implications of these differences were brought home to me vividly in the course of my fieldwork in a Tanjore village. In this village, the Brahmins live separately in their exclusive area of residence called the *agraharam*. The Harijans live apart on the fringe of the village or a little away from it. Even today Harijan men almost never enter the *agraharam*. When a Harijan tenant has to deliver grain to the Brahmin landowner, he stands at the head of the *agraharam* and calls out until somebody (often a non-Brahmin) is sent to bring the grain. The village school is situated in the same *agraharam*, although at one end. It is attended by a number of Harijan children whose movements within the *agraharam* are now hardly noticed. While children freely come and go, a Harijan elder still considers it an act of daring – perhaps even a little impious – to enter the *agraharam*.

It has been noted earlier that there were in the past many differences in culture between the Scheduled Castes and the higher strata. These differences were symbolized in different styles of speech, including vocabulary, diction and accent. Such differences tend to be ironed out today as boys and girls from every caste are brought up together in the atmosphere of a common school.

In Madras State the 'mid-day meals scheme' has been a subject of much discussion and controversy. The scheme provides mid-day meals for all school-going children throughout the State. The children are generally served together irrespective of caste. This sometimes leads to abstention from the meals by boys and girls of the upper castes, particularly the Brahmins. But for all this, the experience is a new one and in view of the central importance of commensality in the Hindu scheme of values, it is likely to have considerable significance for the future.

Western education creates a hunger for white-collar occupations among the younger generation of Adivasis and Harijans. Those who succeed in getting jobs as teachers, accountants or clerks tend to be cut off from their communities. Their position is, in fact, replete with uncertainty. Standing between two worlds, they are often unable to gain a foothold in either. Although their number so far is limited, it is bound to increase and this increase will render more acute the social problems of transition from the most backward sections of society to the new middle class. As Isaacs has put it:

it is the educated ones who are bearing the brunt of the painful experience of change. They have to acquire a whole new identity for themselves, a whole new way of relating to a society that is not yet quite ready to welcome them on any real basis of equality.[24]

The tremendous urge for white-collar jobs among the Scheduled Tribes and Castes cannot be explained solely by motives of economic gain. In every range of Indian society a very high value is attached to non-manual work and a white-collar job is universally viewed as a passport to respectability. This view is sometimes held all the more keenly by the Backward Classes who have until recently been almost wholly excluded from such occupations. Now that white-collar jobs are almost within reach, no price appears to be too high for them.

It is largely for this reason that boys from the Scheduled Tribes and Castes are not attracted in very large numbers to the craft training schools of the Government. A Harijan boy who has been through high school would normally prefer a clerical job even where higher earnings are offered by skilled manual work. Among people who have been tied to social degradation for generations, the appeal of respectability is particularly urgent.

Isaacs has provided a sensitive description of the ways in which educated Harijans use the anonymity of city life to discard their traditional identities. Middle-class jobs enable them to adopt many elements of the Western style of life which is differentiated less by caste than by income, occupation and education. This kind of transition is of course achieved by only a few and then too it is never wholly effective.

Westernization as an alternative means of acquiring status has made inroads also into tribal society. Martin Orans, who has made an intensive study of tribal life in Bihar, writes: 'The aspiring Santal who was well acquainted with Jamshedpur might adopt Western clothing, an automobile or motorcycle, and a *pukka* house . . . rather than vegetarianism, teetotalism, and a sacred thread'.[25]

Thus, the values and status symbols of the upper castes tend to be progressively internalized by the Backward Classes. The

competition for higher social status spreads and becomes intensified. This competition is waged sometimes in the traditional
idiom, e.g. when a lower caste tries to Sanskritize itself and
sometimes in a more modern idiom, e.g. when demands are
made for higher education or Government jobs. In the past it
was generally accepted that different life-styles were appropriate
to different sections of society. Now the social aspirations of
the Backward Classes tend to be pitched at an increasingly
higher level.

It is clear that the competition for status cannot bring the same
kind of success to all sections of society. None the less, this
competition is an important feature of modern Indian society
and its pace is likely to quicken. In the past, social mobility
was slow and gradual because the symbols of high social status
were often not open even in theory to the lower strata of society.
The value system today offers increasingly greater choice to the
individual although it is evident that the channels through which
this choice can be exercised are not equally open to all.

In the past the unit of social mobility was generally not the
individual but a caste or sub-caste. A caste had a more or less
homogeneous culture and it was difficult for an individual to
change his style of life effectively in the absence of corresponding changes in his caste or kin group. Today there is increasing
scope for individual mobility. Western education, the expansion
of caste-free occupations and the possibilities of geographical
mobility – all enable the individual to change his style of life
on his own. And, the criterion of individual achievement is
likely to play an increasingly important part in the emerging
social order.

An increase in the tempo of individual mobility is likely to
bring about a change in the very structure of caste. Closed
status groups based upon birth are likely to yield increasingly to
relatively open status groups based upon education, income and
occupation. There is indeed a noticeable trend in this direction
in large urban centres where the ties of caste are being slowly
but gradually supplanted by those developed in the school, the
office or the club. However, these trends are as yet largely
confined to a small upper layer of urban Indian society. It may
take more than a generation for Harijans and Adivasis to gain

full acceptance in these new status groups based on factors other than caste.

The rapidity with which members of the Backward Classes pass into the newly emerging status groups will depend to a large extent on two factors. It will depend firstly on the extent to which facilities of education and employment are made available to them and secondly on the weakening of the traditional attitudes regarding purity and pollution among the upper castes. There are indications that both these tendencies are beginning to operate but it is unlikely that significant results will be achieved within a short time. And, the rural areas are likely to lag considerably behind the urban centres in the emergence of status groups based primarily upon education, occupation and income.

So far we have been concerned largely with the movement of the Backward Classes along one particular axis, that of social prestige or status. The internalization of the values, idioms and symbols of the wider society, whether through Sanskritization or Westernization, has a certain unifying effect. It tends to pull down the walls which in the past segregated the different sections of society. This it does by replacing clearly differentiated styles of life by ones which are more general and standardized. The different cultures of the multitude of castes and communities tend more and more to be replaced by a single culture in which the same aspirations, values and symbols are shared by an ever-widening circle of people.

The upward movement of members of the Backward Classes is not always a smooth or easy process. Many of the status symbols of the upper strata of society are inaccessible to the Backward Classes if not in principle at least in reality. The channels of mobility whether in the status system or in the system of production are still very restricted in Indian society. On the other hand, the new political system has thrown open many possibilities of advancement to people from the Scheduled Tribes, the Schedules Castes and the Other Backward Classes. Today if a Harijan cannot find a place in a higher status group, he can still hope to become an influential political leader. The adoption of a democratic political order in a highly particularistic society ensures that people from every major section of it can aspire to positions of power and authority. For Harijans and Adivasis political representation is guaranteed by the principle of reservation.

The success of the Backward Classes in the competition for power requires a certain assertion of particularistic ties. A Harijan must assert that he is a Harijan if he is to mobilize the support necessary for his political advancement. And it is here that the demands of power and status come into conflict. Whereas the Backward Classes are prompted to merge their identity with the higher strata to enhance their status, considerations of power and material advantage lead them to define their identity in opposition to the advanced sections of society. This is the dilemma of backwardness. A low caste would like to acquire a high-sounding title, claim Kshatriya status and assume the symbols of high social status; at the same time it would insist on its right to be officially classified as backward.

It would be of interest to examine the conflicting demands of prestige and power from the viewpoint of the Backward Classes. How have these demands been adjusting themselves and what shape are they likely to take in the future? Frustrated in their efforts to gain social acceptance, the Backward Classes are likely to turn increasingly to political action.

The new political system adopted since independence offers vast possibilities to large minority blocks such as the Scheduled Tribes, the Scheduled Castes and the other Backward Classes. It cannot be said that these possibilities have as yet been fully exploited. The process by which the different sections of society get progressively inducted into the arena of politics is a slow and gradual one. In India politics was in the early stages confined largely to a few upper castes. They were the ones to take the lead in forming political associations in order to bargain for power with the British.

But politics has not remained confined to a small coterie of upper castes. It has made its way into ever-widening areas of society. The four general elections since Independence have brought home to every section of the Backward Classes the importance of organized politics. There are many indications that they are going to make increasing use of political action to bargain for a better position in society.

In its formal aspects at least changes in the political order have been much more radical than changes in other spheres of Indian society. And changes in political form do have an impact on the intensity of political participation. As Myron Weiner writes, 'But it is also true that India has become tremendously politicised. Politics has become the avenue for personal advancement in a society in which commercial activities offer little status and administrative posts are relatively few in number'.[26]

There is a clear trend towards increasing participation in the political process by sections of society which have hitherto been excluded from positions of power. It is difficult, however, to assess how far there is as yet a real articulation of interests. There is widespread poverty, ignorance and illiteracy among the Backward Classes, particularly the Scheduled Castes and Tribes. Most members of these communities have as yet only a dim awareness of the nature and strategy of organized politics. It is not unlikely that those who now represent their interests do so in a narrow and short-sighted manner.

However, even the most backward sections of society have by now had the experience of four general elections. Their awareness of political parties, movements, machines and election campaigns has grown steadily over the last fifteen years. By now the experience of being courted during elections by eminent leaders has become familiar even to the hitherto 'exterior' castes. This must in course of time create in them a new awareness of their strength in the political arena.

Recent field studies by social anthropologists often report a change of mood among the Harijans particularly of the younger generation. Bailey[27] indicates how even in a remote hill village in Orissa the Harijan Pans played an active and even aggressive role in the 1957 elections. In Tanjore district where I did field work in 1961-2 the Congress and its ally, the Dravida Kazhagam, drew active support from many Harijan youths for the election campaign.

Participation in election campaigns and contact with party bosses tend to create among the younger Harijans a sense of impatience towards the slow and uncertain process of social mobility through imitation of the life-styles of the upper castes. Young Harijans who are inducted into political machines may feel that they can dispense with Sanskritization. Indeed, for a person who aspires to be a political leader among Harijans and Adivasis, a repudiation of Sanskritization may have a high symbolic value. In Tamilnadu, where the Dravida Kazhagam has had a strong appeal among the Backward Classes, it is not rare for young Harijans to reject explicitly the values and symbols of the upper castes.

Whereas a generation ago an ambitious Harijan might have tried to acquire social respectability by changing his style of life, his counterpart today is more likely to try to build political connections. And young Harijans with ambition, drive and initiative are in demand all round. They are sought by every political party; for, they are not only valuable as vote-banks, but can also be put up as candidates for reserved seats from the Zilla Parishad right up to Parliament.

The scramble for power among linguistic, religious and caste groups has become an important feature of post-independence India. Virtually every region, community and caste claims special benefits for itself. And pressure is exerted at every level for the satisfaction of these claims. The Backward Classes have not lagged behind in this regard. In fact, the policy of protective discrimination pursued by the Government has encouraged them to put forward their demands with special vigour.

The institution of Panchayati Raj is likely to quicken the pace of politicization. Provisions have in general been made for the reservation of seats for the Scheduled Tribes and the Scheduled Castes at all levels of the three-tiered structure. The village *panchayat* is likely to become in many areas an arena for conflicts between Harijan members and those of the 'clean' castes. The latter are rarely prepared to treat on equal terms those who had been until recently excluded from many of the important spheres of social life. So conflict is likely to multiply in the near future. And, perhaps conflict is a necessary condition for the articulation of the interests of the hitherto underprivileged sections of society.

In this context it is well to remind ourselves that there are deep cleavages within the Backward Classes. It is likely that the most stubborn opposition against the attempts of Harijans to improve their social position will come from those who are immediately above them rather than from the top castes. It is a matter of common observation that competition for status is often most acute between segments which are structurally adjacent to one another. This is because such segments operate largely within the same social universe. It is for this reason that castes which are just above the line of pollution are more likely to be jealous of their privileges in relation to the Harijans than the Westernized upper strata of society.

Conflicts between Harijans and caste Hindus over civic rights are likely to play an important part for some time to come. The new generation of Harijans is no longer in a mood to accept with resignation the civic disabilities imposed upon them by the upper castes. Their contacts with politicians and officials have given them a growing awareness of their rights as citizens of a democratic society and they are rapidly becoming jealous of these rights. A show of strength on their part is a likely source of violence in the rural areas where, in spite of a superficial acceptance of democratic values, the structure remains by and large inegalitarian.

In 1957 severe rioting took place in Ramanathapuram district in Tamilnadu between Harijans and Thevars, a locally dominant caste included among the Other Backward Classes. The riots centred around the Immanuel murder case in which a young Harijan was stabbed to death, allegedly for offering rude remarks to a prominent Thevar politician. The setting of the incident was provided by a by-election in which Harijans and Thevars supported rival candidates.

The Ramanathapuram riots provide only a striking example of a phenomenon which is of widespread occurrence and probably on the increase. It would perhaps be unreal to expect the Harijans to become integrated into the wider social system with rights of full and equal participation without any conflict or violence. But the extent to which such violence can be contained will depend in large measure on the effectiveness of our machinery of law and order.

A special correspondent of *The Mail* wrote during the third general elections:

> Shrewd observers draw attention to the new trend in the political
> scene in the State, with emphasis shifting from the outdated
> Brahmin *versus* non-Brahmin to Harijan *versus* non-Harijan as a
> reaction to the numerous concessions made to the Harijans by the
> Government.[28]

These remarks, made with regard to Tamilnadu, seem to
indicate a trend which has general significance.

As Harijans in increasing numbers enter the arena of politics,
conflicts between them and the upper castes are bound to multiply. These conflicts will in all likelihood manifest themselves
most clearly at the level of the village or the small local community. There are now many village *panchayats* where Harijans
have a large representation. In rare cases the domination of the
panchayat by Harijans may lead to the withdrawal of the 'twice
born' from participation.

Where Harijans are more or less evenly matched in numerical
strength with caste Hindus, a certain amount of tension or even
violence is likely to become a part of the system. During my
stay in Tanjore district in 1961-2 several cases of violent
conflict between Harijans and non-Brahmins (particularly of
the dominant Kallar caste) came to notice. There was one
incident in a neighbouring village which culminated in the
murder of a Kallar landowner by the Harijan president of the
village *panchayat*. During the legal proceedings that followed, the
Kallar tried to storm the court room at Tanjore in an attempt to
do violence to the offending Harijan.

Tribal politics differs in many ways from the politics of the
Harijans or the Other Backward Classes. There are certain
special problems in their case which arise partly out of their
geographical isolation and partly out of their ethnic identity
which is even more sharply defined than that of the Harijans.
We noted earlier how the process of Sanskritization was in the
past responsible for the weakening of the cultural identity of
tribal peoples in the different parts of the country. But here also
the process of cultural assimilation is countered by a variety of
forces (principally political in nature) which seek to reassert the
identity of the tribal population.

The shift in emphasis from a ritual idiom of mobility to one which relies more on organized politics has been noted by various observers of tribal society. Discussing the trend of modern leadership in Chota Nagpur, Dr Vidyarthi writes:

> The most significant and obvious fact is the switch over from religious leadership to political leadership. This change corresponds to a difference in aims and a difference in methods. The modern leaders are representing the tribal people to an outside political world. They are not concerned primarily with raising the social status of the tribals by making ritual practices more closely resemble those of the Hindus. Their chief task is to improve the material conditions of the tribals and to obtain government funds and services. Their activities, then, are more within the realm of the civil and political and less within the realm of the religious and the social.[29]

The search for a new identity by leaders of tribal communities is understandable. There are important sections of people outside the tribal world who have warned against the loss of their social and cultural identity. In the case of the Adivasis, assimilation (as opposed to integration) has been viewed as a genuine threat by no less a person than the late Prime Minister. The attitude of 'progressive' Indians towards Harijans is fundamentally different in this regard and less ambivalent. Few voices would be raised in protest against the assimilation of Harijans into the wider social system.

Close observers of the Adivasis have, in consequence, noted the development of a spirit of 'tribalism' among them. This is due to a variety of factors, among which the special treatment policy of the Government and the work of the Christian Missions are of importance. Today the spirit of tribalism can be given expression through the processes of organized politics. The demand for a tribal homeland and the growth of a political party to put it forward indicate the politicization of tribal society. Professor N.K. Bose, until recently Anthropological Adviser to the Government, writes: 'Tribal communities formerly tried to better their condition by either identification with the Hindus or with the ruling class through Westernization and Christianity. Now power can be derived by political organisation into parties'.[30]

Tribal groups may, of course, press their demands through

parties committed to unity and integration or they may form separatist parties to represent their exclusive interests. Separatist demands have been particularly strong in the NEFA and Assam. The Jharkhand Party had also made similar demands. On the other hand, the Congress has shown an extremely high degree of resilience in meeting the special demands of communities of every kind. The recent merger of the Jharkhand Party with the Congress in Bihar seems to suggest that the party in power has many devices for softening the tone of separatist demands.

The kind of compromises which the ruling party is prepared to make is likely to deflect it, to some extent, from its main aims and policies. The Congress is likely to continue its tolerance of tribal exclusiveness partly as a measure of political expediency; an uncompromising attitude is more likely to precipitate a crisis than to overcome it. It seems probable that the special treatment policy will slacken the pace of development for some time to come by creating an atmosphere of apathy and complacency. It is difficult, however, to foresee any radical change in this policy in the immediate future. And the policy remaining broadly the same, the chances of a crisis being precipitated by separatist forces appear rather limited.

It is most unlikely that the 'communal' element will be eliminated from Indian politics for some time to come. N.K. Bose writes, 'under the climate created by special treatment, communal consciousness has been inordinately accentuated'.[31] But the significance of this development can be evaluated in different ways. The growth of 'communal consciousness' need not be viewed as necessarily an unhealthy or disruptive force. It may, on the contrary, be a precondition to the integration of the tribals into the wider body politic. For the measure of integration lies not so much in a passive acceptance of the *status quo* as in the adoption of a body of common political rules through which divergent interests are organized and articulated.

Thus, what has been viewed by some as an increase in communal consciousness may be one step forward in the politicization of Indian society. The years to come are likely to witness a fuller participation in the political process by larger sections of the tribal population, and a more effective articulation between tribal leaders and the masses. The wider political order can be brought close to the tribal masses only when their leaders at every level learn to put forward demands on their own behalf. In a heterogeneous society where particularistic ties are of such importance, it is unreal to expect political integration to come about without large concessions to special demands.

It may be interesting in this context to re-examine the old controversy regarding isolation, assimilation and integration as three alternative lines along which tribal communities might develop. The case for isolation seems to have been abandoned as both unreal and undesirable. The tribal people everywhere are being drawn increasingly into wider social, economic and political networks. In addition to market forces of diverse kinds, the developmental activities of the Government are bound to make steady inroads into the world of the Adivasis. And the Adivasi leaders are rapidly coming to realize that they can gain more for themselves and their communities by coming to terms with the Government and the ruling party than by remaining isolated.

Increasing articulation with the wider social, economic and political system is likely to lead in the long run to the disappearance of many of the distinctive features of tribal life. The process of modernization has a certain standardizing effect and it may be too costly for the Government to keep alive in a hot-house atmosphere the picturesque or artistic elements of tribal culture. The search for an identity on the part of tribal leaders does not always involve a genuine revival of the traditional heritage; more often it is part of an attempt to come to terms with political forces; which in the long run are bound to destroy the very bases of this identity.

The Harijans illustrate even more clearly than the Adivasis the mechanism of integration through the political process. At the height of the Depressed Classes Movement under Dr Ambedkar it had at times appeared as if they might move further and further away from the wider social system. In the years since independence the Congress has successfully absorbed their demands and integrated the bulk of the Harijan leadership into the structure of the party.

The Congress Party seems to have succeeded in winning over the loyalties of the Harijans by making numerous concessions to them. Although such loyalties may not go very deep, it is doubtful whether any other party can compete with the Congress in this regard. Bailey has recorded in some detail the nature of Harijan support for the Congress in Bisipara; which he attributes to 'the ideological pull (or perhaps one should call it "enlightened self-interest") of Congress policy towards the Harijans'.[34] I found confirmation of Bailey's observations in a Tanjore village more than a thousand miles away.

The integration of the Harijans into the wider body politic is, by comparison with the Adivasis, relatively easy. Unlike the latter, they are not geographically concentrated and there is hardly any question in their case of the demand for a separate homeland. But numerically they are far more important than the tribals and, for historical reasons, the problem of untouchability has caught the imagination of the Western educated élite in the country. For this reason the Congress has been compelled to accommodate the demands of the Harijans at every level and these demands are likely to become progressively organized both within and outside the party.

There is a curious dilemma in the position adopted by the Government and the ruling party towards the Harijans. On the one hand, the leaders among the latter are impatient of the limited and tardy nature of the concessions granted to their community. On the other, there is a growing resentment among castes of the middle region against the 'soft' attitude of the Government towards the Harijans. The Congress, in gaining the support of Harijans through accommodation of their demands, is likely to create increasing disaffection in the ranks of the upper castes.

The arguments presented above suggest that the Harijans (as well as other under-privileged groups) are likely in the near future to seize their civic rights with increasing success and perhaps also get increasing representation in political bodies of various kinds. At this point it is possible only to raise the question as to how effective this representation is likely to be.

In the last analysis it may be argued that the fundamental problem facing the Harijans (and also, to some extent, the others) is a material one. It is a problem of landlessness, poverty and unemployment. How well can the Harijans or the Adivasis make use of their position of growing political strength to solve or even tackle some of these basic economic problems?

It is admitted on all hands that the economic transformation of the bulk of the Scheduled Tribes and the Scheduled Castes has been taking place at a creeping pace if at all. The Harijans and Adivasis by and large continue to be poor, indebted and landless. Governmental measures to ameliorate their economic conditions have had, at best, a moral or symbolic effect. Given the magnitude of the problem, it is doubtful whether any substantial change can be brought about solely through measures such as the allotment to a few Harijans of bits and pieces of land or the reservation of a certain number of jobs in the Government for them. The same, of course, applies in a large measure to the tribals.

In the pre-British economic system Harijans had almost wholly been in the position of agricultural labourers. In certain areas their position was no better than that of serfs tied to the soil. British rule and developments since independence have progressively emancipated them from their former servile status. But the change in legal status has rarely been accompanied by any real change in economic position. Most Harijans continue to be landless agricultural labourers. In some ways their economic position has been rendered more insecure than in the past. In the past, traditional obligations assured the Harijan labourer of some source of employment and sustenance. Today with the collapse of traditional obligations, even this is threatened.

The material position of the tribals is not very much better than that of the Harijans. Here, however, the issues and problems are a little different. There is, to begin with, the problem of wasteful techniques of cultivation. Attempts are being made by Government to control these but the problem itself is particularly acute for only a small section of the tribal people.

Land alienation and money-lending are the two most important economic problems which confront the tribals (and indirectly the Government). The two problems are closely related, since the money-lenders are also the ones to whom land is most frequently alienated. They have been sought to be remedied by legislative as well as executive action but the success so far has been very limited. Such action sometimes has the consequence of raising higher the barriers between tribals and non-tribals without bringing about any substantial improvement in the economic condition of the former.

When tribal people do become a part of the wider social order they generally occupy within it the lowest rungs of the economic ladder. They join as landless labourers, often without security of employment, working sometimes on the farms of other people and sometimes eking out a bare existence through the sale of baskets, mats or jungle produce. In such cases their economic problems are not significantly different from those of the Scheduled Castes.

It is rather difficult to visualize any radical transformation in the economic position of the Scheduled Tribes and Castes for some time to come. If such a transformation does come about it is unlikely that it will have its sources within tribal or Harijan society. Any significant change in their economic position will require major changes in the external system, in particular the agrarian class structure of the country as a whole. The Harijans and Adivasis are almost everywhere prevented by their insecure position from initiating any kind of major economic change. Nor can governmental intervention by itself bring about any quick and substantial improvement, the magnitude of the problem being what it is.

Changes in the economic position of the Other Backward Classes are, if anything, even more difficult to assess. For one thing, they appear to be a rather assorted category, including at one end castes which are similar in position to the Harijans and at the other end powerful dominant castes like the Lingayats and Okkaligas. Further, the Other Backward Classes do not form a sharply defined category in the social system, and in the absence of numerical data it is impossible to consider trends of economic change among them separately from such trends in the whole of Indian society.

The Central Government's policy to do away with the 'communal' definition of the Other Backward Classes and its refusal to draw up an all-India list of these communities is bound to affect their position in important ways. These communities had developed a separate identity partly as a consequence of policies pursued by the State Governments of associating them with certain concessions and advantages. When these are given to individuals on the basis of income, and not to whole communities, the boundaries between the latter and the so-called advanced sections of society will cease to have their former social and political significance.

It is not within the scope of this paper to consider the prospects of change in the agrarian class structure of the country. Here it can only be reiterated that the future of the Backward Classes is intimately related to what happens to the economy as a whole. In this paper we have tried to consider the problems of the Backward Classes *qua* Backward Classes, as understood in the Constitution and recognized for specific purposes by the Central and State Governments. Although it is true that the Backward Classes overlap in large measure with certain economic categories, as defined in this country, they are not 'classes' at all but groups of communities.

The distinctive features of the Backward Classes are in large measure related to the very structure of Indian society. When this structure undergoes change, the Backward Classes are likely to lose much of their identity. There is ample evidence to show that Indian society is undergoing profound changes. The traditional segmental structure is losing many of its characters and a greater interpenetration of segments is coming about. Networks of interpersonal relations cutting across the boundaries of caste and community are becoming an increasingly important feature of the new economic and political systems. Finally, ritual values which played a decisive role in keeping alive the concept of structural distance are becoming progressively weakened.

It is true that the forces of modernization are as yet largely confined to a limited sector of Indian society. Their effects are felt primarily among the Western educated middle classes, particularly in the urban centres. The Backward Classes are largely concentrated in the rural areas and the impact of Westernization on them has been less widespread than on the upper castes. It is therefore not unlikely that the Backward Classes and, in particular, the Scheduled Tribes and the Scheduled Castes will retain their identity for some years to come.

8 Equality as a right and as a policy

In an important essay on affirmative action in the United States Professor Ronald Dworkin has urged the need to acknowledge the distinction between equality as a right and equality as a policy, a distinction that, according to him, 'political theory has virtually ignored'.[1] I would like to devote the present lecture to an examination of this distinction for, although the subject bristles with difficulties, something may be gained by bringing to it the approach of comparative sociology. Problems that are very similar to those brought to light by the DeFunis case (and the Bakke case) in America arise frequently and persistently in India in a very different social and cultural setting.

For all its inherent difficulties, one gets a sense of the distinction between equality as a right and as a policy while considering the structure of the Indian Constitution. Due to a variety of historical reasons the concern for equality figures prominently in it. But the equality provisions in the Constitution are not all of the same kind or to be found in the same place. The principal provisions are divided between Part III, entitled Fundamental Rights, and Part IV, entitled Directive Principles of State Policy. Hence a student of the equality provisions in the Constitution of India must sooner or later stumble upon the very distinction that Professor Dworkin has urged us to make.

The equality provisions in the part of Fundamental Rights relate on the one hand to equality before the law and, on the other, to equality of opportunity. Here equality is conceived in terms of *individual* rights and in terms of what has been described as the 'anti-discrimination' principle.[2] All Fundamental Rights, including the right to equality, are enforceable by the courts. As against these, the Directive Principles of State Policy are not enforceable by the courts although they are of great social and political significance. They provide a framework for a policy of greater equality overall in the distribution of resources and in the relations between the different members of society.

There are several reasons why the equality provisions in the Indian Constitution appear stronger and more extensive than in the American. The American Constitution is nearly two hundred years older than the Indian. When it was being written equality was a novel social ideal and the possibility of changing the structure of society through systematic social policy was still to receive serious attention. The Indian Constitution was written in a different age and political climate. When it was being written there was no longer any novelty in the idea itself of the right to equality, whereas a great deal had come to be expected from a policy of greater social equality.

Considering the time at which the American Constitution was written, one would not reasonably expect it to incorporate a framework of policy for removing the social and economic disparities between, say, men and women or whites and blacks. An expectation of that kind would appear normal and natural to those who fashioned the Constitution of India in the middle of the present century. The persistence of gross disparities between castes and communities, and between the sexes was associated with backwardness and, in the case of the former, also with national disunity, and it was believed that the remedy for all this lay not only in the creation of individual rights but also in the formulation of an active social policy.

The makers of the Indian Constitution believed that the individual right to equality and the social policy of equality were complementary and would reinforce each other. That belief is widely shared in contemporary India, and it has to be understood in the background of the continuing hold of the traditional hierarchy over a large part of Indian society. Not only are resources unequally distributed but social customs are set in a hierarchical mould. The right to equality, whether equal protection of the laws or equality of opportunity, would have little security without important changes in the structure of society.

Similar arguments have been made by others elsewhere. More than fifty years ago Tawney had pointed out in the context of British society that equality of opportunity meant little in the absence of what he described as 'practical equality'[3] The idea of practical equality found expression in the welfare state in Britain and other West European countries. In India the problem was of a different magnitude, hence the decision to inscribe the commitment to equality as a policy in the Constitution.

Not everyone, of course, believes that in order to secure equality as a right, it is necessary to promote equality as a policy. Those who are described as libertarians are opposed to equality as a policy although they may be strong champions of the equal rights of individuals. They argue that it is impossible to pursue systematically a policy of equality without continuous and arbitrary interference by the state in the free activities of individuals. Their view is that equality as a policy is subversive of equality as a right, and that one can have either the one or the other but not both.[4] This kind of argument is not commonly encountered in India where a correspondence between the two is widely assumed, and those who are opposed to equality as a policy are likely to be opposed also to equality as a right, although such opposition would not normally be articulated in public.

The Indian experience of the last thirty-five years raises doubts about the presumption of harmony between equality as a right and equality as a policy. Almost immediately after the new Constitution was adopted, two major instruments of the policy for greater equality, agrarian reform on the one hand and benign quotas in education on the other, came up against the provisions on Fundamental Rights. These provisions had to be realigned by the First Amendment to the Constitution so as to accommodate policies designed to reduce disparities between classes and disparities between castes.[5] There has been, since then, some limitation of individual rights, including the right to equal opportunity, in the interest of policies designed to bring about greater equality overall. Individual rights do not have the same depth and firmness in India, the same anchorage in its social structure, that they do in the United States.

In the United States as compared with India there is a much stronger emphasis on equality as a right and perhaps less public support for equality as a policy. In the American tradition equality has been inseparably linked with individualism.[6] Equality is valued to the extent that it is brought into being by individuals through their own unaided effort: it is something to be won for themselves by individuals, not imposed upon them by an external agency, particularly the state. If Indians accept equality they are less troubled by having to accept it under state auspices.

The American approach to equality through individual rights was shaped by those historical circumstances which made America a land of opportunity. In no other country were opportunities thrown open on such a large scale to individuals with ability, drive and initiative. But the tremendous dynamism of American society, with its high rates of geographical and occupational mobility, concealed the massive impediments to equality faced by blacks and other minorities, and by women. Far from there being equality of opportunity in any meaningful sense, in their case there was not even the formal guarantee of equality before the law. Whole segments of society were kept out of the domain within which equality as a right was acknowledged. These segments have developed their own social identities which cannot now be erased by a mere alteration in the structure of legal rights. It is in this context that the need for equality as a policy came to be acknowledged in America, despite the general lack of public sympathy for state intervention in social arrangements.[7]

Dworkin's essay is important because it forces us to consider the tension between equality as a right and as a policy. He, clearly, does not wish to surrender equality as a right but seeks to define and protect its essential core. At the same time, he believes that greater equality overall is desirable in itself and that a policy to achieve it is both legitimate and feasible. He maintains that preferential policies in education and employment do not necessarily violate individual rights although they may cause hardships to individuals. His view is that the rights said to be violated by policies for greater equality overall are more often imaginary than real.

It is obvious that a policy of greater equality overall, though desirable in itself, is not without its cost. Experience has shown in the United States, and even more abundantly in India, that such a policy puts some, or even many, individuals at a disadvantage. But it can be argued, according to Dworkin, 'that in certain circumstances a policy which puts many individuals at a disadvantage is nevertheless justified because it makes the community as a whole better off'.[8] What is actually involved in putting 'many individuals at a disadvantage'? Does it involve putting restrictions on their rights and, if so, what kinds of rights?

The right to equality has been conceived in a number of ways. Dworkin has sought to make a distinction between the right to equal treatment and the right to treatment as an equal. The right to equal treatment is 'the right to an equal distribution of some opportunity or resource or burden', whereas the right to treatment as an equal is the right 'to be treated with the same respect and concern as anyone else'.[9] The second, according to Dworkin, is fundamental whereas the first is derivative. It can certainly be argued that the right to equal treatment can be more easily sacrificed than the right to treatment as an equal; and, further, that every sacrifice of the first does not involve a sacrifice of the second.

The right to treatment as an equal, as Dworkin defines it, is a very important one, but we must acknowledge that in saving it we do not save everything. A policy of reverse discrimination, like other policies for bringing about greater equality overall, requires individuals to forego certain things in regard to which they have normal expectations if not established rights. It would be idle to pretend that there is no hardship here, or, even, that it is easy to balance this hardship to the individual against the benefit to the community as a whole. But the hardship is not all: hardship may be imposed with or without due concern for the loss suffered by those on whom it is imposed; and in societies where very little concern has been shown for those on whom the most severe hardships have been imposed, that is no mean consideration.

I would now like to consider the substance of equality as a right in contemporary India so as to see where it is re-inforced and where it is threatened by policies for greater social equality. This is a very large question and I will have to confine myself to only a few aspects of it, but those will have to be examined in relation to the structure of Indian society and its cultural traditions.

The point of departure in most discussions of the subject is that the right to equality is an individual right.[10] Whether we talk of equality before the law, or of the equal protection of the laws, or of equality of opportunity, the primary referent is the individual. Historians, political theorists and sociologists have shown how in the West the right to equality grew with the growth of individual autonomy.[11] In India, where the bias until recently has been for the collectivity, the rights of the individual have still to contend with age-old traditions, customs and habits. The Indian experience shows that it is one thing to create the right to equality but quite another to make that right secure: it would avail very little to create a right if nothing could be done to give it security.

Traditional Indian society was hierarchical to an unusual degree.[12] Although the hierarchical conception of society was not unknown in the West, the elaborateness, the stability and the continuity it acquired in India is without historical parallel. In a hierarchical society the legal order is structured in terms of the privileges and disabilities of groups rather than the rights of individuals. There was little concern in traditional Indian society over either the equal distribution of benefits and burdens (the equal treatment of individuals) or the equal consideration of interests (their treatment as equals). Whole segments of society were excluded from positions of respect and responsibility without consideration of individual interests.

The most striking inequalities in traditional Indian society, supported by both classical and customary law, were those based on caste and on gender. Though the disabilities of the inferior castes and of women were numerous and pervasive, they did not operate in the same way in the two cases. As a recent observer has noted, 'A paradoxical feature of inequality based on sex was that women suffered greater disabilities the higher they were in the caste hierarchy.'[13] Despite regional variations and historical changes, the system retained the same basic structure for about two thousand years and down to the middle of the last century.

Caste and family governed the activities of individuals to a very large extent, and the subordination of the individual to the family was more marked for women than for men, and more for women of superior than of inferior castes. Among the Hindus, who constitute the great majority of Indians, caste was an inescapable part of civil life. Every individual was born into a particular caste and expulsion from caste deprived him automatically of the right to property and other rights, and amounted virtually to civil death. The first major step in the emancipation of the individual from caste was taken with the passage of the Caste Disabilities Removal Act in 1850 exactly a hundred years before the adoption of the Constitution of India.

The Act of 1850 merely opened the way for enlarging the rights of the individual; it did not do away with all the disabilities of caste. As I have already indicated, these disabilities were manifold and had accumulated over centuries. It would be unreasonable to expect all the accumulated disabilities to disappear as a result of a single act of legislation or of legislation alone, without corresponding changes in the economy and society. A large number of them remained untouched by law for a hundred years, and many survived in practice even after they were legally abolished by the new Constitution in 1950.

Among the many disabilities inherited from the past and continuing into the present, I shall dwell mainly on those that arise from untouchability. The classical legal literature, the *Dharmashastra*, gives detailed accounts of the disabilities suffered by the lowest castes, described variously as Chandalas, Svapachas and Antyajas. While parts of the account are probably fanciful, broadly the same structure of disabilities is revealed in ethnographic descriptions of Indian society in the late nineteenth and early twentieth centuries. However, it is difficult not only to define untouchability but also to specify the number of its real or potential victims. The official category of Scheduled Castes, corresponding broadly to those earlier described as untouchables, accounts for 15.75 per cent of the present population.[14]

The disabilities imposed on the untouchables included residential segregation; confinement to polluting and menial occupations; and denial of access to temples, wells and other civic amenities. These disabilities were maintained to a large extent through a set of religious values in which the ideas of purity and pollution occupied a central place. But physical coercion was also used to keep untouchables as well as others in their place.

With the erosion of traditional ideas of purity and pollution, the use of force has probably increased, since the maintenance of social disabilities is of some economic advantage to landowners and other privileged members of the community. However, the line of untouchability was never very clear, and disabilities were suffered by many inferior castes in addition to those listed as the Scheduled Castes. To add further to the complication, disabilities were commonly imposed by superior untouchable castes on inferior ones.[15]

It is in this background that we have to consider the very generous provisions made for equality as a right in the Indian Constitution of 1950. The three principal rights to equality are: (1) equality before the law, including equal protection of the laws (Article 14); (2) prohibition of discrimination on grounds of religion, race, caste, sex or place of birth (Article 15); and (3) equality of opportunity in matters of public employment (Article 16). It was recognized that these three articles provided necessary but not sufficient conditions for securing the right to equality. A further step in that direction was Article 17 according to which untouchability was abolished, and the 'enforcement of any disability arising out of "Untouchability"' made an offence.

The Constitutional abolition of untouchability underlined the right to equality within the framework of a certain policy. As a recent commentator has said,

> The frame of Article 17 suggests that the rights there conferred are conferred not merely for the benefit of individual(s) but as a matter of public policy because enforcement of any disability arising out of untouchability forbidden by that article is made an offence punishable in accordance with law.[16]

In accordance with the provisions of Article 17, Parliament enacted the Untouchability (Offences) Act in 1955. The scope of the Act was extended and its provisions made more stringent by a major amendment in 1976 which also changed its title to the Protection of Civil Rights Act. These may be viewed as affirmative steps taken by the state to give greater security to equality as a right.

The provisions of the Protection of Civil Rights Act relate to disabilities that may be broadly classified as religious, social and economic. It has often been pointed out that the practice of untouchability had a religious basis, with its roots in the Hindu ideas of purity and pollution. Since some people were considered to be in a permanent state of pollution, they were denied access to temples; denial of access to places of public worship to such people is now punishable by law. Similarly, denial of access to wells, bathing places, cremation grounds, shops, restaurants and other public facilities is also punishable according to the provisions of the Act. There were in the past two kinds of restrictions on the choice of occupation by untouchables: they were not allowed to enter superior occupations and they were forced to perform certain kinds of tasks such as scavenging, flaying, tanning, etc. The imposition of either kind of restriction is now punishable by law.

The Protection of Civil Rights Act has under Section 15A made provisions for a machinery to ensure against the violation of civil rights. These include the supply of legal aid to the victims of untouchability; the appointment of officers for initiating and supervising prosecutions under the Act; and the setting up of special courts for the trial of offences. It also has provisions for monitoring the operation of the Act by agencies specially set up for the purpose. Finally, the Union Government is required to place before both Houses of Parliament Annual Reports on the working of the Act. A perusal of these Reports shows how many kinds of initiative by the state are considered necessary to give support to its provisions. These range from the rehabilitation of scavengers to cash awards for marriages of non-untouchables with untouchables.

Article 17 and the Protection of Civil Rights Act can do something to change the social atmosphere in which untouchables live, but such measures cannot by themselves secure fully their right to equality. The majority of untouchables are ignorant and illiterate, and unaware of the provisions of the Protection of Civil Rights Act and their implications. Most of them live in small rural communities where the distinction between private and public is not always clearly drawn. They are generally poor and often abjectly dependent on the caste Hindu landowners for whom they work. The machinery of the law does not easily reach into a rural community and, where it does, it is heavily compromised in favour of the established interests of the dominant landowning castes.

A case study of the untouchables in India clearly shows that disabilities cannot be abolished or the right to equality established at a single stroke. Nobody would seriously claim, thirty-six years after the Constitution was adopted, that untouchables enjoy in the average Indian village the same rights as the other members of the community. But if there is still such a long way to go in securing the right to equality, this is not because of a policy of equality, but in spite of it. That policy has helped a little in securing the right, but hardly enough.

It would be a mistake to believe that overcoming disabilities and securing the right to equality are slow and painful processes for the untouchables alone and that for all others they are smooth and easy. What is true for the untouchables is true, though in a rather different way, also for women. It is also true in more or less the same way, though not to the same extent, for various inferior castes and other disadvantaged groups in addition to the untouchables. It is for the benefit of all these various groups – untouchables and others – that a policy of greater equality overall has been made a part of the Directive Principles of State Policy.

I have tried to show that there are historical circumstances in which it is difficult to secure the right to the equal protection of the laws without some affirmative action by the State. Is it possible to secure the right to equal opportunity under those circumstances without any affirmative action? Even if we argue that it is not, we must keep in sight the fact that the implications of affirmative action for securing the right to equality are not the same in the two cases. Hence, those who support affirmative action for the removal of disabilities need not support it for the equalization of life chances.

Equality of opportunity is an important component of the right to equality in most contemporary societies. But it must be emphasized that the scope of equality of opportunity varies greatly from one society to another. It has a limited scope in many societies, including some in which there is a considerable measure of substantive equality. Many tribal societies, including those in the Islamic world, are egalitarian in a certain sense, yet the concept of equality of opportunity is not fully applicable to them. Equality of opportunity becomes a value where a high value is placed on the individual, especially on individual achievement. It is possible for societies to value equality while disregarding individuals and their achievements.[17]

Traditional Indian society emphasized neither equality of condition (as many tribal societies do) nor individual achievement (as most industrial societies do). It was considered right, proper and desirable there for the individual to remain in the station of life into which he was born, and this is to some extent true of all predominantly agrarian civilizations. Competition, individual achievement and equality of opportunity have a specific institutional setting, being associated both historically and sociologically with a particular occupational structure. Equality of opportunity is an issue in the office or the factory in a way in which it is not in the cottage or the farm.[18]

In India a modern occupational structure has emerged but it does not have the same reach and scope as in an advanced industrial society. The majority of people continue to live by agriculture and related activities, although the traditional occupational structure has lost much of its coherence. Only a minority of people have employment in settings where equality of opportunity can be reasonably expected to work. Not only does equality of opportunity have a different significance here as compared to, say, the United States, but the problem of ensuring it is also different in nature. Employment policy in India tends to be directed towards creating more jobs in those sectors where individual mobility is relatively free from the constraints of tradition.

In India the constraints on individual mobility are enormous, but even the constraints generally regarded as traditional are not all of the same kind and do not all operate in the same way. In the traditional village the organization of work according to caste left little room for individual mobility between occupations, whether within a lifetime or between the generations. An oilpresser could not become a carpenter, or a washerman a blacksmith, on account of customary sanctions against the change of occupation which operated for centuries and until quite recent times. These sanctions no longer enjoy the support of law but it would still be regarded as unusual for people to wish to change their occupation within the context of their own village. To change their occupation they have to move to a different context, and this is by no means an easy thing to do.

A certain amount of movement was possible even in the traditional context, but it was limited in various ways. Those who were classified as untouchables were confined to menial and polluting tasks, and they were strictly excluded from every kind of superior non-manual occupation. It is difficult to exaggerate the cumulative effect on the untouchables of the twin processes of confinement and exclusion. They have put them at a severe disadvantage not only in material terms but also in terms of motivation. That kind of disadvantage can scarcely be cancelled by the mere removal of the legal constraints on occupational mobility.

Although the new occupations in the office and the factory are in principle caste free, the association between caste and occupation is carried over from the traditional to the modern occupational setting.[19] The various castes are not represented in the new occupations according to their proportions in the population. The inferior castes in general, and the Scheduled Castes in particular, are very thinly represented in the superior administrative and managerial occupations. In a society which has adopted the principle of equality of opportunity but whose members remain acutely conscious of caste distinctions, these disparities are now a source of anxiety and concern. This concern finds expression in the policy to redress such disparities between groups, but the policy in turn impinges on the equal rights of individuals, particularly their right to equality of opportunity.

There are several reasons why untouchable and other inferior castes are so thinly represented in the higher occupations. While Article 15 prohibits discrimination on grounds of caste and Article 16 guarantees equality of opportunity in public employment, there is, in fact, widespread prejudice against the inferior castes in general and the untouchables in particular. This prejudice is not easy to measure and by its nature it is difficult to establish in the individual case. It operates more actively at the lower levels of employment where recruitment, tenure and promotion are to a large extent personalized than perhaps at the higher levels where these processes are organized in a more impersonal way. But there is reason to believe that some candidates are at every level rejected on account of prejudice even when they have the necessary qualifications.

There is, in addition, a marked decline in the number of qualified candidates as we move down from the upper to the lower levels of the caste hierarchy. This is a result of poor material conditions, and more of past than of current social prejudice, or of a kind of prejudice for which it is impossible to assign individual responsibility. It has been an objective of social policy to expand the pool of qualified candidates among the disadvantaged sections of society through freeships, scholarships and other educational inputs. This objective finds its justification in the argument that equality of opportunity depends 'not merely on the absence of disabilities, but on the presence of abilities'.[20]

Although the pool of qualified candidates among the untouchables and other inferior castes has expanded somewhat, it has now become apparent that this expansion is a slow and long-drawn process. Even while it takes its course, special measures may be adopted for recruiting more members of these disadvantaged groups into higher occupations by relaxing the conditions of appointment in their favour. A policy of positive discrimination has, in fact, been extensively used for increasing the numbers of persons belonging to inferior castes in public employment. It is at this point that the tension between equality as a policy and as a right is most clearly revealed, for it is difficult to create and maintain on a large scale special opportunities for some without taking something away from the equal opportunities of all.

Article 16 of the Constitution on equality of opportunity in public employment contains a clause by which the state is enabled to make special provisions 'for the reservation of appointments or posts in favour of any backward class of citizens'. Further, Article 335 stipulates that the claims of members of the Scheduled Castes and Scheduled Tribes are to be 'taken into consideration, consistently with the maintenance of efficiency of administration, in the making of appointments to services and posts in connection with the affairs of the Union or of a State'. Article 15, which prohibits discrimination on grounds of religion, race, caste, sex or place of birth, incorporated through the First Amendment a clause by which the state is enabled to make special provisions 'for the advancement of any socially and educationally backward class of citizens or for the Scheduled Castes and the Scheduled Tribes'.

It should be clear that positive discrimination in India differs in scale, if not in principle, from affirmative action in the United States. There is a great deal of disagreement in India, leading sometimes to violence, about how the policy should be made to work and how far it should be extended, but the principle behind the policy is widely accepted as an important part of the commitment to equality. In the United States there appears to be far greater ambivalence about accepting the principle itself. This, no doubt, is partly because of the distinctively American conception of equality which, as Professor Fiss has pointed out, is based on the 'anti-discrimination' rather than the 'group-disadvantaging' principle.[21] In India, where collective identities are so much more marked, disparities between groups figure prominently where equality is a consideration.

American courts, even while accepting affirmative action, have been hostile to racial or ethnic quotas.[22] In India quotas or reservations are accepted by all branches of government as a necessary part of a policy of greater equality overall. It must be pointed out that, as far as employment is concerned, the Constitution has only enabling provisions for reservation, but caste quotas in employment have been created extensively by legislative and executive action, and the courts have in general accepted them.[23] Caste quotas in admission to educational institutions, particularly to medical and engineering colleges, have also been accepted as a part of the programme of positive discrimination.

Caste quotas in education and employment were introduced during British rule and, in some parts of the country, all positions in certain sectors of employment and education were reserved according to caste and community. These quotas were designed more in the interest of political balance than of social equality. Comprehensive caste quotas have been struck down by the courts as being against the Constitutional provisions for the right to equality.[24] Caste quotas are now admitted only if they can be shown to be required by a policy of equality, not by a policy of balance. This means that there can be quotas for inferior but not superior castes.

Quotas in education and employment are everywhere allowed in favour of the untouchables – and also the tribals – because of their marginal position in traditional Indian society. Such quotas have also been extended, though not uniformly for the different parts of the country, to various other castes and communities on the ground that they too are disadvantaged or backward. It has, indeed, been argued that such groups have developed a vested interest in remaining 'backward', and political pressure is often used by them to get themselves so classified. It is at this point that a policy of greater equality in the long run yields to calculations of immediate political advantage.

As I have said, the Constitution has enabling provisions for reservation on the basis of caste in education and employment where such reservation serves the policy of greater social equality. Further, reservation has received the support of the legislature, the executive and the judiciary although the support has not been equally enthusiastic or equally consistent in the three cases. There has also been public opposition to caste quotas in education and employment. The grounds of opposition are various and it is not easy to separate them from each other. Some – perhaps the silent majority – are opposed to the very idea of greater social equality. Others may favour greater equality but feel that this cannot or should not be brought into being by state intervention. Yet others may feel that, while there should be a policy of greater social equality, positive discrimination in general and job reservation in particular are not good policies.

It is a remarkable fact that in India, where a hierarchical way of life was created very early, and maintained and justified for centuries, there is no public defence of hierarchy today. To be sure, people practise inequality extensively and justify their practice in private, but anyone who speaks against equality in public is bound to lose his audience. In independent India the language of equality has caught the imagination of not only politicians and professors but also judges and civil servants.

Granted that it is difficult to determine the extent of genuine concern for equality, it is likely that those who are in favour of it will be, on the whole, inclined to favour an active policy of greater social equality. Those who speak the language of equality cannot but be struck by the wide disparities in social conditions between Brahmans and Harijans, landowners and landless, or men and women. They have seen some of these disparities being reduced in their own lifetime and are likely to believe that much more can be done by concerted and co-ordinated effort. These beliefs and sentiments are commonly held by those who are closest to the centres of planning and policy-making. It is true that there has been a certain loss of faith in planning and policy-making in India, but that has not been replaced by an increase of faith in the individual's capacity to change his circumstances by his own unaided effort.

Those who are in favour of a policy of equality are not all equally in favour of positive discrimination. Some of them feel that positive discrimination contributes little if anything to social equality and has serious negative consequences, while others feel that it is at best a weak instrument of social transformation. These latter argue that a policy of greater equality overall will be much better served by agrarian reform, or the eradication of poverty, or the removal of illiteracy. They maintain that a great deal more can and should be done for the disadvantaged, but that the disadvantaged ought to be defined by rational economic criteria and not by caste.

Even those who feel that all untouchables deserve special attention as against, say, all landless labourers, may not wish to put the main emphasis on reservation in public employment or higher education. In other words, it may be possible to conceive of positive discrimination in somewhat broader terms than those of reservation, by linking affirmative programmes more closely with the removal of disabilities. An example would be the supply of drinking water, on a preferential basis, to untouchable hamlets in the rural areas. Other facilities, such as primary education, primary health care, house sites, etc., may also be made available to untouchables and tribals on a preferential basis. There is clearly some discrimination in diverting scarce resources in favour of such groups and to the possible detriment of very poor or destitute individuals not belonging to them, but its negative effect may be offset by the wide diffusion of basic facilities to millions of people who have strong claims on them.

Those who favour reservation in the narrow sense would certainly concede that there are costs in it, but they would argue that its social costs are in the aggregate outweighed by its benefits in the form of greater equality overall. It is difficult to measure these costs and benefits, and they are perhaps perceived differently in different societies, depending upon their traditions and circumstances. If I might hazard a quick generalization, I would say that in the United States the costs are weighed largely in terms of individual rights, whereas in India they tend to be weighed more in terms of national unity.

In an article on the Bakke case, Professor Dworkin adverted in passing to the argument, which he dismissed, that affirmative action might lead to the balkanization of the United States.[25] Problems of 'balkanization', 'separatism' and disunity do not present themselves with the same urgency before every nation or in every phase in a nation's life. America in the 1980s can perhaps take a somewhat distant view of the threat of balkanization. In contemporary India, on the other hand, what is called 'national integration' is a major policy preoccupation. To the extent that caste quotas appear as a threat to national integration, they are bound to be counted on the debit side.

Whether caste quotas become a threat to national unity or not will depend upon the scale on which they are adopted. Moreover, the political auspices under which they are introduced and extended also affect people's perception of their desirability. Caste and communal quotas were first introduced, and in some areas on a very comprehensive scale, by the colonial administration in India, and they were perceived by the nationalists, whether rightly or wrongly, as divisive in intention. Immediately after independence, when the new Constitution was being written, caste quotas acquired a bad odour, and some of the existing ones were struck down by the courts.

What is turning once more into a source of anxiety is not simply the fact of reservation but its scale. While caste quotas in selected occupations in favour of untouchables and tribals might be tolerated if not supported by many, the extension of such quotas to large numbers of other castes and communities acquires a different political complexion. It is one thing to offer special concessions to groups because they are socially stigmatized but quite another to have to yield such concessions to them because they are politically powerful. The culmination of that process is the creation of preferential policies by powerful majorities for their own advantage. This has happened in India in regard to language and locality, but on a smaller scale than in some other countries such as Malaysia.[26]

While defending reverse discrimination in America, Professor Dworkin argued that DeFunis (or Bakke) had no Constitutional right to a legal (or medical) education of a certain quality that could be said to be violated by a policy of preferential admissions. He would go further and argue that DeFunis did not have even the right to equal treatment in the matter of allocation of places in law school, although he did have a right to treatment as an equal. Dworkin would make a distinction between benefits like legal (or medical) education which can be provided to only a few and those like elementary education which can be provided to all and to which, therefore, the right to equal treatment might be admitted.

DeFunis could seek remedy in the courts only under the equal protection clause introduced into the United States Constitution by the Fourteenth Amendment. As Dworkin has pointed out, that Constitution 'does not condemn racial classification directly',[27] nor does it provide specifically for equality of opportunity.

The Indian Constitution differs from the United States in both respects. It directly prohibits discrimination 'on grounds of religion, race, caste, sex or place of birth' (Article 15); and it has a clause that guarantees equality of opportunity (Article 16) in addition to the one that guarantees equal protection of the laws (Article 14). On the latter, it has been pointed out that 'the Constitution envisages the right to equal opportunity as an independent right and not as a subsidiary right flowing from Article 14 or as an incident or amplification of it'.[28] It is true that equality of opportunity is guaranteed only in public employment and that the prohibition of discrimination is qualified in a number of ways, but the provisions are in both cases explicit.

The Indian Constitution, unlike the United States, was designed in full awareness of the negative as well as the positive implications of preferential policies in education and employment. The subject was debated extensively in the Constituent Assembly and elsewhere in the country. Dr Ambedkar, regarded widely as the architect of the Indian Constitution, pleaded for some quotas as well as for equality of opportunity, and maintained that the former could, up to a point, be accommodated within the latter. He was a strong advocate of quotas for the Scheduled Castes and Scheduled Tribes, but warned that extensive quotas would 'eat up' the very principle of equality of opportunity.[29]

In India thousands of qualified candidates are every year rejected for admission to medical and engineering college and appointment to government service because they have to make room for other candidates, apparently less qualified than they, in whose favour caste quotas operate. Can we say that the rejected candidate has no ground for complaint, even when he is apparently better qualified, because he has no constitutional right to the place he has been denied and that the right to equal treatment does not apply in such matters? To be sure, he has still the right to treatment as an equal, and that right may be saved by treating his interest with concern and sympathy even while rejecting him. But what would it mean, in such circumstances, to treat someone's interest with concern and sympathy?

It may certainly be argued that those rejected are only apparently better qualified and that candidates from inferior castes, though they perform badly in written tests and interviews, are in a deeper sense better qualified because of the range of their social experience, their sensitivity to social issues, their capacity to withstand adversity, and so on. While this may possibly be true in the aggregate, it is impossible to establish the facts in the case of each individual candidate accepted or rejected, for in the circumstances in which such selections are made, the law of large numbers prevails. At any rate, no serious attempt is made to weigh and assess these additional criteria as against the ones ordinarily in use. Hence, the individual candidate who is rejected, despite better scores, inevitably feels that he has been passed over to make room for another on account of caste and not some definable individual ability that he lacks and the other has.

Where caste quotas come to be extensively used, definable individual ability will tend to be at a discount. This may not be a bad thing for countries that have long suffered from the Protestant ethic, but its implications will be otherwise for countries like India which have a different cultural tradition. There, in view of the long tradition of the subordination of the individual to family, caste and community, individual ability needs to be nurtured rather than restrained. It is freely acknowledged that in public sector employment in India ability and efficiency count for rather less than they should. While it would be absurd to attribute this solely to reservation, caste quotas certainly contribute to the general devaluation of individual ability.

The urge to smooth out disparities speedily leads the Government to act at times in ways that not only devalue individual ability but also discredit its own procedures. Tests of ability for recruitment or promotion to particular posts are devised, and then waived or relaxed in favour of candidates belonging to the Backward Classes. A judge might on occasion seek to rescue the Government from its embarrassment.

The case of N.M. Thomas provides an interesting insight. Lower division clerks in a particular branch of the Kerala government were required to pass within a fixed time certain departmental tests in order to be eligible for promotion as upper division clerks. The limit of time for passing the tests had been extended by successive orders of the Government in favour of candidates belonging to the Scheduled Castes and Scheduled Tribes while they were already enjoying the benefits of promotion. Moreover, as many as thirty-four out of a total of fifty-one vacancies had been filled in this manner. The Kerala High Court struck down the rule under which the orders were passed. On appeal the Supreme Court reversed the judgement on the ground that the extensions were necessary to give fuller representation to the Scheduled Castes and Scheduled Tribes among upper division clerks. Making light of the qualifications expected from junior functionaries of the Government, Justice Krishna Iyer observed, 'After all, here is a pen-pushing clerk, not a Magistrate, accounts officer, forest officer, sub-registrar, space-scientist or top administrator or one on whose initiative the wheels of a department speed up or slow down'.[30] Then, again, 'And, after all, we are dealing with clerical posts in the Registration Department where alert quilldriving and a smattering of special knowledge will make for smoother turn-out of duties'.[31]

Where individual ability is widely discounted, individual rights cannot remain secure. It would be going too far to say that the individual had no rights in traditional Indian society, but we must at the same time acknowledge that such rights as he had were very different in kind from those that the Constitution has sought to establish. There has been some drift away from the security originally given to individual rights by successive amendments to the Constitution. The Twenty-fifth Amendment, enacted in 1972, is regarded as a turning point:

> 'Prior to the 25th Amendment, the notion was that Fundamental Rights prevailed over the directive Principles of State Policy.... The 25th Amendment introduced a radical change in the concept, in the interest of promotion of social justice and egalitarianism envisaged under the Constitution'.[32]

In other words, within a quarter-century of being established, equality as a right began to yield to equality as a policy.

Although the Twenty-fifth Amendment was occasioned by the need to protect state laws designed for agrarian reform, the insecurity of individual rights is most clearly revealed in the context of positive discrimination, for here the individual has to yield not only before the state but also before caste and community. Positive discrimination and the group-disadvantaging principle on which it is based, bring to our attention the problem of disparities between groups as against that of inequalities between individuals. It can be shown that increased opportunities for individual mobility do not lead at once or automatically to the reduction of disparities between castes or between races.[33] Strong advocates of caste quotas have in that light argued that

equality between castes must first be established before there
can be equality between individuals.[34]

It may well be the case that no individual has a Constitutional
right to a place in a medical or an engineering college, or in
a particular service of the Government, but a comprehensive
system of caste quotas raises another kind of question. Do castes
and communities have claims to particular shares of such places?
What kinds of claims are these, and how are they to be weighed
against the claims of individuals? These are not speculative
questions because caste quotas are adjusted and re-adjusted
through intense political bargaining in a language whose implicit
assumption is that castes and not just individuals have claims.

The language of bargaining over caste quotas reflects an
important part of the Indian social reality. In the traditional
Indian village rights and obligations were to an extent defined
by caste. The barber, the washerman, the potter, the carpenter
and the blacksmith provided services not merely as individuals
but as members of their respective castes. If a particular barber
or potter was unavailable it was the obligation of the local caste
group to provide a substitute, and each of these groups had
its own rights in the village and its total produce which it
protected from encroachment by individuals from other groups.
The system of quotas introduced by the colonial administration
reinforced, against countervailing tendencies, the belief that
every caste or group of castes could claim a share of what was
at the disposal of the State.

I would not like to leave the impression, while concluding,
that nothing has changed in India, for I do believe that a great
many things have changed. There is widespread antipathy to
the excesses of hierarchy and some genuine sympathy for
equality. But collective identities have withstood this change of
orientation from hierarchy to equality without being substantially
weakened. For that reason, although the concern for equality
may be both genuine and strong, that concern has a somewhat
different orientation in India as compared with the West.

In the distinctively Indian orientation more emphasis is likely
to be given to equality as a policy than to equality as a
right. The Twenty-fifth and the Forty-second Amendments
appear to be signposts in that direction.[35] Indians who regard

themselves as forward-looking have been prepared to accept some restriction of individual rights in the interest of a more equitable distribution of property. It is not yet clear how far they will agree to such restriction in the interest of greater parity between castes.

9 Individualism and equality

The relationship between individualism and equality is a large subject which social anthropologists have only recently begun to explore systematically. It has, however, been discussed in a variety of contexts for a century and a half by scholars in different intellectual disciplines: philosophers, political theorists, lawyers, historians, economists, and others. Many of the social theorists of the nineteenth century were struck by the simultaneous emergence of the desire for equality and the appreciation of the individual, and they sought to establish a relationship between the two. Alexis de Tocqueville was one of the first to argue that individualism and equality were both new values and that they were inseparably linked in their origin and development. The intimate connection between the two was also stressed, though in other ways, by the jurist Henry Maine and the historian Jacob Burckhardt.

Individualism, equality, and their relationship have so far been discussed almost entirely within the context of Western culture. It is desirable to extend the discussion to cover not only those societies in which these values were first clearly articulated but also others to which they have spread and in which they have found some room for themselves. The social anthropologist can bring to bear, perhaps a little more fully than others, a comparative perspective on the subject. He is trained not only to look for differences among cultures but also to appreciate and respect these differences. It is necessary to ensure, however, that we do not, out of a false sense of appreciation of or respect for other cultures, stress the differences beyond their true proportions. While cultures undoubtedly differ, and differ in important ways, they are in the modern world also closely interconnected. This is particularly relevant in the context of equality, for as an ideal and a value it has acquired a certain appeal in every part of the modern world.

A second important requirement of the approach of social anthropology or comparative sociology is to study ideas and values in their concrete social setting, to take into account, in the language of Durkheim, both collective representations and social morphology and to relate them to each other. We need to examine not only the strength and consistency of the ideal of equality in a particular society but also the institutional arrangements and the interpersonal relations through which that ideal is expressed. It is equally necessary, though more difficult, to do this for individualism, which has so far received less attention from the sociologist or social anthropologist than from the historian of ideas (see Dumont, 1983).

Both individualism and equality are large, vague, and ill-defined ideas. I will not try at this point to define them even in a preliminary way, but it is necessary to note that each of them can be and has been conceived in more than one sense. Equality and individualism can be shown to reinforce each other when conceived in certain ways; when conceived in other ways, they can be shown to limit or, in the extreme case, even to exclude each other. Those who argue that equality and individualism are, as it were, two sides of the same coin generally leave it unsaid that by stressing other aspects of equality or of individualism than the ones they stress, it is possible to formulate a very different kind of relationship between the two.

Many of those who have written about individualism have acknowledged that it has been conceived in more than one way. However, they have often adopted a partisan attitude, arguing that one of the available conceptions – the one to which they subscribe – is the true conception and some other conception, which may be equally popular, a false one (see Hayek, 1980 (1946); Durkheim, 1969 (1898)). On closer examination it might well turn out that a conception of individualism rejected as false spells out some of the implications and presuppositions left unstated in the one accepted as true.

Broadly the same thing may be said about equality, of which more than one conception usually prevails in the same society. The philosopher or historian of ideas is apt to pick out a particular conception of equality and to build his argument from the premise that it is widely endorsed in a given society, ignoring the fact that there are other conceptions of equality, not unrelated to the first, to which some or many members of the same society may be indifferent or even hostile.

Thus, defining individualism is one thing, and demonstrating that it has a central or unique place in the collective consciousness of a given society is another. We need not take at face value the kind of statement which says that the individual counts for nothing in some societies and for everything in others.[1] When we say that individualism is a value in a given society we mean that its people hold the individual to be as important as, or more important than, clan, caste, estate, race or nation, and that they act in ways which enable us to infer that they assign him such significance. With something as large as individualism, however, it becomes evident that even in the same society people hold divergent beliefs and act in divergent ways. At any rate, as Lukes (1973) has cogently demonstrated, in countries like Britain, France and Germany, which are recognized as the natural habitat of individualism, some misgiving about over-emphasis on the individual has always been expressed by Catholics, Conservatives, Socialists, and various others.

One might think that there would be agreement at least in contemporary Western societies on the value to be placed on equality as a principle of social life, but that would be far from the truth. Tocqueville pointed out some of the negative social consequences of equality even while drawing attention to the providential nature of its progress. Voices have been raised against the pursuit of equality, certainly in Britain and also in other Western countries, throughout the nineteenth century and in the twentieth. It is true that these voices have been muted or muffled at times and in places, but they have begun to make themselves heard again in the last ten or fifteen years on both sides of the Atlantic (see Letwin, 1983a). It might have caused Tocqueville some surprise to have learnt that the strongest arguments against equality were to come in the last decades of the twentieth century from America.

It is obvious that the commitment to equality – as also the value assigned to the individual – varies within the same society between classes, between racial, religious, and linguistic groups, and between men and women. While we cannot take all

these variations into account in every study, we have to be
cautious about characterizing a whole civilization in terms of
a single value or a single pair of values and about making such
characterizations the basis of a radical opposition between whole
civilizations.

The difficulties of identifying the dominant values of a large
and complex society are well known to the social anthropologist.
We might take up a normative text, such as a constitution, but we
know that the values which people actually live by are at variance,
and sometimes widely at variance, with their constitution. We
might take up representative thinkers, but their selection bristles
with difficulties. Limiting ourselves only to England in the
second half of the nineteenth century, whom should we regard
as a representative thinker on equality? Matthew Arnold (1903),
who castigated his countrymen for their 'religion of inequality'?
Or T.H. Huxley (1890), who, in his essay 'On the natural
inequality of man', argued that they yielded too readily to the
rhetoric of equality? Clearly, we have to adopt an approach which
seeks continually to relate ideas, values and norms to the social
arrangements in and through which people live and work.

Our understanding of many of these issues has been advanced
considerably by the writings of Louis Dumont (1977; 1983).
The point of departure of Dumont's work is the contrast,
at the level of values, between societies governed by holism
and hierarchy on the one hand, and by individualism and
equality on the other (Dumont, 1972). Dumont's work has
had a marked impact on Indian studies, since a great deal of
what he has written in his books and in the journal founded
by him, *Contributions to Indian Sociology*, has been about India.
Despite the force and subtlety of this work, it has certain
limitations. It has concentrated on the structure of traditional
Indian society and on holism and hierarchy in it, leaving
largely unconsidered many of the issues that are of concern
in India today. Whatever might have been the emphasis of
traditional Indian culture, both equality and the individual are
central concerns in the contemporary constitutional and legal
systems; and it is impossible to understand what is happening
in India today without taking into account Constitution, law, and
politics.

My own interest in these questions derives less from a preoccupation with speculative theory than from a concern with the realities of society and politics in contemporary India. More specifically, it has grown out of a consideration of the problems of the Backward Classes and the presuppositions and implications of the policy of positive discrimination. Positive discrimination challenges certain common assumptions about equality, for it sets out to achieve equality by not only taking collective identities into account but assigning them a certain pre-eminence over individual identities. And these questions about equality and about individuals and collectivities have a certain comparative significance, for they now arise not only in India but also elsewhere, notably in the United States.

The assumption of a relationship between individualism and equality has been since the nineteenth century a part of the collective wisdom of a large section of the Western intelligentsia. This is not to say that everybody accepts that assumption; it is nevertheless widely acknowledged. The work of Tocqueville (1956 (1835-40)), which was a landmark in this regard, has influenced generations of writers on the subject. 'Individualism', he wrote, 'is a novel expression, to which a novel idea has given birth' (vol. 2, p. 98). And he added, 'individualism is of democratic origin, and it threatens to spread in the same ratio as the equality of condition'. Tocqueville himself was too close to the values of an earlier age and had too finely tuned a mind to view the growth and spread of individualism – or of the passion for equality – with unmixed pleasure.

In the work of Burckhardt (1954 (1860)) we are taken back to an earlier period of European history for tracing the origins of individualism, that of the Renaissance in fifteenth- and sixteenth-century Italy. What Burckhardt emphasized was not so much 'equality of condition' in Tocqueville's sense as a new appreciation of quality, excellence and distinction wherever found in individual human beings, irrespective of birth or estate. He too was struck by the relationship between this new individualism and what he called the 'equality of classes' (see especially pp. 265-72), but it must be pointed out, as I have done elsewhere (Béteille, 1984), that his ideas about social equality are vague and inconsistent.

Here a word of caution needs to be introduced, because how far back we can go in tracing the origins of individualism or of equality will depend on how strictly or broadly we define these terms. Historians have noted the presence of individualism, social mobility, and the spirit of equality in pre-modern times (Macfarlane, 1978), and anthropologists have recorded evidence of all three in the simplest of tribal societies (Malinowski, 1926, Béteille, 1984). It is well to remember what Maitland said in his monumental work on English law in the Middle Ages: 'we may have seen enough to give us pause before we assent to any grand dogma which would make "communalism" older than "individualism". The apparent communalism of old law covers an individualism which has deep and ancient roots (Pollock and Maitland 1968 (1895), p. 688).

Dogmas aside, we cannot fail to notice certain basic differences in legal ideas and concepts between past and present societies. In some societies the caste, the clan, or the family overshadows the individual to a large extent. In others the individual is given a kind of pre-eminence as the bearer of rights and capacities, as citizen, as voter, as earner, and as consumer. There are specific social and legal arrangements under which the autonomy of the individual and respect for him are fostered and promoted. Maitland's senior contemporary, Maine (1950 (1861); 1914 (1875)), showed how the emancipation of the individual from the family and other such groups was historically linked with the progress of equality, including equality between men and women.

These and similar ideas have been brought together in Dumont's impressive body of work. The guiding thread of this work is the contrast between hierarchical and egalitarian societies, between *homo hierarchicus* and *homo aequalis*. For Dumont, hierarchy is the social expression of a fundamental value which he calls 'holism', and equality is the expression of its opposite, individualism. His work on India (1972), which provides a detailed analysis of hierarchy, promised a subsequent and complementary work on Europe, to be devoted to equality. His work on Europe (1977), though it bore the title *Homo aequalis*,[2] turned out to be more on individualism than on equality. There need not be any objection to this, provided we accept the premise that individualism entails equality; but it is the premise itself that I would like to submit to examination and criticism.

Dumont's contrast between *homo hierarchicus* and *homo aequalis* may be seen as a reformulation of Tocqueville's contrast between aristocratic and democratic societies (Béteille, 1979), but there are important differences. Dumont's interest is in contrasting two different societies, separated in space and having distinct historical traditions. Although his work shows both imagination and insight, it lacks the historical spirit which animates the work of Tocqueville. While Tocqueville pushed hard the contrast between democratic society and aristocratic society, his fundamental concern was to show how the one grew out of the other. Dumont's preoccupation is with *difference*, whereas Tocqueville takes pains to establish *continuity*.

A study of the relations, whether of opposition or agreement, between hierarchy, equality, the individual, and the group cannot be made without a historical awareness of the changes taking place throughout the modern world. Basic legal and political ideas are no longer insulated within their original matrix in the way in which they were in the Middle Ages or earlier. Societies and cultures which were different and separate until a century or two ago have become mutually implicated as never before. The contemporary social significance of ideas and values has to be considered separately from their historical origin, however important the latter might be. It cannot be argued - certainly not in the modern world – that ideas and values that have been current for merely four or five generations are necessarily less significant or effective than those which held the field for a millennium or more.

Nor is it a question of the passage from one part of the world to another of only ideas and values. A whole range of new institutions – offices, factories, trade unions, political parties, schools, colleges, universities – has arisen in societies in which until very recently hierarchical values and collective identities prevailed. These institutions cannot even begin to work unless some attention is paid to the claims of individuals for equal treatment. Conversely, collective identities have shown remarkable durability in societies in which both equality and individualism have long been established as fundamental values. Equality, individual rights, and the claims of collectivities are all part of the language of contemporary politics, and this language has now acquired a certain universal currency.

The difficulty of arriving at a clear judgement on these issues becomes apparent as soon as we begin to look into a living society in the contemporary world. The most striking feature of Indian society today is the co-existence of divergent, even contradictory, beliefs and values. Hierarchical values are in evidence everywhere: yet people proclaim loudly, and not always insincerely, that equality should be placed above every other consideration. Individuals compete with each other and claim their dues as individuals in a growing number of fields: yet loyalty to caste, tribe, sect, clan, lineage, and family have a continuing, and in some fields an increasing, hold over people.

A convenient place to begin an enquiry into these fundamental concepts is the Constitution of India. What the Constitution actually signifies for the different sections of Indian society – educated and uneducated, urban and rural, men and women, Hindus, Muslims, and Christians, the high- and the low-born – is a separate question that cannot be examined here. All that we need to acknowledge at this point is that it signifies something for at least some sections of Indian society. If there is an overall design in the Constitution, that design may be said to put equality in the place of hierarchy and the individual in the place of caste. Hierarchical values are repudiated, and the commitment to equality is strongly asserted; but the repudiation of collective identities of the kind on which the traditional hierarchy rested is not as clear as the repudiation of hierarchy itself.

In the Indian Constitution the individual is the principal, though not the sole, bearer of rights and responsibilities, and citizenship is an unmediated relationship between the individual and the state. This has to be contrasted with what prevailed in the past, when the civil status of the individual derived from his caste or his family. Until 1850 expulsion from caste, at least for Hindus, who constitute the vast majority of the population, amounted virtually to civil death.[3] The rights of individual citizens are equal rights, and there is in that sense a convergence in the idea of citizenship of the values placed on equality and those placed on the individual.

The right to equality is a part of the Fundamental Rights made available to all citizens by the Constitution (See Tripathi, 1972). The three most important among these relate to equality before the law (Article 14), the prohibition of discrimination on grounds of religion, race, caste, sex or place of birth (Article 15), and equality of opportunity in matters of public employment (Article 16). All these articles bring out the centrality of *individual* rights, treating religion, race, caste, sex, etc., as possible impediments to their full exercise. To settle the issue more fully, Article 17 abolishes untouchability, while the remaining article on equality in the section on Fundamental Rights attends to an issue of only historical interest, the abolition of titles.

The Constitution, however, does not give attention to the individual alone. His rights are to some extent qualified and limited by other considerations. Chief among these, from the point of view of equality, are the special claims of certain tribes, castes, and other communities together designated as the Backward Classes.

Part XVI of the Constitution is devoted to 'Special Provisions relating to Certain Classes'. Some of these provisions are very specific, others general or even vague. The most specific are those relating to political reservations: seats are reserved in the lower house of Parliament and in the corresponding houses of the state legislatures for the Scheduled Castes and Scheduled Tribes, roughly in proportion to their strength in the population. The constitutional provisions relating to reservation in the services of the government are vague and general but none the less important. They have invariably been interpreted in executive orders and judicial decisions to mean that the Scheduled Castes and Scheduled Tribes have special claims in regard to public employment on a par with their claims to seats in the legislatures.

The Scheduled Castes and Scheduled Tribes, which together make up 23.5 per cent of the population, comprise only the most clearly defined part of the Backward Classes. The Constitution mentions other backward classes but does not specify what they are or what provisions are to be made for their benefit. A large number of states have, however, made special provisions for them which are in some regards comparable to those in existence for the Scheduled Castes and Scheduled Tribes. The courts have upheld some of these provisions, and there has been a fair amount of political support for them. Indeed, parties in office have until recently tended to assume that by making or extending such provisions they can enhance their electoral appeal.[4] There is also public opposition to the extension of caste quotas in employment and education to the Other Backward Classes.[5] It is difficult to infer solely on the strength of political support for or opposition to reservation how strongly Indians belonging to different sections of society regard as legitimate the respective claims of individuals and of collectivities. There clearly is some tension if not contradiction here between two principles: equal opportunities for all on the basis of citizenship and special opportunities for some on the basis of caste or community (see Galanter, 1983; Béteille n.d). The courts have repeatedly pointed to this, and there is growing awareness of it in public life.[6]

I ought to point out that caste or, rather, communal quotas in employment and education were introduced into some parts of India during British rule and were already in existence when the Constitution of 1950 came into effect. These quotas were bound to come into conflict with the rather strong provisions for equality of opportunity in the new Constitution, and they did. Article 16, guaranteeing equality of opportunity in public employment, had a clause enabling special provisions to be made in favour of the Scheduled Castes and Scheduled Tribes. Article 15, prohibiting all forms of discrimination, had no such safety clause. Almost immediately after the Constitution came into force, caste quotas in admission to medical college in the state of Madras were challenged. The Supreme Court struck down the standing order of the government of Madras on quotas on the ground that it was *ultra vires* of the Constitution (Galanter, 1983).

The Constitution had to be amended in 1951 to make reservation in both education and employment legally valid. This did not mean that caste quotas could no longer be challenged in the courts. They have been challenged over and over again, but now for violating the spirit rather than the letter of the Constitution (Galanter, 1983). The courts have responded differently to reservations for the Scheduled Castes and Scheduled Tribes and for the Other Backward Classes. Till around 1962 they were generally inclined to ask for what may be described as strict scrutiny in regard to caste quotas for the Other Backward Classes. Since then they have been somewhat more accommodating towards programmes of reservation operated by the state governments.

The political movement for selection on the basis of caste quotas as against open competition has definitely gained strength, at least in North India since 1977, although more recently there has been indication of a reaction against it (Government of India, 1981). The recent agitation over reservations, both for and against, has revived suspicions that, despite professions to the contrary, what Indians really care about is caste; and caste, one hardly needs to point out, is the antitheses of the individual and of equality.

It is in this light that we must examine the question, often raised, about the significance to be attached to the commitment to equality in the Constitution of India. The commitment is no doubt vigorously expressed, but is it seriously meant? Indians themselves often say that the talk about equality in the Constitution, in the law courts, or on political platforms is mainly rhetoric - that there is no genuine commitment to it at any level of Indian society. One may point out, in support of this kind of scepticism, that the Constitution itself and the laws sustain the basic units of a hierarchical society by acknowledging in a large number of cases the special claims of castes and communities.

When we survey the politico-jural domain in India since independence, we are struck by two things: continued assertions of the commitment to equality and continued concessions to collective identities. Two related questions arise out of this: (1) Is equality possible without the assignment of social pre-eminence to individual rights? (2) Is equality possible where collective identities appear so compelling? These are both important questions, but they cannot be seriously considered so long as we adhere to the dogma of the inseparability of equality and individualism. We shall see in what follows that the relationship between the two is a complex one: they reinforce each other in some respects, but in other respects their paths diverge.

I would like to argue that, no matter how deeply loyal he may be to his caste or community, the educated Indian today also values Article 15 of the Constitution, which prohibits discrimination on grounds of religion, race, caste, etc., and Article 16, which guarantees equality of opportunity in public employment irrespective of those considerations. He does so not only because of his direct exposure to Western or modern values but also because of the compulsions of the social arrangements by which he has to live and work. As more and more Indians make use of the new educational system and the new occupational system, more and more of them begin to appreciate that, no matter what the proper considerations might be in the village or the home, considerations of caste and community ought not to prevail, under normal conditions, in the school, the college, the university, the office, or the factory. I am not saying that they believe that these considerations do not in fact prevail, only that, ideally, they ought not to prevail.

Evidence of a shift in people's perceptions of right and wrong ways of doing things may be found in the recent literature on factory employment in various parts of the country. People know, of course, that jobs are secured in all sorts of ways, among them by using influence, including the ties of kinship and caste, and even bribery, but there is a sense in which they also feel that the best way of obtaining a job is 'on merit'. Holmstrom (1984, p. 210) writes about selection on merit on the basis of his fieldwork among factory workers in Bangalore: 'Workers and managers talk as if it is the morally superior way to find work: workers who got their jobs on "merit" are proud of it, those who used influence are on the defensive'. And again, ' "merit" is an ideal standard against which to measure the other ways people get jobs'. All this represents a shift in the never stable balance 'between values of hierarchy and equality, or between fixed roles and competitive individualism' (p. 283).

It is important to note the institutional accompaniments of equality of opportunity. Equality of opportunity – which represents equality in one sense and not in every sense – acquires its full significance in the modern occupational and educational systems. Equality of opportunity would signify very little in a tribal community or even a peasant community, although such a community might in other respects be markedly 'egalitarian'. Indians today can no longer regard the modern educational system or the modern occupational system in the same way in which their forebears thought of traditional learning or of traditional crafts and trades. That every individual – or at least every male – should have, irrespective of caste or community, an opportunity to go to school or enter government service is now widely, though not universally, acknowledged as a principle. Why this does not happen and what can be done to make it happen in practice are questions that have to be considered separately.

The idea of treating individuals on merit is in some sense a new one, but we must not exaggerate its novelty. No matter how disguised, it may be recognized in every major religious tradition, Hinduism not excepted. It is true that the old social practice emphasized the distinctions of caste and community, but the requirements of a new social practice might give new life to the moral claims of individuals as individuals. This can be clearly seen in the writings of a large number of nineteenth-century Indian intellectuals, who began to take a keen interest in equality (Ganguli, 1975).

The claim that in public life individuals be treated on merit, irrespective of outward differences, was made early in modern India in relation to race.[7] The British brought with them a new social theory based on equality, but colonial social practice was often markedly at variance with this theory. Indians in privileged positions in the traditional order, who discriminated extensively against their fellow Indians on the basis of caste, were irked by being discriminated against on the basis of race. They experienced or imagined such discrimination in every sphere of public life: in the civil service, in the law courts, and in virtually every profession. A new Indian intelligentsia, not very different in its social composition from the old, came into being in the nineteenth century and established an important place for itself in society. It became a matter of principle with this intelligentsia to demand equality of opportunity, for Indians and Europeans alike, in the civil service and in the professions. Entry into the Indian Civil Service, which represented the pinnacle of prestige and power, became a key issue: the Indians did their best to secure equality of opportunity, and the British did their worst to subvert it.[8] It would hardly appear reasonable on the part of these Indians to seek to repudiate the distinctions of race if at the same time they sought to uphold the distinctions of caste. Precisely this point was made in an essay on self-rule and alien rule by one of the leading intellectuals of nineteenth century India, Bankimchandra, who also published a tract on equality (Bankimchandra, n.d. (1382 Bengali calendar)).

The most conspicuous impediment to equality of opportunity is the presence of legal disabilities based on race, caste and gender. In India the disabilities of the inferior castes and of women were very many and of very long standing (Sivaramayya, 1983). These legal disabilities were gradually whittled down over a hundred-year period and finally abolished under the new Constitution of 1950. However, a great deal of discrimination against the lower castes and against women, enjoying the sanction of custom, if not law, survived the legal abolition of disabilities. This too was an impediment to equality of opportunity and seen as such. In the villages, where traditional occupations prevailed, the question of equality of opportunity hardly arose. It did arise for those who sought to leave the village and its traditional occupational setup to enter the new world of schools, colleges, universities, offices, and factories, and more and more people wanted to do precisely that.

It is not surprising in this light that B.R. Ambedkar, a principal architect of the present Constitution and himself an untouchable and a lawyer, should have argued strongly in the Constituent Assembly for making the individual the basic unit in the new scheme of things (Constituent Assembly Debates 1950, p. 39). In arguing for the individual, Ambedkar was arguing for equality and against the constraints of caste and community. There were some in the Constituent Assembly who advocated making the village the basic unit, but he resolutely opposed them on the ground that the village was the seat of caste and faction and would allow little room for individuals to develop their abilities.

Ambedkar was not the only one who saw the link between equality and the primacy of the individual. Others also recognized individual mobility as a good thing in itself and as a solvent of the traditional barriers of caste and community. But how far could one count on individual mobility alone to transform the very structure of a hierarchical society? It has to be stressed that what Ambedkar and others like him wanted was a change not merely in the positions of some individuals but in the structure of society itself. A society which permits some individual mobility may at the same time tolerate large social disparities.

The plain fact is that, despite equality of opportunity and despite individual mobility, there are large social disparities between upper castes and lower castes in India, between whites and blacks in the United States, and, to some extent, between men and women everywhere. What is obvious to us today and was not as obvious a hundred years ago is that by ensuring equality of opportunity between individuals we do not immediately or automatically reduce disparities between groups. Formal equality of opportunity combined with free competition between individuals may, in fact, lead to an increase rather than a decrease in such disparities. It may no doubt be argued that what leads to the reduction of inequalities between individuals will, in the long run, lead also to the reduction of disparities between groups, but there is little reason to believe that this will happen on its own in the short run. And in the modern world, members of disadvantaged groups – blacks, untouchables, perhaps also women – have lost the taste for enjoying the gift of equality posthumously.

It would thus appear that certain collective identities may have to be acknowledged or even emphasized as a part of the concern for equality. This is seen in the United States in the context of affirmative discrimination in favour of blacks and certain other minorities. It is true that the American courts have in general treated racial classifications as suspect, but such classifications have also been admitted in a number of important cases in which the issue has been the removal or reduction of social disparities (see Rossum, 1980). Fiss (1977) has criticized the American courts for adhering to too narrow a conception of equality, one that takes into account only discrimination against individuals,

when a more adequate conception would take into account also
the disadvantages of groups.

In India affirmative or positive discrimination has been written
into the Constitution itself, both in Part IV on Directive Principles of State Policy and in Part XVI on Special Provisions
relating to Certain Classes. The 'classes' in question comprise
a variety of groups with pre-existing collective identities, mainly
the tribals and the untouchables. Ambedkar, who spoke strongly
in support of the individual in the Constituent Assembly,
pleaded also for the recognition of the special claims of certain
groups. What was at issue was not simply equality as a right
available to all individuals but also equality as a policy aimed
at bringing about certain changes in the structure of society (see
Dworkin, 1977).

It is far from my intention to argue that the claims to equality
of individuals and of collectivities are nicely balanced in the
Constitution of India or that they can be nicely balanced. Law
and politics in India have, in fact, been bedevilled by these
conflicting claims ever since the Constitution came into effect.
It cannot be too strongly emphasized that the Constitution treats
the provisions in favour of the Scheduled Castes and Scheduled
Tribes as special provisions. Ambedkar himself argued in the
Constituent Assembly that these special provisions should not
be allowed to 'eat up' the general provisions for equality of
opportunity for all individuals alike (Constituent Assembly
Debates, 1950, pp. 701-2). These special provisions continue to
be   in
force, and it cannot be argued that, because they take collective
identities into account and perhaps even strengthen them, they
are by definition hostile to the spirit of equality.

I myself have misgivings about the extent to which the ends of
equality can be served by stressing collective identities of the
kind based on race and caste (Béteille, 1981), but it is not
because I believe that those ends are secured by a single-minded
pursuit of individualism. I would now like to turn the coin
over and examine, on its other side, the disjunction between
individualism and equality.

Some of the most penetrating insights into the relationship
between individualism and equality we owe to the writings of

Simmel (1971, 1950 (1917)). Simmel saw quite clearly that individualism might lead to either an appreciation of human equality or a preoccupation with the inequality of man, and he distinguished between what he called the 'individualism of equality' and the 'individualism of inequality' (1971, pp. 251-93). It is not enough merely to distinguish the two kinds of individualism, for one might go on to argue that they are different and separate and are mistakenly given the same name (see, for example, Hayek, 1980 (1946); Durkheim, 1969 (1898)). It is a part of Simmel's argument, unlike, for instance, that of Durkheim on the same subject, that the two kinds of individualism are historically related and products of the same social process.

According to Simmel, the individualism of equality came into its own in Europe in the eighteenth century. This kind of individualism, as Durkheim too had pointed out, found its most complete expression in the moral philosophy of Kant: 'treat each man as an end in himself, and never as a means only' (Williams, 1962, p. 17). What was important in this conception was the claim of moral autonomy for each individual and his freedom from the constraints of estate, guild and church. And every individual had, as a moral agent, an equal claim to autonomy and respect. While Simmel was undoubtedly right in drawing attention to the eighteenth century contribution, these ideas have much broader appeal. They were echoed in the debates over citizenship, equal protection of the laws, and equality of opportunity in the Constituent Assembly in mid-twentieth century India.

This coupling of individualism and equality was inherently unstable and bound to come apart as soon as the stress shifted from what was common to all individuals to what was unique to each individual. Simmel argues that this is what happened in the West in the passage from the eighteenth to the nineteenth century. We need not take this periodization at face value. The stress on the uniqueness, the incomparability, of individuals was already present in the civilization of Renaissance Italy, and it went with a belief in natural distinctions among men no less than the belief, stressed by Burckhardt, in human equality.

Simmel traces the passage from the individualism of equality to that of inequality in the following terms: 'First there had been the thorough liberation of the individual from the rusty chains of guild, birth right, and church. Now, the individual that had thus become independent also wished to distinguish himself *from other individuals*' (Simmel, 1950 (1917), p. 78). To use the well-worn language of textbook sociology, inequality based on ascription was, after an interval, replaced by inequality based on achievement. 'Yet,' as Simmel puts it, 'this new inequality was posited from within'.

The nineteenth century saw not only the emergence of a new idea of human inequality but its systematization in a new scientific theory. Evolutionary biology achieved pre-eminence around the middle of that century, particularly in Britain, and it influenced anthropology, sociology, psychology, economics, and virtually every science whose subject was man. It provided a new framework for explaining and justifying inequality in the animal kingdom as well as the social world. In England Galton (1950 (1869)) and that great popularizer of evolutionary biology, Huxley (1890), both presented strong arguments in support of the inequality of man. Huxley even appealed to religion in opposing the case for equality, arguing (p. 13) that the only kind of equality admitted by either Judaism or Christianity is 'the equality of men before God – but that is an equality either of insignificance of or imperfection'.

Every student of anthropology is familiar with the argument, supported by nineteenth century biology, that the different human races are unequally endowed. That argument came into its own in the heyday of colonial rule and slavery. It did not end, however, with the demise of either slavery or colonial rule but tends to reappear with unfailing regularity, to the surprise of many well-meaning anthropologists. One reason it dies hard is that it is not a separate argument but part of the general argument about natural inequality (Béteille, 1980). Human beings are unequally endowed; these inequalities are more marked between individuals of different race, but they are also present between individuals of the same race. The natural inequality of the sexes is another part of the same general argument.

The argument about natural inequality is more than a scientific argument; it has also an important normative component. Huxley and others like him argued against egalitarianism not only because they thought it scientifically untenable but also because it appeared morally flabby. They had great faith in men of unusual ability, natural geniuses (hereditary or otherwise), and regarded the idea of levelling as contrary to both nature and morality. Individualists believe in equality of opportunity, no doubt, but they also believe in competition and inequality of reward, and they are strong opponents of levelling. If it is argued that Stalin too was an opponent of levelling, or *uravnilovka* (Ossowski, 1963, pp. 112-13), it will only strengthen my point that 'individualism' appears in many guises to many people.

The moral argument against levelling that has probably the widest appeal is the one which relates it to envy. 'I have no respect for the passion for equality', wrote Justice Holmes (quoted in Hayek, 1960, p. 85), 'which seems to me merely idealizing envy.' Nozick (1974, p. 239) has recently sought to establish a relationship between equality, self-esteem, and envy in somewhat more abstract terms: where there is scarcity of a desirable object or quality, 'the envious man prefers neither one having it, to the others having it and his not having it'. But individuals are, in fact, unequal, such individualists would argue, in their qualities as well as their possessions, and to yield to the passion for equality would be to reduce humanity to its lowest common denominator.

A society whose individual members are reduced to the lowest common denominator can only stagnate; it cannot progress. Whatever affinity there might have been in the past between individualism and equality, individualism is in the contemporary world linked more with the idea of progress than with that of equality. It has always been a central part of the capitalist creed that the ultimate source of all progress is the individual. Different individuals cannot all move forward at the same pace. This being so, inequality is built into the dynamic structure of every progressive society, and the suppression of it must sooner or later bring to a halt the engines of progress (Hayek, 1960, especially chapter 3).

Individualists who espouse the idea of natural inequality thus have various arguments against levelling. They say, first, that it is impossible or unworkable. In the economic field they draw attention to entrepreneurship and in the educational field to intelligence and try to show how, in the end, men of ability come out on top in either case despite all the obstacles placed in their way, since it is impossible to suppress natural talent. It may also be argued against levelling that it can be maintained only through the arbitrary use of coercive force. It is not worth paying the price of this, the argument goes, to maintain a kind of equality that in no way corresponds to the natural scheme of things. What is true of levelling in the totalitarian state is true of it, though in a milder and less visible form, also in the welfare state. There are, of course, many who would maintain that levelling is both impossible to achieve and futile to attempt. We thus come back to a central dogma of libertarian capitalism – that equality as a policy (though not necessarily as a right) is bad because it does violence to liberty as well as efficiency.

Dumont's contribution to our understanding of both hierarchy and individualism, despite its importance, has ignored almost completely what may be called, after Simmel, the individualism of inequality. This is surprising, because it is that form of individualism which is today most conspicuous in Dumont's own chosen field of enquiry, the field of economic doctrine.

What is original about Dumont's work is not that it has established for the first time the affinity between individualism and equality, for that affinity, as we have seen, had been noted by many before him. Its originality lies in the way in which it has established the affinity within a particular field of ideas, the field of economic doctrine. There Dumont has shown how from Mandeville to Marx the rise of economic doctrine brought into focus the twin concerns for the individual and for equality. Now, while there is much to be said about the affinity between the two in past economic doctrine, it is the disjunction between them that strikes us in the economic doctrine of the present. Among contemporary economists the strongest enthusiasts for individualism are precisely those who are either indifferent or hostile to equality.

Contemporary economists who are strong individualists may not reject equality as such, but they take a narrow view of it as being co-extensive with equality of opportunity. Moreover, they define equality of opportunity itself in a narrow way, as 'formal' rather than 'fair' equality of opportunity (see Rawls, 1973). Now, one may choose to define equality in such a way as to deprive it of all content and to make the very idea of it vacuous. It has indeed been argued that the term 'equality' is misplaced in phrases such as 'equality of opportunity' or 'equality before the law', for what is at issue is a principle not of equality but of universality (Letwin, 1983b, p. 46).

Equality of opportunity can be made into a principle of universality and nothing more by being delinked completely from all considerations of distribution. The crucial question about equality today turns on the way in which we view the relationship between equality of opportunity and distributive equality. There are those who would seek a balance between the two, and there are those who would define the first so as to exclude the second (Béteille, 1986). In a recent book, two British intellectuals, one of them a member of the Conservative cabinet, have said, 'Equality of results is itself the enemy of equality of opportunity' (Joseph and Sumption, 1979, p. 28). It would be quixotic to describe this position as egalitarian, although the authors certainly take their stand on individualism.

The most far-reaching argument about the incompatibility of egalitarianism and individualism has been presented, among contemporary economists, by F.A. Hayek, although similar points have been made, if anything even more forcefully, by Milton Friedman. In an early essay entitled 'Individualism: true and false'. Hayek drew attention to the threat to true individualism presented by socialism, with its preoccupation with equality and distributive justice. Men are born unequal, they start from unequal positions: the state should not intervene to alter all this *even for the sake of equality of opportunity*:

From the point of individualism there would not appear to exist even any justification for making all individuals start on the same level by preventing them from profiting by advantages which they have in no way earned, such as being born to parents who are more intelligent or more conscientious than the average (Hayek, 1980 (1946, p. 31).

Hayek stresses the point that liberty and the rule of law are bound to produce inequality. We must both treat individuals alike and recognize their disparate abilities, accepting the inequality of result that follows: 'From the fact that people are very different it follows that, if we treat them equally, the result must be inequality in their actual position'. And further, 'The equality before the law which freedom requires leads to material inequality' (Hayek, 1960, p. 87). Hayek is strongly opposed to the imposition of any preconceived pattern of distribution and, indeed, to any attempt to create such a pattern through conscious social intervention. He does not object to 'equality as such' if it emerges as a by-product of unfettered competition under the rule of law. But this concession to equality does not amount to very much where it is accompanied, as it is in Hayek's work and that of others, by a rooted conviction that natural talents are unequally distributed.

Hayek is an individualist, not an egalitarian. He believes in equality of opportunity in so far as it is compatible with or required by the rule of law and no farther. As an individualist, he is opposed to nationalism and, above all, to socialism, but it is interesting that his antipathy to the nation and the state does not extend to every kind of group. True individualism, he says:

> recognizes the family as a legitimate unit as much as the individual; and the same is true with respect to other groups, such as linguistic or religious communities, which by their common efforts may succeed for long periods in preserving for their members material or moral standards different from those of the rest of the population (1980 (1946), p. 31).

Thus, 'true individualism' may compromise with the family and up to a point also with ethnicity and caste but never with state power. This point of view of one of the most influential economists of our time is markedly at odds with Dumont's views about both individualism and equality.

Friedman's position is in many ways similar to Hayek's. He is a strong proponent of equality of opportunity but deeply mistrustful of distributive equality. In his opinion, taking from some to give to others in the name of social justice is detrimental to the freedom and autonomy of the individual. The ends of distributive justice and those of individual freedom necessarily collide, and one must choose: 'One cannot be both an egalitarian, in this sense, and a liberal' (Friedman, 1962, p. 193).

It is quite clear that neither Friedman nor Hayek would like to pass for an egalitarian. They are both strong individualists, Friedman unequivocally so, and both might have been considered egalitarians in an earlier age, say, in the age of Mandeville. An egalitarian today is not simply someone who believes in or advocates equality of opportunity as admissible under the rule of law. He must show some concern for distribution and, in addition, some commitment to the principle of redress – 'the principle that undeserved inequalities call for redress' (Rawls (1973, p. 100).

The concept of equality as understood today – and this is true both of the United States and of India – incorporates a component of distributive equality, even at some cost to formal equality of opportunity. Here it is important to keep in mind the distinction, to which Dworkin has drawn attention, between equality as a right and equality as a policy. The principle of redress, which has become a part of equality as a policy, is opposed by strong individualists on two grounds. The first, which is the more general ground, is that it involves some expansion of state power at the expense of individual autonomy. The second, which relates specifically to positive discrimination or affirmative action, is that it sacrifices the claims of individuals to those of collectivities based on race, caste, and ethnic identity (Glazer, 1975; Goldman, 1979).

We have to make a distinction between those who 'do not object to equality as such' provided it is available without cost and those who are committed to equality as a value. As I have more than once suggested, equality means many things to many people, but we can hardly describe equality as a value where there is no readiness to forego or sacrifice anything for a fuller realization of it. This is not to say that what is sacrificed – liberty, for instance, or efficiency, or progress – is itself of no value, for in that case we would not call it a sacrifice. It is doubtful that equality as a value in the specific sense has become established as a universal feature of any modern society, and there is reason to suggest that the strongest impediments to its establishment today are presented by those whom we may legitimately describe as individualists.

If we are to take equality seriously, we must enlarge the concept of equality. As soon as we do that we recognize that the different components of the concept do not harmonize well with each other. We recognize also that the pursuit of equality limits the attainment of other ends such as those of efficiency, liberty, and even the self-realization of the individual. This should not lead us to assert either that the 'central argument for Equality is a muddle' (Lucas, 1965, p. 299) or that 'equality of opportunity is a false ideal' (Coleman, 1973, p. 135). It is the task of social theory to recognize the diversity of human ends and to understand and interpret the ways in which each society seeks, according to its own historical circumstances, to reach a balance between the different ends it values. Social equality and individual autonomy may not be as inseparably linked as they were once believed to be, but it is difficult to see how any modern society can discard or neglect either of these two ends.

On 'Individualism and equality': reply to Dumont

'Individualism and equality', along with comments by a number of authors and my reply to them, was published in *Current Anthropology* in April 1986. About a year later Professor Dumont sent a separate comment to the journal in which he criticized me for misrepresenting his view on the relationship between individualism and equality. He also explained his concept of value and his approach to the comparative study of values. Below is my reply to Dumont which was published, together with his comment, in *Current Anthropology* in December 1987.

In the Preface to *From Mandeville to Marx*, Dumont recalls how at the end of *Homo hierarchicus* he had outlined his new intellectual project, a work on the modern equalitarian type of society. 'I added, somewhat lightheartedly,' he said, 'that this might be done in a book called *Homo aequalis* (Dumont, 1977, p. vii). On reflection he seems to have thought better of this, for he goes on to say in the very next sentence: 'I have now come to a soberer assessment of the situation'. This, one might reason, is why he gave the book the title it bears, for *From Mandeville to Marx* sounds distinctly soberer than *Homo aequalis*. That, however, was not the end of the matter, for he published the same book in French under the very title he had lightheartedly chosen, *Homo aequalis*. The dispassionate reader will perhaps concede that this alternation between sobriety and lightheartedness on Dumont's part might give rise to some misunderstanding among his readers. Why should he choose two completely different titles for the same book published simultaneously in Chicago and Paris? Why should he write a book on individualism, call the book *Homo aequalis*, and then appear to disclaim responsibility for the view that individualism entails equality (see the first two sentences of his second paragraph)?

For all that he may have written in fine print, Dumont does not like to miss an opportunity to indulge his taste for symmetry. *Homo hierarchicus*, *Homo aequalis*; holism versus individualism; hierarchy versus equality; India as against the West; others as opposed to ourselves. Take a system, stand it on its head, and you get another system. Take a model, turn it around on itself, and you get another model. This craving for symmetry is far more than Dumont's personal weakness; it is a disease of a whole intellectual climate.

One can well understand that after finishing his book on India Dumont should wish to write a book on Europe that would be symmetrical with it. One cannot reproach him for having failed to achieve his purpose. That he did fail must have been apparent to him before it became apparent to others. He neither acknowledged nor explained his failure but simply confused the issue by presenting the book as *Homo aequalis* to one set of readers and as *From Mandeville to Marx* to another.

Dumont has sought to defend himself – against Srinivas

– by saying: 'Beteille has chosen to give the terms at issue a sense different from mine'. That is indeed the case, for my main concern was to examine the relationship between individualism and equality and not to present an exegesis of Dumont's work. In examining that relationship I referred to the views of several scholars – Tocqueville, Simmel, Hayek, and others – and not just Dumont. Dumont ignores all views that are not in agreement with his own. To take one example: Hayek is a major contemporary theorist who has written on identically the same subject but from a different angle. One will look in vain in Dumont for any reference to such points of view.

Since I am told by Dumont that I have given my terms a sense different from his, I would like to know what exactly is the sense he has given the term 'equality'. It is not simply that he has ignored the large and controversial literature on equality; he has not even bothered to define what he means by it. The astonishing thing in a book called *Homo aequalis* is that it has so little to say about equality. The whole subject is disposed of in the first few pages, and even there all that we get is truisms to the effect that equality is the opposite of hierarchy, that modern societies are egalitarian, that other societies might value equality but not in the same way, and so on. There is nothing remotely comparable here to the discussion of hierarchy in *Homo hierarchicus*. *Homo aequalis* is not a book on equality, and a book on individualism cannot be passed off as a book on equality because the relationship between the two is not what Dumont asserts it to be. There is something fictitious about the symmetry of the design of which the book is a part.

There is a large literature on the subject of equality. Anyone familiar with this literature must know that it is a difficult and ambiguous concept, signifying different things to different persons. One who asserts so categorically the primacy of equality as a value in modern societies might take the trouble to examine its principal meanings to see where they converge and where they diverge. It is an essential part of my argument that the concept of equality is inherently ambiguous. Dumont has nothing to say on this, either in his book or in his rejoinder to my essay. All that he does is to reassert that equality is the paramount value in modern as against pre-modern societies. To strengthen his argument he tells us that in Germany at present university professors do not have two votes as they had in England in the past. Can one be more banal?

Dumont concedes 'that the identification of paramount values is of course open to debate and is not supposed to be always easy'. I am not sure that he realises how much he is giving away by making that concession – or perhaps he feels that he has covered himself adequately with phrases like 'supposed to be' and 'always'? In any case, I would be the last to demand as a condition for discussing paramount values that such values should be easy to identify. But where a task is difficult, or even 'supposed to be difficult', should we not discuss these difficulties candidly? Should we not try to look for a method that will make the task less difficult? Where has Dumont discussed the difficulties of formulating a method for identifying the paramount values of one's own society? His whole approach is different. He merely asserts the paramountcy of a certain value and, when challenged on the point, says that the subject is not an easy one and is open to debate. Why take as self-evident a subject on which scholarly opinion is known to be divided?

It has been argued that by denying the hierarchy of values I deny value itself. This is tendentious. I do not believe that there is any society in which *all* values are of *equal* significance, and I doubt if any sociologist believes in such nonsense. But that does not oblige me to agree that *all* values can be arranged in a *single* hierarchy of the kind specified by Dumont. Why should I agree to this when I find that, on being challenged, Dumont himself turns out to be shaky about 'the identification of paramount values'?

I am not impressed by Dumont's fascination for 'hierarchy', which is of a piece with his craving for symmetry. Values must fit nicely together. Something that does not fit has no significance and is therefore not a value. As I have stressed elsewhere, hierarchy is a theological rather than a sociological concept, and Dumont argues about value in a manner that is close to the theological.

Dumont invests what he calls the modern ideology with a unity which those who live in the modern world are not always able to find in it. Where he sees unity and harmony, others find contention and strife not only among individuals and groups but also among values, including fundamental if not 'paramount' values. This difference between Dumont and others is partly a matter of faith and conviction and partly a matter of perspective. It is easier for the anthropologist and the historian of ideas who views a system at a distance to discover unity in it than for the sociologist who views it at close quarters. Those who live in the modern world can see the difference between a formal endorsement of the principle of equality and a commitment to equality as a value even at the cost of other values. Dumont accuses me of denying value itself because I refuse to accept his construction of the hierarchy of values. I view the matter differently. For me something is a value for people only if they are prepared to forego some other thing to secure it.

Not only the modern ideology as a whole but the idea of equality itself lacks the unity that Dumont would like to impute to it. I start with the idea of equality and am struck, like most modern writers on the subject, by the variety of meanings it has been made to bear. My paper considers the various meanings of equality in order to bring to light the tensions between them. These issues, which I consider to be central to an understanding of equality as a value, have all been swept under the carpet by Dumont both in his book and in this rejoinder. How is it possible to discuss the significance of equality as a value without so much as mentioning the various meanings given to the term by both the proponents and the opponents of equality?

Let us take first that aspect of equality on which there is likely to be least disagreement: equality before the law. We can agree that equality should mean at least this and that equality in this sense is generally valued today even by those who may be opposed to it in other senses. Furthermore, regard to equality in this sense is distinctive of modern societies such that even where women and racial or ethnic minorities were denied equality before the law, that denial could not survive very long against the force of the general principle. Finally, equality in this sense is very closely linked with and perhaps inseparable from individualism. I have said all this in my paper, and on this I agree with Dumont even though he might disagree with me.

Then there is equality of opportunity, but here we are

already on shifting sands. The idea of careers open to talent
had a certain significance as a pledge of the commitment to
equality in the transition from feudalism to capitalism, but it
is doubtful that it has the same significance today. It is easy
to see that what Rawls (1973, p. 100) describes as a 'callous
meritocratic society' can be at the same time fully committed
to equality before the law and formal equality of opportunity.
Could we describe equality as the paramount value of a callous
meritocratic society? The question is not easy to answer, and it
seems not to have occurred to Dumont to ask it.

Despite formal equality – equality before the law and careers
open to talent – large inequalities in fact continue to exist in
modern societies. I should imagine that the test of equality as
a value would lie in the orientations of people towards these
inequalities. Some accept them as inevitable or even desirable
whereas others maintain that they should be reduced even at
some cost to individual members of society. This difference is
an extremely important part of what Dumont calls the modern
ideology. I see very little justification for confusing these two
very different orientations on the ground that they can both be
related to a positive evaluation of equality in some sense.

If it be agreed that there is a genuine difference of orientation
between those who believe that the inequalities that survive the
institution of formal equality are inevitable and should be left
undisturbed and those who maintain that something should be
done for the redress of such inequalities, then it should be clear
than individualism is associated more with the first than with the
second orientation. This was the basic argument of my essay. I
would have valued Dumont's observations on it, for I regard his
work on individualism very highly, but his zeal for vindicating
himself has prevented him from making any such observation.

The question I have raised is a large one, but it may be
pursued into Dumont's chosen field of investigation, that of
economic doctrine. How were individualism and equality related
as values in the economic doctrine of the eighteenth century?
How are they related in the economic doctrine of today? I believe
that Dumont's answer to the first question is substantially true
but that the generalization he draws from it about the whole of
modern ideology is false. Had he paused to consider the second

question he might have hesitated to make the generalization, but then he would not have been able to accomplish in its full symmetry the task he set for himself at the end of *Homo hierarchicus*.

Leaving aside for the moment the question of paramount value, contemporary economic doctrine is not uniformly egalitarian. There is a part of it that is indifferent if not hostile to substantive as against formal equality. We need not enquire here whether that part is a large or a small one. What is striking is that individualism is a marked feature of precisely that part of contemporary economic doctrine that is most opposed to substantive equality. There may be as much to learn on this score from Hayek and Friedman as there is from Bernard de Mandeville.

Dumont points out that he uses individualism in a sense different from mine. Here he is on much firmer ground, because, in contrast to the case of equality, he has taken some pains to explain what he means by individualism. But he has been too quick to take offence; my essay was meant not to denigrate his work but to raise certain questions set aside by him. The distinction between the two meanings of individualism – one derived from Kant and the other from the utilitarians – was pointed out by Durkheim (1969 (1898)) nearly a hundred years ago. What I tried to do in my essay was to link the second meaning of individualism with the defence of inequality in certain forms of modern ideology.

In the very last paragraph of his comments Dumont seems to admit that modern ideology may not after all be made of whole cloth, but I would like to repudiate the perception he seeks to attribute to me 'that modern ideology has become more complicated through Germany's acculturation from the end of the 18th century onwards'. My essay had nothing to do with 'Germany's acculturation' but sought to explore tensions within modern ideology that may be perceived in France, England and the United States as well as in Germany. Dumont is welcome to his own theory about the peculiarities of the Germans: why should he wish to saddle me with it?

The argument about 'Germany's acculturation' strikes me

as unconvincing. The rise of national socialism in twentieth-century Germany is too complex an issue to be settled in terms of the late emergence of individualism. Individualism may have emerged late in Germany, but that can hardly be said about Italy. We have Burckhardt's classic study (1954 (1860)), in which the development of the individual is placed at the heart of the ideology of the Renaissance in Italy. Why did fascism find such a congenial home in Italy in the present century? I am sure that some *ad hoc* argument can be found within Dumont's scheme to explain that as well.

I find the argument that the modernization of Germany has been marked by 'a synthesis of individualism and holism' rather lame. What, within Dumont's conceptual framework, would such a synthesis amount to? First we are told about the radical heterogeneity of 'individualism' and 'holism' and then, when something perculiar, or apparently peculiar, turns up, we fall back upon their 'synthesis'. I should have thought that within the kind of framework on which Dumont insists there can be no synthesis of individualism and holism but only their co-existence. As far as I am concerned, the co-existence of contradictory values is a common feature of all societies, and there is nothing peculiar to Germany in this.

Dumont prescribes strict conditions for the study of values but himself overlooks these very conditions. In his conceptual universe values do not merely co-exist, they have to be valorized *inter se*. He has taken great pains to explain that the central truth about value (in the singular, and not in the plural) is not the content of individual values but their arrangement in a hierarchy (Dumont, 1980b). And has he not castigated me for denying value itself because of my failure to acknowledge the hierarchy of values? How does one hierarchize such radically heterogeneous values as individualism and holism? If I have understood Dumont's argument about value – and it is not an easy argument to understand – Germany has values, but not Value. This seems to be the implication of his stance, although elsewhere he might be profuse in expressing his warmth and sympathy for German society and culture.

Dumont says that he has not disparaged India but, in contrast, 'vindicated India in the very aspects that made her looked down upon by many in the West'. I do not wish to question his good faith, but it seems to me that what he has tried to vindicate is the world that Indians have left behind, not the one that they are trying to create. He should not feel too surprised, therefore, if some Indians do not find his attempts at vindicating India entirely to their taste. Dumont's own sympathies lie all with traditional India and hardly at all with modern India. I can see that he has, out of his deep concern with traditional India, tried to forge a method for the study of his own society, but it is that very method that has stood as an obstacle to his understanding of contemporary India.

Contemporary India is even less amenable than modern Germany to Dumont's method of study. That method places not merely values but values in their hierarchical order – i.e. Value – at its heart and centre. Over and over again Dumont has contrasted Indian ideology with modern ideology, and I would say that it is that basic contrast that animates his work. At the same time, he recognizes that India also exists in the contemporary world and, in that sense, partakes of modernity. Surely, hierarchy and holism no longer exist in their complete and pure forms in contemporary India, and some room has had to be made there for the basic modern values that are 'compelling for everyone in the present world'. What exactly is the hierarchical arrangement of all this in contemporary India? Is such a hierarchical arrangement possible? No matter what he may say in extenuation, Dumont's conception of value, if he takes it seriously, must oblige him to regard modern India as lacking in coherence and unity.

Dumont's lack of ease with modern India is writ large in his work, although it does not shine as brightly as his enthusiasm for traditional India, which is partly an India of his own construction. In this construction traditional India is made of whole cloth. Modern Europe, at least Western Europe – and with strong reservations about Germany – is also made of whole cloth, though of a somewhat inferior texture. Modern India, in Dumont's construction, is not made of whole cloth; it is a thing of shreds and patches.

When Dumont writes about the unique configuration of values characteristic of modern ideology, India, clearly, is far from his thoughts. India is the exemplar of holism and hierarchy, which are at the opposite pole from modern ideology, although, when pressed to the point, one has to admit that India also 'partakes of modernity'. This makes of modern India a kind of anomaly that is easily forgotten when basic and fundamental questions relating to Value or the hierarchy of values are at issue. Dumont's two basic contrasts are between India and the West and between pre-modern and modern ideologies. Modern India does not serve well to illuminate either of these contrasts.

The anomalous position of modern India accounts for a peculiar feature of Dumont's comparative method. He moves easily and without warning from the contrast between India and the West to that between pre-modern and modern ideologies. For him the two contrasts are for all practical purposes the same. This can be made possible only by bracketing or discounting modern India. Dumont cannot but acknowledge the existence of modern India on the plane of facts, and his few essays on the subject bear witness to that, but he does not fully admit to its existence on the plane of Value. I do not ascribe this to bad faith but see it as a necessary outcome of what he calls his comparative method.

Dumont's comparative method is severely constrained by the symmetry of his own construction. By conscious choice that method assigns priority to contrast over comparison, to difference over similarity, and to discontinuity over continuity. It deals with the varieties of society not as they actually exist but in so far as they exemplify certain constellations of value in their pure form. From the viewpoint of this method not all societies are of the same value: societies are valorized in the very acts of comparison and contrast.

I am unable to understand what Dumont means by attributing to me the rejection of the comparative method. If I made my comparisons with an open mind about both similarities and differences, both continuities and discontinuities, does that mean that I 'ignore comparison' or 'eschew...the idea of comparison'? It is absurd to describe my rejection of a rigid and artificial scheme of contrasts as a denial of the comparative method. I believe that it is an abuse of that method to highlight difference and discontinuity by suppressing evidence of similarity and continuity.

A comparison of *Homo hierarchicus* with its counterpart *From Mandeville to Marx* will show that the two books differ widely not only in subject matter but, what is more germane to my argument, in type of data and method of analysis. The book on India is markedly anthropological, and that too in a specific sense of the term: it relies mainly on contemporary ethnographic data and on insights derived from a reading of classical texts. The passage from the one to the other, spanning a period of 2,000 years, is smooth, easy, and almost effortless. To be sure, Dumont does not deny that India has a history, but historical analysis is quite marginal to the techniques by which he has identified holism and hierarchy in India. In that sense these values and Indian civilization itself are made to appear timeless and ahistorical.

Far from being marginal, the historical method is at the heart and centre of Dumont's analysis in *From Mandeville to Marx*. A historical sequence is clearly established, and the data are carefully arranged to accord with that sequence. *From Mandeville to Marx* pictures a world on the move, not one in which the operation of time stands suspended. If the book on India is an exercise in anthropology, this one is an exercise in the history of ideas. In the first book the secondary material is drawn mainly from studies by ethnographers, in the second from studies of a quite different kind. It is not as if anthropologists had not made ethnographic studies of European communities, but one will look in vain for accounts of their work in Dumont's study of 'modern ideology'. I need not remind readers of *Current Anthropology* that there are dozens of ethnographic studies made by anthropologists in every part of Europe. What makes these studies inappropriate as raw material for a work devoted to European ideology? What makes similar studies conducted in India by anthropologists similarly trained and using similar techniques appropriate as raw material for a work on the civilization of India? In what way can the two constructions be regarded as comparable? I may not have achieved great success in my use of the comparative method, but I have not used two different scales for weighing the data on the societies I have compared.

Dumont has been less than candid in facing up to the problems involved in comparing his own society with societies that are distant in space, time, or moral texture. If the anthropologist is, in Lévi-Strauss's (1963, p. 378) picturesque phrase, 'the astronomer of the social sciences', how does the astronomer come to terms with the historian and the political economist? The difficulties are formidable, and they cannot be disposed of with clichés such as 'the reversal of perspectives' or 'the approach to a civilization through its own values'. Where the same subject is being studied, and must be studied, by people in different existential situations, very little progress can be made without candour about one's own views and consideration for the views of others.

It has been suggested that I value tradition too little and modernity too much. That is a harsh judgement against which I do not wish to defend myself here. I cannot question someone else's right to his own preference, although I know only too well how generations of Western sympathizers of India have used their admiration for Indian tradition to mask their allergy to the India of their experience. As to modernity, there is very little in that today - whether in India or in the the West - to make the imagination soar. But I belong to the modern world, and I would be untrue to my vocation as a sociologist to disown the world to which I belong.

10 Individual and person as subjects for sociology

Some thirty inches from my nose
The frontier of my Person goes,
And all the untill'd air between
Is private *pagus* or demesne.
Stranger, unless with bedroom eyes
I beckon you to fraternize,
Beware of rudely crossing it:
I have no gun but I can spit.

W.H. Auden

The terms 'individual' and 'person' evoke and express a great variety of ideas, and it is not possible at the outset to assign a single, unvarying meaning to either of them. Some might find it safer to take only one of the two concepts – and each is broad enough – but my first objective is to draw attention to the confusion of tongues that marks the discussion. I will make my own observations about the changing position of the individual in contemporary Indian society, but they will come later. For the present, one might add to 'individual' and 'person' the concept of 'self' for that also has figured prominently in sociological discussion of a certain kind, particularly in the United States:[1] the same concept, though in a different form, has been a perennial, not to say an obsessive, concern in certain traditional systems of Hindu philosophy.[2]

Individual and person are not neutral or uncharged scientific terms; they represent important values on which there are sharp and passionate disagreements, expressed as well as unexpressed. Hence, even when their meanings are discussed in apparently scientific terms, there is often an undercurrent of polemic.

Some scholars who are deeply attached to these values adopt a possessive attitude towards them, arguing that they are exclusive to their own social and cultural tradition. Others who have inherited a different tradition then bring forward a mass of evidence – not always germane to the issue – to demonstrate that they have an equal, if not a better, claim to the same values. A very common feature of contemporary discussions on individual, person and self is for scholars to talk past each other.

The variety of referents of each of these terms is not necessarily the outcome of partisanship, but it enables partisanship to flourish. While the terms in use and their meanings are various, their usage is not carefully specified. The disciplines which use the concepts of individual, person and self are many: metaphysics, legal and political philosophy, history of ideas, psychology, sociology and cultural anthropology. Scholars working in a given discipline have generally felt free to kidnap terms, concepts and arguments from other disciplines, leading more often to confusion than to clarity. Standardization of terminology is, in any case, very difficult, but partisanship compounds the difficulty.

Although authors have their preferences, it is a common tendency, at least among sociologists, to use individual and person, or person and self, interchangeably. This is governed partly by the conventions of the language being used. In English one can make 'individuality' and 'individualism' out of 'individual', but corresponding derivations cannot be constructed as easily out of 'person'; 'personeity' sounds archaic and not quite right, although 'selfhood' or even 'personhood' is frequently used, at least in philosophy. Durkheim wrote most typically about the individual, although he also used 'person' and 'personal'; Mauss wrote about the person, but also used 'the self' to cover broadly the same range of meanings.

Let me illustrate with a passing example the kind of terminological problem that frequently arises. Individual and group are generally opposed in the sociological literature, and that opposition was an important part of Durkheim's argument in his first book[3] as well as in his later writings. Now, while sociologists might use individual and person interchangeably, and contrast both with the group or collectivity, in jurisprudence the legal person can be either an individual or a group. It is well known that in India, for instance, a group such as the Hindu undivided family was, and continues to be, regarded as a legal person. There are innumerable examples in archaic societies of groups of almost every conceivable kind being treated as legal or moral persons. This should not lead us to overlook the simple fact that the individual might also be treated as a legal person in such societies, or, conversely, that English law recognizes the legal personality of groups and not only individuals.

Sociologists differ in their conception of the individual or person not only because they deal with facts from different societies, or with different facts from the same society, but also because they differ in their philosophical and moral orientations. The philosopher uses methods and techniques of analysis that are both different from those of the sociologist and highly specialized. Durkheim pointed out at the beginning of the present century that 'the philosophical analysis of the idea of person [was] far ahead of the sociological analysis'.[4] This is perhaps still the case today, and the sociologist must watch very carefully for the snares and pitfalls he will encounter in his attempt to catch up with the results of philosophical analysis.

Sociological accounts of the individual and the person have taken shape largely within the orbit of contemporary Western thought. Philosophical accounts of the person and the self have a place also in other intellectual traditions with whose technical apparatus those working within the framework of modern social science are not always fully familiar. Students of comparative sociology generally devote themselves to such topics as social structure, social differentiation and social stratification. These are large topics in themselves, and few who deal with them acquire mastery over the relevant literature for the full range of human societies. Not only is this literature highly uneven, but for any given society or civilization there is no necessary correspondence, in terms of quality, richness and reliability, between the sociological literature and the philosophical one. Even a very competent comparative sociologist is rarely at home in philosophical cultures that are distant from his own in space and time. In dealing with them he yields sooner or later to the temptation of applying his common sense to the solution of problems that are simple only in appearance.

A civilization may choose, in so far as such choices are made by civilizations, to confine its preoccupation with the self or the person to the world of ideas – metaphysics, ontology and epistemology – without giving it much scope for expression in the economic and political domains. This should not lead to the settled conclusion, to which Mauss appears to have been led in regard to India and China, that the concept then loses its social efficacy for ever.[5] There are other possibilities to consider, including the possibility that an ideal, insulated for centuries from the everyday concerns of society, may be brought back to life by the challenge of new historical conditions. The present may relate itself to the past not only by replication but also dialectically.

Since a variety of disciplines is engaged in the study of individual, person and self, the approaches to the study are many and diverse. Even within sociology, as Niklaas Luhmann has recently pointed out, there are two rather different currents which treat the individual as an emerging unit. In one of these, best represented by G.H. Mead and his successors in the United States, the individual is viewed as emerging 'from social encounters', while in the other he is viewed as emerging 'from history'.[6] The first is psychological in its orientation, while the second is historical and comparative. It is with the second that I shall be mainly concerned here.

In comparative and historical studies of the individual one notices close interconnections among concept, theory and method. As I shall be concerned mainly with such studies, I would like to make a few observations on theory and method since they bear closely on the selection of the facts presented for comparison and contrast. What is striking about the comparative study of the individual by sociologists and social anthropologists is the correspondence between theory and method; the correspondence is not only very close, it is of the particular kind in which method is constrained by theory. Now, there are two kinds of theory about the place of the individual in human society and culture. According to the first, the individual or person is present everywhere although his social role might vary enormously from one case to another. According to the second theory, 'the individual as a value' or 'the category of the person' is a unique feature of modern Western civilization or of Western civilization as such, being absent or very weakly developed in non-Western civilizations as well as in tribal societies. Adherents of the first theory make their comparisons in such a manner that human beings always and everywhere come out as basically similar. Adherents of the second theory arrange their comparisons with an eye to the uniqueness of a particular society, usually their own; in its extreme form it is a method of contrast rather than comparison.

It seems to me that one of the two approaches, the one which emphasizes difference and contrast is the one that prevails today in studies concerned with the individual in Indian society. Since I am not wholly in sympathy with that approach, I would like to spend a little time in exploring the roots of the difference between the two approaches. I will begin with a brief consideration of the place assigned by anthropologists of different persuasions to the individual in primitive societies. This is necessary in so far as one of the most influential views about the individual in Indian society are linked directly to theories of the individual in 'archaic' societies, a term used loosely to cover both primitive societies and the ancient civilizations of China and India.

If we look among anthropologists of an earlier generation, we will find the two theories of the individual (or the person) in the writings of Mauss (1872-1950) on the one hand and Malinowski (1884-1942) on the other. These two anthropologists are exemplary not only for their own work, but also as exponents of two distinct traditions in the study of man. Mauss and Malinowski were almost exact contemporaries and they both enjoyed great influence. Malinowski's reputation was perhaps the greater in his own lifetime, but it declined sharply after he died, undermined to some extent by his own students.[7] The reputation of Mauss, by contrast, remains undiminished, not least because of the steadfast loyalty of his pupils and disciples.[8] It is remarkable all the same that when the individual or person is discussed today so much respectful attention should be paid to

Mauss and so little – indeed, hardly any – to Malinowski, even by anthropologists in Anglo-Saxon countries.[9]

Mauss's essay on the person is well known among anthropologists. It was delivered as the Huxley Memorial Lecture before the Royal Anthropological Institute,[10] and it was the subject of a recent Oxford symposium. Two separate English translations of it have been published within the last ten years.[11] Instead of trying to summarize the essay, I shall begin by drawing attention to two of its important features. The first relates to its theoretical line of descent and the second to its ethnographic base of support. The central theoretical argument of the essay has retained a remarkable sameness in French sociology from Durkheim who was Mauss's teacher to Mauss's own pupils and successors. That argument was first formulated at length by Durkheim in *The Division of Labour in Society*;[12] it was repeated in a somewhat different form in a polemical essay published by him five years later;[13] and it can be picked up at various points in his *The Elementary Forms of the Religious Life*. Echoes of all these works can be clearly heard in the essay by Mauss.

Durkheim's argument in his very first book, *The Division of Labour in Society* was that, contrary to the views of both utilitarians and contract theorists, the individual was not the starting point of social evolution; he was its end product. The nineteenth-century view of individualism as an emergent property was grounded in evolutionary theory, most notably in the work of Herbert Spencer. It is true that Durkheim took issue with Spencer in all his major writings that dealt with the individual, but the alternative theory that he offered of the emergence of the individual was also an evolutionary theory. Although his style is far less assertive than Durkheim's, Mauss's theory of the person is also set firmly within an evolutionary framework. This is as one would expect, for he presented his own essay as a sample of the work of the French school of sociology whose adherents derived both their theory and their method from Durkheim. It is this evolutionary framework that encouraged Mauss to proceed at 'inordinate speed' from the Zuni and the Kwakiutl to contemporary Europe without casting more than a glance at the 'very great and ancient societies' of India and China.[14]

Now, as Evans-Pritchard often pointed out, the kind of evolutionary theory to which Durkheim and Mauss subscribed (Mauss more circumspectly than Durkheim) relied on a characteristic artifice of method, which may be called the artifice of inversion. No matter what the institution under consideration might be – religion, marriage, family or whatever – the end point is taken as being given in the form current in one's own society; the starting point is then constructed deductively by an inversion of the features known in advance to have prevailed in the end.[15] Both Durkheim and Mauss placed a very high value on the individual in their own society on moral as well as scientific grounds; and, if the individual was to count for everything in the most advanced society, as both of them believed and hoped, then it stood to reason that he should count for nothing in the most primitive ones. Although in an evolutionary series societies are placed on a continuum, from the most primitive to the most advanced, Durkheim, and to some extent also Mauss, frequently uses his typology to contrast the most advanced society in which the individual is valued above everything with all other societies in which he is of little or no value.

Durkheim's contrast between the rigidly structured societies of the past where 'the collective consciousness completely envelops our total consciousness' so that 'our individuality is zero'[16] with the more fluid and flexible modern societies where the collective consciousness withdraws to make room for the morally autonomous and responsible individual is well known. In making the contrast he frequently uses examples from both primitive tribes and ancient civilizations to illustrate what he calls the 'alveolar' system of society. Mauss follows him in this when, for example, he says in the opening pages of his celebrated work on *The Gift* ;

> For it is groups, and not individuals, which carry on exchange, make contracts, and are bound by obligations; the persons represented in the contract are moral persons – clans, tribes and families; the groups, or chiefs as intermediaries for the groups, confront and oppose each other.[17]

Durkheim was a master of the artifice of inversion, and he presented his argument about the evolutionary primacy of the group over the individual with superb dialectical skill. What he sought particularly to impress upon his readers was that he had facts whereas his adversaries – whether utilitarians or contract theories – had only their opinions. Now, it is well known that Durkheim's ethnography, in *The Elementary Forms of the Religious Life* and even more in *The Division of Labour in Society*, is highly defective. Between *The Division of Labour* and the essay on the person by Mauss there was an interval of nearly half a century which saw a tremendous advance in knowledge about simple societies through intensive fieldwork in Oceania, Africa and elsewhere. This research not only presented new facts about primitive societies, it created a new image of primitive man – quarrelsome, amicable, generous, mean, aggressive, timid, treacherous or steadfast – much as human beings are anywhere in the world.[18] Intensive fieldwork appeared to have an in-built bias for the individual both in the collection of data and in their presentation.

Malinowski was the pioneer of the new ethnography, and he felt himself to be more than a match for any armchair anthropologist with pretensions to general theories of evolution. He knew how to choose his targets, and he hit hard. He took up the cudgels on behalf of the 'individualism' of primitive man, and he set about to overwhelm the sceptics with a profusion of facts fresh from the field. The idea of primitive men and women as mere actors in a play of masks, as represented in Durkheim's *The Elementary Forms* and even more pointedly in Mauss's essay on the person, was precisely the one he set out to demolish. 'The opposition of primitive "group sentiment", "joint personality" and "clan absorption" to civilized individualism and pursuit of selfish ends appear[s] to us', he wrote, 'altogether artificial and futile'.[19]

Malinowski attacked Durkheim and Mauss openly. Criticizing the views of Steinmetz, he wrote:

His views are fully endorsed by the great French sociologists Durkheim and Mauss, who add besides one more clause: that responsibility, revenge, in fact all legal reactions are founded in the psychology of the group and not of the individual.[20]

His own conclusion was as follows: 'The savage is neither an extreme "collectivist" nor an intransigent "individualist" – he is, like man in general, a mixture of both'.[21] Characteristically, he did not take much trouble to enquire whether it was the same mixture in every case.

The stricture on 'clan absorption' entered by Malinowski in 1926 went straight past Mauss when he presented his paper to the Royal Anthropological Institute in 1938. What is remarkable about that paper is that it ignores altogether the new ethnography which in Britain and elsewhere was transforming the study of primitive society. There is no reference to any of Malinowski's monographs or to any of the monographs that the first batch of his pupils – Bateson, Firth, Evans-Pritchard – had already begun to publish. The ethnographic sources used by Mauss are of the old type: Frank Hamilton Cushing, Barbara Freire Marecco, Elsie Clews Parsons, and articles by Boas and others in the *Annual Reports of the Bureau of American Ethnology*. They are in the main the same as the ones used by Durkheim in *The Elementary Forms*, and by Durkheim and Mauss in *Primitive Classification*.

For a time at least, Malinowski appears to have been wholly successful in his effort at 'bringing the men back in'. But did he overwork his argument about universal individualism? The general consensus among anthropologists today is that he clearly did. In a penetrating critique, Edmund Leach argued that Malinowski's empiricism reached the point of theoretical sterility very quickly because of his dogmatic insistence that all human beings were alike in acting as pragmatic individuals. 'Malinowski's biggest guns are always directed against notions that might be held to imply that, in the last analysis, the individual is not a personality on his own possessing the capacity for free choice based in reason'.[22] And again, 'It was dogma for Malinowski that all human beings are reasonable (sensibly practical) individuals'.[23] This kind of dogma made it impossible to examine differences between societies and cultures in a serious or systematic way.

Without taking anything away from Leach's critique of Malinowski, we can still say that the ethnographic record flatly contradicts Durkheim's thesis about the position of the individual in primitive society and Mauss's thesis about the place of the person in primitive consciousness. Those who have contributed to this record include anthropologists like Evans-Pritchard and Godfrey Lienhardt who are sceptical about, if not opposed to, empiricism and pragmatism. Gregory Bateson, who published his remarkable study of the Iatmul of New Guinea in 1936, though trained by Malinowski in field methods, had serious reservations about his theoretical approach. But about the Iatmul themselves, he tells us that they have 'a highly individualist culture and will readily respect the law-breaker if he have but sufficient force of personality'.[24] Personal pride and its public expression are recurrent features of the Iatmul way of life. Further, 'A man achieves standing in the community by his achievements in war, by sorcery and esoteric knowledge, by shamanism, by wealth, by intrigue, and, to some extent, by age'.[25]

But the most decisive evidence comes from Evans-Pritchard whose professed theoretical sympathies were all against Malinowski and all in favour of Mauss. He has left us vivid accounts of the Nuer which alone, in all the ethnographic literature, can compare with Malinowski's accounts of the Trobriand Islanders. 'The Nuer constitution', Evans-Pritchard tells us, 'is highly individualistic and liberatarian'.[26] In talking about Nuer character, he remarks upon 'their profound individualism'.[27] Then he says, 'The Nuer has a keen sense of personal dignity and rights'.[28] And, again, it is difficult to see how the Nuer can be said to commit sin or suffer misfortune if they lack a concept of the person.[29] Finally, we have Godfrey Lienhardt's recent essay on the Dinka which tells us with exquisite irony that if we cannot see the person behind the individual Dinka, it may be our failing rather than their lack.[30]

Returning for the last time to Malinowski, it is certainly true that some anthropologists represent the others about whom they write a little too closely in their own image, and we must be watchful about this. But we must be watchful also about those anthropologists who represent others not as copies but as inversions of themselves. The objective should be to avoid the extremes of both variants of the comparative method, one of which overlooks difference while the other dwells only on difference.

In his essay on the person Mauss uses the ancient civilizations of India and China as a bridge to pass from the primitive to the modern Western world. But it is a slender and precarious bridge, hardly equal to the burden of conflicting evidence that it has to bear. He mentions, *en passant*, the classical Hindus' ideas of *aham* and *ahamkara*, but not in a manner calculated to divert attention from the main argument that the 'category of person' as against the mere 'sense of person' comes into its own only in modern Western society.

We have seen that, contrary to Durkheim and Mauss, in the simplest societies the individual was by no means completely absorbed by the group or completely devoid of a sense of personal identity and worth. The individual might, in fact, enjoy considerable freedom of action in such societies, and his sense of personal dignity and worth might sometimes be quite acute. Can we say from this that the individual or person must have had considerable significance in Indian society since that society represented a more advanced type than any primitive society? Such an inference would be fully in keeping with Durkheim's and Mauss's evolutionary perspectives, but it would be mistaken. The lessons we learn from primitive societies can be useful in the study of Indian society, but they cannot be conclusive.

Despite its high level of intellectual culture and the considerable mental agility of its philosophers, traditional Indian society provides better evidence of Durkheim's 'alveolar system' than any one might encounter in the world of primitive man. It was here if anywhere that boundaries between groups were clear and sharp, and individuals confined to bounded social spaces to such a degree that one might plausibly assert that the group predominated over the individual. Durkheim's description of the alveolar system seems to correspond remarkably with the model of traditional Indian society, whereas along the Sepik or the Amazon we are very far removed from any such type of society.

However, the prominence of the alveolar system – of groups clearly demarcated from each other – did not prevent the development of a highly articulate consciousness in regard to individual, person and self. Durkheim clearly believed that the segmental type of society went hand in hand with an absence of individual consciousness or the awareness of the individual as a morally significant agent. In such a society the individual played a part or enacted a role, but was not the object of metaphysical or ethical valuation. Mauss took over the argument from Durkheim, and only the grip of that argument can account for the astonishing statement at the beginning of his essay: 'I shall show you how recent is the philosophical term "self" '[31], astonishing because Mauss enjoyed a reputation as a Sanskritist.

In writing about non-Western societies neither Durkheim nor Mauss showed much awareness of the variety of ways in which consciousness and thought might be related to the social order. The Iatmul might tolerate or even encourage many acts of individual deviation from social convention, and yet lack an articulated consciousness of the meaning of individual freedom. The Hindus might demand strict conformity to social convention from the individual, and yet develop complex philosophical arguments about the nature and significance of the self or person.

Instead of bypassing the philosophical discussion of the self in the Hindu literature as Mauss did, one might dwell on the obsessive concern with the self in it, and still reach the same conclusion as Mauss did about the individual or person in Indian society. It goes without saying that the conception of the self in Advaita Vedanta is very different from the conception in modern Western thought. Nevertheless, it does cause some anxiety to see the ease with which the conclusion is reached that Indians, including modern Indians, lack an appreciation of the individual or person.

Hindu conceptions of the self cannot be studied in the same way as Iatmul or Nuer ideas about the individual. The method has to be different because the nature and sources of data are different. In the case of the Nuer or the Iatmul the same person studies social structure on the one hand, and religion and ideology on the other, whereas the case is very different with traditional Hindu society. In the Hindu case there are several traditions of discourse regarding individual, person and self and some of them reach far back in time. The discourse has been kept alive by intellectual specialists who have disputed with each other with the aid of a complicated, not to say an esoteric, technical apparatus for two thousand years or more. This is not a subject which the general anthropologist with a strong dose of common sense can handle on his own.

It is not uncommon for Indian and Western philosophers to talk past each other on the subject of the individual or person. Professor Kalidas Bhattacharyya, one of the ablest of contemporary Indian philosophers, wrote in an essay which is a model of scholarship, 'Regarding the Indian attitude toward the individual, Westerners hold certain views which are not wholly correct'.[32] After listing four such views, he went on to observe, 'Of these four views, the last one is wholly incorrect, and the first, second and the third are correct only insofar as they represent the standpoint of the Advaita Vedanta'.[33] Not all philosophers pay heed to such admonitions, and the anthropologist is either unaware of them or is unable to see the reason behind them.

Most contemporary Indian philosophers who have written on the subject have stressed that there was not one traditional view of the individual or person but several. Bhattacharyya observed: 'in fact, there is no *one* Indian view of the status of the individual'.[34] He distinguished the view of the individual in Advaita Vedanta from the views in other philosophical systems such as Nyaya, Samkhya and Mimamsa, and pointed out that the denial of the plurality of individuals and the assertion of their oneness, which was a characteristic of the former, was not a feature of other philosophical systems, including other systems of Vedanta. He also maintained that the prominence enjoyed by Advaita Vedanta was a result of recent historical factors. Professor Raju, writing about the individual in Indian epistemology, also stressed the plurality of perspectives, concluding thus: 'All advanced cultures are in this sense pluralistic, their members leaning toward one or the other perspective according to circumstances'.[35]

These different philosophical systems co-existed not only with each other, but with popular conceptions, legal institutions, social regulations and economic arrangements of the most bewildering variety. In course of time the social and economic arrangements became increasingly rigid, leaving the individual less and less space for movement outside his allotted positions in society, and changes also took place – to some extent in tune with the ones described – in legal institutions and modes of thought. But the alveolar system of society was not a primitive condition; it was a later development and it did not extinguish the concern for the individual in the realm of abstract ideas. Rather, that concern became more and more detached from the ongoing institutional arrangements of society. The individual or person, as both agent and value, has once again become significant with the effort to find a new place for him in these very arrangements under greatly altered historical conditions in which the distinction between 'endogenous' and 'exogenous' factors has lost its old significance.

Historically, the great impetus for rethinking the individual came with the introduction by the British in the nineteenth century of new legal and economic arrangements, and new ideas about the rights and responsibilities of the individual. There can be no doubt that these legal and economic arrangements were substantially new, and therefore the place of the individual in them had to be thought of anew. Indians not only acquired new ideas from western sources, but they went back to their own sources to seek out new meanings from old ideas. Many of those who wrote about the individual or person – and they included poets and philosophers as well as social and religious reformers – genuinely believed that they were engaged in a rediscovery of their own past. The view that traditional India 'knew nothing of the individual' must either ignore their effort or treat it as a kind of self-delusion.

Two of the makers of modern India, Tagore and Gandhi, each stressed in his own way the respect due to the individual and the responsibility due from him, not only in some ultimate metaphysical sense but also as a member of society. There is no doubt that both Tagore and Gandhi, as indeed others of their generation and the two preceding ones, had been greatly influenced by Western ideas, but it would be quixotic to maintain that they had become disconnected from their own traditions of religious and philosophical thought.

Tagore was one of the most influential poets of his generation, remembered to this day by two independent nations to whom he gave their national anthems. He was a poet and not a social theorist, but his critique of caste and untouchability is among the most profound and moving examples of its kind. Tagore was unusual among Indians of his time in so far as he stood clearly against nationalism.[36] The nation, he argued, was an artificial construction which should never be placed on the same plane of value as the individual or humanity. He wrote extensively about the human personality which he felt should be set free from artificial social restraints including those of caste. He was a cultivated person who read widely, Walt Whitman being one of his favourites, but he always referred back to the Upanishads in making his case for the person.[37] The point is not whether his was the correct interpretation of the Upanishads but that it was the interpretation of a person whose voice was acknowledged by millions of Bengalis and other Indians.

The same argument may be made about Gandhi who was in other respects a very different person from Tagore. Although he was an indefatigable writer of newspaper articles, pamphlets, letters, memoranda, etc., he influenced people less by his writing than by his life which many regarded as exemplary. Gandhi believed very strongly in the dignity of labour and in individual self-reliance, and he required everyone who lived with him to do some manual work. The anthropologist N.K. Bose, who was closely associated with him for a time, has left an invaluable account of the life and work of Gandhi.[38]

An intellectual ferment had been going on in India for a hundred years when Mauss wrote his essay on the person. Why did he and other anthropologists of his persuasion who brought India into their discussion of the individual or person pay so little attention to the history of ideas in India in the nineteenth and twentieth centuries? Mauss himself provides a clue that is highly revealing. At the end of his essay on the category of the person, he wrote: 'It was formed only for us, among us'.[39] The same possessiveness towards what is without doubt one of the major values of modern Western civilization is to be found, though it is not as clearly revealed, in Durkheim's essay on individualism as well as in more recent writings on the subject by European scholars.

The possessive attitude towards individualism as a value is not infrequently expressed in an arrogant and aggressive manner. Nationalist Indians respond to that with a characteristic mixture of vehemence and bombast. After all, their present Constitutional and legal order commits them to placing a certain value on the individual, and they do not like being told that that value is the exclusive possession of a totally different intellectual tradition. Hence, the more strident among them set out to demonstrate that they not only have a claim on that value but that they have an older and a better claim on it than anyone else. One's faith in the comparative method must be very strong indeed to survive such onslaughts from both sides.

The search for an authentic identity for the individual in India's traditional culture should not be taken to indicate a failure to recognize the subordination of the individual to the group in contemporary Indian society. That recognition was clearly articulated by Jawaharlal Nehru. Writing about Indian social structure, he underlined the primacy of the group: village, caste and joint family. He observed, 'In all these three it is the group that counts; the individual has a secondary place'.[40] And again, 'An individual was only considered as a member of a group; he could do anything he liked so long as he did not interfere with the functioning of the group'.[41] Nehru's attitudes towards the individual and the group were mixed: he was wholly against caste, but he believed that something of value might be preserved in the village and the joint family. He strove to create more room for the individual in society, not just more scope for self-realization in a metaphysical sense but more opportunity for movement across the entire social space. To be sure, he was repelled by untempered individualism as an economic doctrine of the utilitarian kind; but so, indeed, was Durkheim.

It is obvious that family, kin and community signified, and continue to signify, something very different for Indians in all walks of life in comparison with what they signify in modern Western society. Indians in general, and to some extent irrespective of region and religion, retain strong feelings of obligation towards family, kin and community, although we should not ignore altogether the changes being brought about by modern education, professional employment and urban living. Also, we should not over-stress the moral obligation to the group, for those who are fully at ease in the idiom of caste and community may use these instrumentally to attain individual ends, as in the case of the managers of political machines whether in India or the United States.

The joint family is a favourite subject for discussion among Indians. It is, according to inclination and circumstance, condemned by some for destroying individuality and extolled by others for keeping in check the excesses of individualism. It is true that most Indians, including most Hindus, do not live in joint families in the sociological sense of the term, but family and kin count for much more among them than they do in the West. There are two aspects of this: firstly, a wider range of relatives is recognized, and, secondly, the obligations due to them are more numerous and more varied. It is often pointed out that one does not choose one's relatives, and in India this is largely true also of one's spouse. But to what extent is one allowed, within the system, to treat the relative as a person, according to his personal qualities and irrespective of the formal structure of rights and obligations? This is an important question on which, unfortunately, very little systematic information is available.

Societies differ not only in the extent to which they offer a choice of roles outside the domain of kinship, but also in the extent to which they respect privacy within that domain. Privacy within the family has been valued in England and certain other European countries for a long time, and the high value placed on it there, but not necessarily elsewhere in the West, probably antedates the major changes in the division of labour and the occupational structure associated with the Industrial Revolution.[42] On the other hand, what Indians value is not privacy within the family but gregariousness among relatives. It is very likely that there is a link between the value placed on privacy and the respect for the person, but that link has to be demonstrated by careful comparative research and cannot be asserted as an established truth.

The village is a very different kind of group – if 'group' be the right word – from family and caste which are both based on kinship in some sense of the term, or at least on the sentiment of kinship. While it would be misleading to argue that the Indian village lacks 'sociological reality', loyalty to it does not interfere very seriously with the pursuit of individual opportunity when it makes itself available. Indians have moved increasingly from villages to towns and cities in search of education and employment in sectors of the economy where individual initiative and individual success count for much more than in the traditional village. It is true that most Indians continue to live in villages, but that may be as much a question of opportunity as of value.

The disintegration of the Indian village from the onslaught of British imperialism became a favourite theme with nationalists who constructed a rosy picture of the traditional village as a haven of unity, harmony and co-operation. Nostalgia for the harmony of village life was often very strong among precisely those Indians who had left the village and achieved success in professional life in towns and cities.[43] Some of them sought to give flesh and blood to their nostalgia with plans for the reconstitution of the Indian polity on the basis of village autonomy.[44] They argued in the Constituent Assembly, invoking the authority of Gandhi, that the village and not the individual should be the irreducible unit of the new Constitution of India; but they failed.

Not everyone subscribed to the nostalgia for the Indian village or the myth of village unity and harmony. Dr B.R. Ambedkar, hailed as the principal architect of the Constitution, relentlessly exposed the hiatus between the myth and the reality of the Indian village. In a celebrated speech in the Constituent Assembly he attacked the villages as cesspools of bigotry, superstition, petty strife and merciless oppression. He warned against attempts at reviving the spirit of the traditional village and pleaded, successfully, for making the individual and not the village (or any other group) the principal bearer of rights and capacities.[45]

While many might speak up for the Indian family system and some even for the village community, the defence of caste has proved to be a far more difficult endeavour, at least since the end of the last century. Even Mahatma Gandhi, whose foibles his countrymen treated with unusual indulgence, had in the end to give up his defence of caste.[46] I regard this collapse of the public defence of caste to be a turning point in India's ideological history. To be sure, Indians continue to live by caste in a variety of different spheres. But in public life, they will at best justify the use of caste by saying that it is a means to an end, not an end in itself.

Caste had a very different place in the Indian consciousness in earlier times. The social subordination of the individual to caste is best seen in the *Dharmashastra* which may be regarded as the charter of the traditional Hindu social order. But even here one has to proceed with caution. As Professor Kane has pointed out, the traditional authors were familiar with both *sadharana* or *samanya dharma* (i.e. *dharma* common to all mankind) and *varnashrama dharma* (i.e. *dharma* specific to caste and stage of life). Kane observes, 'In the midst of countless rules of outward conduct there is always insistence on the necessity to satisfy the inner man (*antara-purusa*) or conscience'.[47] However, he makes it plain that the writers of the *Dharmashastra* concerned themselves principally with *varnashrama dharma* and not with *samanya dharma*.

In everyday affairs the individual was expected to go along with his caste, and a combination of economic and religious constraints kept each caste in its allotted place. No single individual or group of individuals could easily upset the massive and elaborate architecture that became gradually established. Religious movements emerged from time to time whose leaders sought to free the individual from the constraints of everyday life, but their long-term impact was small. N.K. Bose argued that these movements could have very little social impact so long as the economic structure of society remained unchanged. Attributing the failure of the 'tremendous upheaval created in society by Chaitanyadeva' to the fact that 'the economic organization of the village remained in its ancient form', he concluded: 'I think that it is this that ensured the triumph of Raghunandan in regard to both social practices and religious beliefs'.[48]

British rule not only exposed Indians to new moral and intellectual currents, it also imposed new economic and political arrangements on them. Western ideas, beliefs and values posed a challenge of unprecedented magnitude. Indian intellectuals were quick to respond to the challenge. They wrote novels, pamphlets, tracts and, of course, poetry, and they started newspapers in both English and the vernaculars to express their ideas. The response, as one would expect, was highly various. Some were totally opposed to the 'new individualism'; a few embraced or professed to embrace it wholeheartedly; the rest were more cautious in their response.

An important part of the historical development of the individual is his development as a legal person. British rule played a major catalytic role in initiating the development of a legal personality for the individual unencumbered by the burden of caste. This happened despite the great caution with which the British proceeded, after a first phase of enthusiasm, in regard to the personal laws of their Indian subjects. As Srinivas has pointed out, the rulers of independent India were able to dispense with the circumspection that the British felt was necessary and desirable in their case.[49]

A watershed in the legal emancipation of the individual from his caste was the passage in 1850 of the Removal of Caste Disabilities Act. Particularly among Hindus of the higher *varnas* many of the legal rights of the individual were acquired by virtue of his birth in a particular caste, and expulsion from caste amounted in such cases to civil death. The Act of 1850 gave some protection to the individual in such matters, but it did not by any means do away with all the disabilities due to caste. These disabilities were progressively whittled down in the next hundred years, and the Constitution of 1950 sought to replace a legal order based on the privileges and disabilities of groups by one based on the rights and responsibilities of individuals.

This is not the occasion for discussing in detail the place assigned to the individual in the Constitution of India which is a large subject on which I have commented elsewhere.[50] What I would like to stress here is that the making of the Constitution, which took more than two years, was itself a historical process of great importance. The Constituent Assembly brought together Indians from different sections of society representing different points of view, and they put forward claims on behalf of units of every conceivable kind. Primacy was in the end assigned to the rights of the individual, save where provisions had to be made for protecting the interests of minorities and Backward Classes.

Some place has thus been found for groups as well as individuals in the Constitution of India. The provisions for the former are of two different kinds. There are those which seek to protect the religious, linguistic and cultural interests of minorities; their justification is sought in the value assigned to pluralism by both traditional Indian culture and modern democratic theory. Provisions of the second kind relate to positive discrimination in the interest of the Backward Classes or weaker sections of society; these bring out more openly the conflict between individual and collective interests because they restrict to some extent the rights of individuals to equality of opportunity. The continued and even the increasing force of these latter provisions has led some to argue that, far from eliminating the traditional identities of caste and community, the new Constitution has in some ways reinforced them.

I have tried to make in the foregoing two points regarding the historical development of the individual in India from the middle of the last century till the present. Firstly, this development did not begin in the nineteenth century on a *tabula rasa*: the encounter with the West introduced new ideas but also raised echoes of old ones, and they all contributed to the process of development. Secondly, such development as there has been, has been neither uniform nor continuous; it has been greater in some domains than in others, and in some phases the group has not only held its own against the individual but even enhanced its strength.

Having stressed the uneven development of the social personality of the individual in contemporary India, I would like to examine very briefly in this concluding section some of the factors that make the development uneven and discontinuous. Although there are different ways of looking at the individual or the person – and I have stressed this all along – what the sociologist cannot fail to note are the points of tension between individual and collective identities. It was a part of Durkheim's argument that socially the individual comes into his own with the attenuation of collective identities of the kind based on race, caste and community, and that this attenuation could be seen as a uniform and continuous process at least in contemporary Western societies.[51]

Collective identities have proved to be far more durable in the modern world than was envisaged by the sociological theory of the nineteenth century. This is true almost everywhere – Europe, America and the Soviet Union – but I shall take only the case of India. Since I have written more fully elsewhere about the persistence of collective identities,[52] I shall confine myself to a few brief observations here.

Tribe, caste, sect and denomination did not vanish from the public domain with the coming of independence; they appear, in some sense, to have become even more strongly entrenched there. The Muslim identity has survived the partition of India without significant loss of strength, and the Sikh identity is now probably at its strongest. The makers of the Indian Constitution were a little like Durkheim in their belief that a new economic and political order would create more opportunities for the individual and greater confidence in him; and they also believed that India was firmly set on the course of rapid technological and economic change.

The experience of most contemporary societies suggests that short-term fluctuations in the strength of collective identities tend to obscure such long-term trends in their growth or decline as might operate below the surface. Since there is no single convincing theory of these long-term trends, the short-term fluctuations are often seized upon as evidence of the direction of change. A common view of the resurgence of collective identities is that it represents a return to the initial condition of Indian society after a brief and superficial encounter with the Western values of individualism, liberty and equality. This view appeals naturally to those who stress the differences between civilizations, regarding each civilization as an irreducible whole.

There is, however, another view of the same phenomenon which maintains that the group – tribe, caste, sect or denomination – acquires a new lease of life because of the insecurity experienced by the individual in an unstable and intractable social environment. The proponents of this view point out that the sense of collective identity is often more acute in towns and cities, particularly industrial cities, than in the more traditional rural areas. According to N.K. Bose:

> In Calcutta the economy is an economy of scarcity. Because there
> are not enough jobs to go around everyone clings as closely as
> possible to the occupation with which his ethnic group is identified
> and relies for economic support on those who speak his language,
> on his coreligionists, on members of his own caste and on fellow
> immigrants from the village or district from which he has come.
> By a backwash reliance on earlier modes of group identification
> reinforces and perpetuates differences between ethnic groups.[53]

Here the phenomenon is seen more as an aspect of transition
than as a return to an original condition.

Dr Ambedkar, who spoke so forcefully in the cause of the
individual in the Constituent Assembly, persuaded the same
Assembly to make special provisions to safeguard the interests
of the Scheduled Castes and Scheduled Tribes. He asked for
special provisions on the ground that the individual members
of these groups remained severely disadvantaged because of
the disabilities to which they had been collectively subjected
for centuries. He saw that there might be a conflict between
the special claims of particular groups and the general claims
of all individuals, and he urged restraint in regard to the
former, saying that they should not be allowed to 'eat up'
the latter.[54] The provisions were intended to enable these
highly-disadvantaged sections of society to catch up with the
rest, particularly in matters of education and employment, and
not, as were those in favour of religious or linguistic 'minorities',
to safeguard their distinctive identities for all time.[55]

The public recognition of the Backward Classes and of the
minorities, and the allocation of quotas in their interest go back
to the period of British rule, and were not innovations designed
by the Constitution of 1950. In fact what that Constitution
sought to do was to restrict rather than expand the claims
of such groups in the public domain. To take one example,
in much of South India quotas in education and employment
had been instituted in the 1920s for religious minorities and the
upper castes as well as for the lowest castes and communities.
The Constitution did away with quotas or reservations for
religious minorities and upper castes, retaining them only for the
Scheduled Castes and Scheduled Tribes, and, somewhat more

ambiguously, for Other Backward Classes or weaker sections of society.[56] The main purpose behind this restriction was to provide more scope to the rights created for individuals – equality before the law and equal protection of the laws, equality of opportunity – in the part on Fundamental Rights.

Why should the claims of any kind of group be admitted in a Constitution whose basic objective is to secure the rights of individuals? And, what kinds of groups are these? In general, exceptions are made in favour of groups only when they can be justified by a policy of greater equality overall.[57] Thus, there can be quotas for inferior castes but not, as there also were in the past, for superior castes. This is the policy of reverse discrimination for which the Constitution of India has a variety of provisions. They represent interesting departures, by no means unknown outside India, from the classical liberal idea of equality which was defined solely in terms of the claims of individuals.[58]

Advocates of positive discrimination do not deny the value in principle of equality of opportunity between individuals, but they insist on the distinction between real and formal equality of opportunity.[59] They argue that to have real equality of opportunity we require measures for the redress of the disadvantages inherited by certain groups on which severe disabilities had been continuously imposed in the past. That argument generally concedes that such measures, being measures of redress, have a specific purpose. In other words, the benefits accruing from them should be restricted to limited sections of the population and the measures themselves should be time-bound and not perpetual.

What has been the record of positive discrimination in the forty-odd years since independence? How have the rights of the individual guaranteed by the Constitution withstood the special claims of groups acknowledged by the same Constitution? It can hardly be denied that developments in the last forty years have belied the expectations of the Constitution makers in some important ways. The groups securing the benefits of positive discrimination have expanded instead of contracting, and in some states they now make up well over half of the total population.[60] Moreover, their claims have become so secure that it does not appear now that the measures can be reversed in the foreseeable future.

Public policy in India is governed increasingly by considerations of social justice in which parity between groups receives more attention than equality between individuals. Critics of the policy view it as an accommodation to the struggle for power between organized groups, but it also appeals to a conception of social justice which probably lies very deep in the Indian consciousness. However, public policy is not the only force in India today, and, in any case, it operates in a greatly altered environment where competition between individuals as well as groups is widespread if not universal.

It is true that middle-class Indians value group-based quotas in education and employment both from considerations of security and out of a sense of social justice. But they also value the sweets of success in competition between individuals, and it is a prejudice, contradicted by the Indian experience, that those who appreciate quotas for groups on grounds of security and social justice cannot, at the same time, value competitive success as a measure of individual ability and achievement.

In India the Government plays a large part in providing education and employment in what may be called the organized sector, and parity between groups is always an important consideration for it. But even here one finds significant variations. Some state Governments, as in Karnataka, are particularly responsive to the demands of castes and communities; others, as in West Bengal, are more responsive to the demands of organized labour which represents a different kind of collectivity. Moreover, education and employment are also available in the private sector where other considerations prevail. Government has never shown a very strong inclination to suppress the private sector even where it is regulated by considerations which depart from its own conception of social justice. Indeed, there are indications that it has in the last few years encouraged the development, outside the area of its own immediate control, of a sector in which the main accent is on competition, efficiency and individual initiative. Capitalism has its own compulsions, and even Indian society cannot remain wholly immune to them.

The protagonist of competitive capitalism in its pure form

is a very different kind of individual or person from the one about whose emancipation Nehru or Tagore wrote. The birth of the 'new individualism' is due as much to a transformation in the moral awareness of people as it is to a transformation in the economic structure of society with the attendant changes in material and moral density about which Durkheim wrote. Historically, the two transformations have been very closely intertwined. Durkheim's vision of a society in which the utilitarian individualism of Spencer and the economists will be separated out from the moral individualism of Kant was a utopia which will perhaps always remain out of the reach of human societies as they are actually constituted. It is not that there is no individual in contemporary Indian society, but we should not expect to find him everywhere or in only a particular idealized form.

Notes and sources

Introduction

1. A. Béteille, 'Some observations on the comparative method', *Economic and Political Weekly* xxv, 40, 6 October 1990, pp. 2255–63.
2. E. Durkheim, *The Rules of Sociological Method* (Macmillan: London, 1982) p. 157.
3. C. Lévi–Strauss, *Le regard eloigné*, (Plon: Paris, 1983); translated as *The View from Afar* (Basic Books: New York, 1985).
4. See also M.N. Srinivas, *Social Change in Modern India* (University of California Press: Berkeley, 1966).
5 For a brief personal account of this department, see A. Béteille, 'A career in a declining profession', *Minerva* XXVIII, 1, Spring 1990, pp. 1–20.
6. M.N. Srinivas, 'Itineraries of an Indian social anthropologist', *International Social Science Journal* XXV, 1–2, 1973, pp. 129–48.
7. N.K. Bose wrote on a very broad canvas. See, for instance, his *The Structure of Hindu Society* (translated from the Bengali with an Introduction by A. Béteille). (Orient Longman: Delhi, 1975).
8. M.N. Srinivas (ed.), *India's Villages* (Government of West Bengal: Calcutta, 1955); M. Marriott (ed.), *Village India* (University of Chicago Press: Chicago, 1955).
9. A. Béteille, *Caste, Class, and Power* (University of California Press: Berkeley, 1965).
10. See my Introduction in N.K. Bose, *The Structure of Hindu Society* (Delhi, 1975).
11. For a brief but interesting contrast between the two 'structuralisms', see M. Sahlins, *Culture and Practical Reason* (University of Chicago Press: Chicago, 1976), pp. 1–54.
12. L. Dumont, *A South Indian Subcaste* (Oxford University Press: Delhi, 1986) (Originally published in French by Mouton in 1957).
13. L. Dumont, *Hierarchy and Marriage Alliance in South Indian Kinship* (Royal Anthropological Institute: London, 1957).
14. L. Dumont, *A South Indian Subcaste* (Delhi, 1986), p. 4.
15. The opening number of *Contributions to Indian Sociology* (1, 1957) had a joint statement by the two editors that had something of the character of a manifesto. The first three numbers were principally the joint work of the two editors who, through a series of reviews and commentaries, spelled out their own position on the study of Indian society and culture. Although it soon

opened its pages to other contributors, it has remained, by and large, faithful to its original inspiration.

16. L. Dumont, *Homo hierarchicus* (Paladin: London, 1972), p. 74.

17. M. Marriott (ed.), *India through Hindu Categories* (Sage: New Delhi, 1990).

18. A. Béteille, 'Sociology and ethnosociology', *International Social Science Journal* XXVI, 4, 1974, pp. 703–4.

19. A. Béteille, 'Some observations on the comparative method', *Economic and Political Weekly* XXV, 40, 1990.

20. J. Fabian, *Time and the Other* (Columbia University Press: New York, 1983).

21. A. Béteille, 'The problem', *Seminar* 157 (*The Social Sciences*), September 1972, pp. 10–14.

22. J. Baechler, *La Solution indienne* (Presses Universitaire de France: Paris, 1988).

23. N.K. Bose, 'The Hindu method of tribal absorption', *Science and Culture* VII, 1941, pp. 188–94.

24. A. Béteille, 'Homo heirarchicus, homo equalis', *Modern Asian Studies* 13, 4, 1979, pp. 529–48; see also my 'Some observations on the comparative method', *Economic and Political Weekly* XXV, 40, 1990.

Chapter 1 : Race, caste and gender

1. If I were to specify a turning point, I would choose the symposium on Caste and Race organized by the CIBA Foundation and held in London on 19, 20 and 21 April 1966. The conference was chaired by Gunnar Myrdal, and papers were presented by G.D. Berreman, Louis Dumont, Edmund Leach and Surajit Sinha, among others. These papers, along with a record of the discussions, were published in a book, *Caste and Race* (de Reuck and Knight, 1967). I had been invited to the conference, but in April/May 1966 I was lecturing at the Centre of Indian Studies in Paris at the invitation of Professor Dumont; I decided to stay behind in Paris, although Professor Dumont himself went to the conference.

2. This is Leach's phrase, applied by Dumont to the work of Berreman and others in his contribution to the CIBA volume, (De Reuck and Knight, 1967, p. 28).

3. Statistics of atrocities against the Scheduled Castes and Schedules Tribes are published annually in the *Report of the Commission for Scheduled Castes and Scheduled Tribes* (Controller of Publications: New Delhi). Atrocities are grouped under Murder, Violence, Rape, Arson and Others, and figures are arranged state-wise. Atrocities have also been listed in Kamble (1981). For

an account by a sociologist of the exploitation of Scheduled Caste women, see Trivedi, 1976.

4 See, for instance, the March 1987 issue of *The Lawyer's Collective*. The 4th National Conference on Women's Studies held at Andhra University, 28–31 December 1988 discussed several papers on the subject; these are, however, not yet available in published form.

5 Davis, Gardner and Gardner could trace ten of the sixty-five black holdings worth $900 or more to gifts by white fathers to their coloured offspring or commonlaw wife. However, they also note that 'The evidence definitely indicates that in the great majority of cases where real estate has been given to coloured individuals by whites the relation from which the gift resulted was based not upon kinship but upon sexual partnership' (1941, p. 298). The point simply is that there is a code governing the relationship between father and natural child, not that it is the same code as the one governing the relationship between father and lawful child.

6. Traditionally, only sons could be adopted, and only by men, the choice of the son to be adopted being governed by the idea of *putrachhaya* (*putra* son, *chhaya* shadow), i.e. that he must bear the likeness of a real son. All this has changed under the Hindu Adoptions and Maintenance Act, 1955 which, among other things, ignores caste.

7. The literature on race and intelligence is voluminous and controversial. Much of the recent controversy has centred on the question whether the belief in the black's inherently inferior intelligence has a scientific basis. Some say that it has and others that it does not have, but few would contest that the belief itself is widespread. See Kamin, 1974.

8. I refer in particular to Marriott's various essays on village Kishan Garhi, published in the 1950s and 1960s. Dumont's monograph on the Pramalai Kallar, first published in French in 1957, and now available in English (Dumont, 1986), is by any account one of the best monographs on any Indian community. It is, however, notable that in his general work on India, *Homo hierarchicus*, he has hardly referred to his own fieldwork, relying on the fieldwork of others with which he could not have been equally familiar and which he must often have judged to be inferior to his own.

SOURCES

AIR, *All India Reporter* (Government of India: New Delhi, 1976).

Berreman, G.D., 'Caste in India and the United States', *American Journal of Sociology* 66, 1, 1960, pp. 120–7.

Berreman, G.D., 'Caste in cross-cultural perspective' in *Japan's Invisible Race*, G. De Vos and H. Wagatsuma (eds) (University of California Press: Berkeley, 1966).

Berreman, G.D., 'Stratification, pluralism and interaction" in *Caste and Race*, A. Reuck and J. Knight (eds) (J. & A. Churchill: London, 1967).

Berreman, G.D., 'The concept of caste' in *International Encyclopaedia of the Social Sciences*, D.L. Sils (ed.), vol. 2, 1968.

Cayton, H. and St C. Drake, *Black Metropolis* (Harcourt Brace: San Diego, 1945).

Davis, A., B.B. Gardner and M.R. Gardner, *Deep South* (University of Chicago Press: Chicago, 1941).

Davis, K., 'Intermarriage in caste society', *American Anthropologist* 43, 1941, pp. 376–95.

de Reuck, A. and J. Knight (eds), *Caste and Race, Comparative Approaches* (J. & A. Churchill: London, 1967).

De Vos, G. and H. Wagatsuma (eds), *Japan's Invisible Race: Caste in Culture and Personality* (University of California Press: Berkeley, 1966).

Dollard, J., *Caste and class in a southern town* (1937) (Doubleday: New York, 1957).

Dumont, L.,'Caste, Racism and "stratification"', *Contributions to Indian Sociology* 5, 1961, pp. 20–43.

Dumont, L. *La civilisation indienne et nous* (Armand Colin: Paris, 1964).

Dumont, L., *Homo hierarchicus* (Gallimard: Paris, 1966).

Dumont, L., 'Caste: a phenomenon of social stratification or an aspect of Indian culture?' in *Caste and Race*, A. de Reuck and J. Knight (eds) (J. & A. Churchill: London, 1967).

Dumont, L., *A South Indian Sub-caste* (1957) (Oxford University Press: Delhi, 1986).

Fortes, M., *Kinship and the Social Order* (Routledge: London, 1969).

Freeman, J.M., *Untouchable* (Stanford University Press: Stanford, 1979).

Freeman, R.B., *The Black Elite*. New York: (McGraw Hill: New York, 1976).

Ghurye, G.S., *Caste and Race in India* (1932) (Popular Prakashan: Bombay, 1969).

Glazer, N. and D.P. Moynihan (eds), *Ethnicity* (Harvard University Press: Cambridge Mass., 1975).

Hughes, E.C., 'Anomalies and projections', *Daedalus* 94, 4, 1965, pp. 1133–47.

Inden, R.B. and R.W. Nicholas, *Kinship in Bengali Culture* (University of Chicago Press: Chicago, 1977).

Kamble, N.D., *Atrocities on Scheduled Castes* (Ashish Publishing House: New Delhi, 1981).

Kamin, L.J., *The Science and Politics of IQ* (Lawrence Erlbaum Associates: Hillsdale, N.J., 1974).

Kane, P.V., *History of Dharmasastra* (Bhandarkar Oriental Research Institute: Poona, 1974) vol. 2, part 1.

Kapferer, B. (ed.), *Transaction and Meaning* (Institute for the Study of Human Issues: Philadelphia, 1976).

Lévi-Strauss, C., *Structural Anthropology* (Basic Books: New York, 1963).

Manu, *The Laws of Manu*, tran. G. Bühler (Motilal Banarasidas: Delhi, 1964).

Marriott, M. 'Hindu transactions' in *Transaction and Meaning*, B. Kapferer (ed.) (Philadelphia, 1976).

Marriott, M. and R.B. Inden, 'Caste systems' in *Encyclopaedia Britannica*, 15th edn, 1980 Macropaedia, vol. 3.

Mayer, A.C. 1960. *Caste and Kinship in Central India.* (Routledge: London, 1960).

Montagu, A., *Man's Most Dangerous Myth* (Oxford University Press: New York, 1974).

Myrdal, G., *An American Dilemma, The Negro Problem in Modern Democracy* (Harper & Row: New York 1944).

Myrdal, G., 'Chairman's Introduction' in *Caste and Race*, A. de Reuck and J. Knight (eds) (J. & A. Churchill: London, 1967).

Parsons, T., 'Some theoretical considerations of the nature and trends of change of ethnicity' in *Ethnicity*, N. Glazer and D.P. Moynihan (eds) (Harvard University Press: Cambridge Mass., 1975).

Pinkney, A., *The Myth of Black Progress* (Cambridge University Press: Cambridge, 1985).

Risley, H.H., *The People of India.* (W. Thacker: Calcutta, 1908).

Schneider, D.M., *American Kinship* (Prentice-Hall: Englewood Cliffs, 1968).

Shils, E.A. and H.A. Finch (eds), *Max Weber on the Methodology of the Social Sciences* (The Free Press: Glencoe, 1949).

Trivedi, H.R., *Scheduled Caste Women.* (Concept: New Delhi, 1976).

Warner, W.L., 'American caste and class', *American Journal of Sociology* 42, 1, 1936, pp. 234–7.

Chapter 2 : Race, caste and ethnic identity

1. For an interesting discussion see *Caste and Race, Comparative Approaches*, A. de Reuck and J. Knight (eds) (London, 1967).

2. Among the more notable community studies going back to this period are John Dollard, *Caste and Class in a Southern Town* (New Haven, 1937) and Allison Davis, Burleigh B. Gardner and Mary R. Gardner, *Deep South, A Social Anthropological Study of Caste and Class* (Chicago, 1941).

3. G. Myrdal, *An American Dilemma, The Negro Problem in Modern Democracy* (New York, 1944), pp. 667, 688.

4. P.L. van den Berghe, *Race and Racism, A Comparative Perspective* (New York, 1967), speaks of whites, Africans, Asians and coloureds as constituting the four 'castes' or 'colour-castes' of South African society.

5. G. Myrdal, *An American Dilemma* (New York, 1944).

6. A. Béteille, *Castes: Old and New, Essays in Social Structure and Social*

Stratification (Bombay, 1969), p. 3.

7. I. Karve, *Hindu Society: An Interpretation* (Poona, 1961), p. 16.

8. For American examples see the case studies by J. Dollard (*Caste and Class in a Southern Town* (New Haven, 1937)) and by A. Davis, B. Gardner and M. Gardner (*Deep South, A Social Anthropological Study of Caste and Class* (Chicago, 1941)); for an Indian case study see E.K. Gough, 'Caste in a Tanjore village' in *Aspects of Caste in South India, Ceylon and North-west Pakistan*, E.R. Leach (ed.) (Cambridge, 1960), p. 49.

9. G.D. Berreman, *Hindus of the Himalayas* (Berkeley, 1963), pp. 243–5.

10. See A. de Reuck and J. Knight (eds), *Caste and Race, Comparative Approaches* (London, 1967).

11. L. Dumont, 'Caste, racism and "stratification": reflections of a social anthroplolgist', *Contributions to India Sociology* 5, 1961, pp. 20–43.

12. E.R. Leach, 'Introduction: What we should mean by caste' in *Aspects of Caste in South India, Ceylon and North-west Pakistan*, E.R. Leach (ed.) (Cambridge, 1960).

13. S.J. Tambiah presents this opposition as a 'gross simplification' in a discussion reported in *Caste and Race*, A. de Reuck and J. Knight (eds) (London, 1967), pp. 328–9.

14. W. Lloyd Warner, 'Introduction: Deep South – A Social Anthropological Study of Caste and Class' in *Deep South, A Social Anthropological Study of Caste and Class*, A. Davis, B. Gardner and M. Gardner (eds) (Chicago, 1941), pp. 3–14.

15. G. Myrdal, *An American Dilemma* (New York, 1944).

16. W. Lloyd Warner, 'Introduction' in *Deep South, A Social Anthropological Study of Caste and Class*, A. Davis, B. Gardner and M. Gardner (eds) (Chicago, 1941), pp. 3–14.

17. G. Myrdal, *An American Dilemma* (New York, 1944), p. 113.

18. Kingsley Davis, 'Intermarriage in caste society', *American Anthropologist* 43, 1941, pp. 386–7.

19. L. Dumont, 'Caste: a phenomenon of social structure or an aspect of Indian culture?' in *Caste and Race*, A. de Reuck and J. Knight (eds), pp. 28–38.

20. L. Dumont, *Homo hierarchicus* (Paris, 1966).

21. I. Karve, *Hindu Society: An Interpretation* (Poona, 1961).

22. E.R. Leach (ed.), *Aspects of Caste in South India, Ceylon and North-west Pakistan* (Cambridge, 1960).

23. G.D. Berreman, *Hindus of the Himalayas* (Berkeley, 1963), pp. 243–5.

24. A. Béteille, 'The politics of "non-antagonistic" strata', *Contributions to Indian Sociology*, New Series 3, 1969, pp. 17–31 (see Chapter 5). One way in which conflicts between castes were structured in the past was through the opposition between the 'right-hand' and the 'left-hand' castes prevalent in many parts of South India; see J.H Hutton, *Caste in India: Its Nature, Function, and Origins* (Bombay, 1961).

25. G.D. Berreman, 'Caste in cross-cultural perspective', in *Japan's Invisible Race: Caste in Culture and Personality*, G. De Vos and H. Wagatsuma (eds) (Berkeley, 1966), p. 297.

26. G.D. Berreman, 'Caste in cross-cultural perspective', in *Japan's Invisible Race*, G. De Vos and H. Wagatsuma (eds) (Berkeley, 1966), p. 297.

27. P.L. van den Berghe, *Race and Racism, A Comparative Perspective* (New York, 1967).

28. For typical village studies see A.C. Mayer, *Caste and Kinship in Central India, A Village and its Region* (London, 1960); and A. Béteille, *Caste, Class, and Power, Changing Patterns of Stratification in a Tanjore Village* (Berkeley, 1965).

29. A. Béteille, *Caste, Class, and Power* (Berkeley, 1965).

30. A. Béteille, *Caste, Class, and Power* (Berkeley, 1965).

31. McKim Marriott, 'Caste ranking and food transactions: a matrix analysis' in *Structure and Change in Indian Society*, M. Singer and B.S. Cohn (eds) (Chicago, 1969), pp. 133–71.

32. R. Dahrendorf, *Class and Class Conflict in an Industrial Society* (London, 1959).

33. M.N. Srinivas, 'Varna and Caste' in M.N. Srinivas, *Caste in Modern India and Other Essays* (Bombay, 1962), pp. 63–9.

34. I. Karve, *Hindu Society: An Interpretation* (Poona, 1961).

35. G.S. Ghurye, *Caste and Race in India* (London, 1932).

36. I. Karve, *Hindu Society: An Interpretation* (Poona, 1961).

37. I. Karve and K.C. Malhotra, 'A biological comparison of eight endogamous groups of the same rank', *Current Anthropology* 9, 1968, pp. 109–16.

38. A. Béteille, *Caste, Class, and Power* (Berkeley, 1965).

39. A. Béteille, *Caste, Class, and Power* (Berkeley, 1965).

40. H.H. Risley, *The People of India* (Calcutta, 1908), p. 29.

41. H.H. Risley, *The People of India* (Calcutta, 1908), p. 29.

42. P.C. Mahalanobis, 'A revision of Risley's anthropometric data', *Samkhya* I, 1933, pp. 76–105; G.S. Ghurye, *Caste and Race in India* (London, 1932).

43. G.S. Ghurye, *Caste and Race in india* (London, 1932), p. 111.

44. G.S. Ghurye, *Caste and Race in India* (London, 1932), p. 107.

45. D.N. Majumdar and C.R. Rao, *Race Elements in Bengal: A Quantitative Study* (Calcutta, 1960).

46. D.N. Majumdar and C.R. Rao, *Race Elements in Bengal* (Calcutta, 1960), p. 102.

47. D.N. Majumdar and C.R. Rao, *Race Elements in Bengal* (Calcutta, 1960), p. 103.

48. I. Karve and K.C. Malhotra, 'A biological comparison of eight endogamous groups of the same rank', *Current Anthropology* 9, 1968, pp. 109–16.

49. I. Karve and K.C. Malhotra, 'A biological comparison of eight endogamous groups of the same rank', *Current Anthropology* 9, 1968, p. 115.

50. L.D. Sanghvi and V.R. Khanolkar, 'Data relating to seven genetical

characters in six endogamous groups in Bombay', *Annals of Eugenics* 15, 1950–1, pp. 52–76.

51. L.D. Sanghvi and V.R. Khanolkar, 'Data relating to seven genetical characters in six endogamous groups in Bombay', *Annals of Eugenics* 15, 1950–1, p. 62.

52. A. Béteille, 'Race and descent as social categories in India', *Daedalus* 96, 1967, pp. 444–63.

53. In a discussion reported in *Caste and Race*, A. de Reuck and J. Knight (eds) (London, 1967), pp. 110–11.

54. A. Béteille, 'Race and descent as social categories in India', *Daedalus* 96, 1967, pp. 444–63.

55. H.S. Morris, 'Ethnic Groups' in *International Encyclopaedia of the Social Sciences*, David L. Sills (ed.), vol. 5, 1968, p. 167.

56. N. Glazer and D.P. Moynihan, *Beyond the Melting Pot: The Negroes, Peurto Ricans, Jews, Italians, and Irish of New York City* (Cambridge, Mass., 1963).

57. J.S. Furnivall, *Colonial Policy and Practice: A Comparative Study of Burma and Netherlands India* (New York, 1956).

58. F. Barth, 'Introduction' in *Ethnic Groups and Boundaries, The Social Organization of Culture Difference*, Fredrik Barth (ed.) (London, 1969, p. 14).

59. H. Eidheim, 'When ethnic identity is a social stigma' in *Ethnic Groups and Boundaries*, F. Barth (ed.) (London, 1969), pp. 39–57.

60. F. Barth, 'Introduction' in *Ethnic Groups and Boundaries* (London, 1969), p. 10.

61. I am indebted for this information to Jonathan P. Parry who has made an intensive study of the hill Rajputs in Kangra district.

62. L.I. Rudolph and S.H. Rudolph, *The Modernity of Tradition: Political Development in India* (Chicago, 1967); A. Béteille, 'Caste and politics in Tamilnadu' in *Castes: Old and New* (Bombay, 1969) (see Chapter 4).

63. N. Glazer and D.P. Moynihan, *Beyond the Melting Pot* (Cambridge, Mass., 1963).

64. R. Kothari (ed.), *Caste in Indian Politics* (New Delhi, 1970).

65. L.I. Rudolph and S.H. Rudolph, 'The political role of India's caste associations', *Pacific Affairs* 33, 1960, pp. 5–22.

66. S.S. Harrison, 'Caste and the Andhra communists', *American Political Science Review* 50, 1956.

67. O.L. Lynch, *The Politics of Untouchability* (New York, 1969).

68. A. Béteille, 'The future of the Backward Classes: the competing demands of status and power', *Perspectives, Supplement to the Indian Journal of Public Administration* 11, 1965, pp. 1–39 (see Chapter 7).

69. C. von Fürer-Haimendorf, 'The position of the tribal population in modern India' in *India and Ceylon: Unity and Diversity*, P. Mason (ed.) (London, 1967), pp. 182–222.

70. D.N. Majumdar and C.R. Rao, *Race Elements in Bengal: A Quantitative Study* (Calcutta, 1960).

71. C. von Fürer-Haimendorf, 'The position of the tribal population in modern India' in *India and Ceylon: Unity and Diversity*, P. Mason (ed.) (London, 1967), p. 188.

72. See, for instance, the issue of *Seminar* 24, August 1961, devoted to Communalism.

73. A. Spear, 'The position of the Muslims, before and after partition' in *India and Ceylon: Unity and Diversity*, P. Mason (ed.) (London, 1967), pp. 33–4.

74. D.N. Majumdar and C.R. Rao, *Race Elements in Bengal* (Calcutta, 1960), p. 102.

75. S.S. Harrison, *India: The Most Dangerous Decade* (Bombay, 1960).

76. See, for instance, the issue of *Seminar* 23, July 1961, devoted to North and South.

77. R.L. Hardgrave Jr., *The Dravidian Movement* (Bombay, 1965).

78. A. Béteille, 'Race and descent as social categories in India', *Daedalus* 96, 1967, pp. 444–63.

Chapter 3 : The concept of tribe with special reference to India

1. R. Redfield, *Peasant Society and Culture: An Anthropological Approach to Civilization* (Chicago University Press: Chicago, 1956); see also his *Papers* 2 vols, M.P. Redfield (ed.) (Chicago, 1962–3).

2. Kroeber's interest in civilizations is expressed in many of his writings, published over a long period. A good sample is to be found in A.L. Kroeber, *Configurations of Culture Growth* (University of California Press: Berkeley, 1944).

3. See R. Redfield, *Peasant Society and Culture* (Chicago, 1956). The phrase is due to A.L. Kroeber, *Anthropology* (Harcourt Brace: New York, 1948), p. 284.

4. N.K. Bose, *The Structure of Hindu Society*, Translated with Introduction by A. Béteille (Orient Longman: New York, 1975). K.S. Singh, *Tribal Society in India: An Anthropo-historical Perspective* (Manohar: New Delhi, 1985).

5. L.H. Morgan, *Ancient Society* (1877) (Belknap Press: Cambridge, Mass., 1964).

6. E. Durkheim, *The Division of Labour in Society* (1893) (The Free Press: New York, 1933) was, as Sahlins has noted, the starting point of the anthropological discussion of segmentary systems. See also E. Durkheim, *The Rules of Sociological Method* (1895) (New York, 1938), especially Chapter 4.

7. N.K. Bose, *Tribal Life in India* (National Book Trust: Delhi, 1971); S. Fuchs, *Aboriginal Tribes of India* (Macmillan: London, 1973); C. von Fürer-Haimendorf, *Tribes of India* (University of California Press: Berkeley, 1982).

8. The phrase was popularized by D.N. Majumdar, *A Tribe in Transition: A Study in Culture Pattern* (Longman: Calcutta, 1937).

9. E.R. Service, *Primitive Social Organization* (Random House: New York, 1962).

10. M.D. Sahlins, 'The segmentary lineage: an organization of predatory expansion', *American Anthropologist* LXIII, 1961, pp. 322–45; *Tribesmen* (Prentice-Hall: Englewood Cliffs, 1968).

11. M.D. Sahlins, 'The segmentary lineage', *American Anthropologist* LXIII, 1961, p. 325.

12. E.E. Evans-Pritchard, *The Nuer* (Clarendon: Oxford, 1940).

13. M. Fortes and E.E. Evans-Pritchard (eds), *African Political Systems* (Oxford University Press: London, 1940).

14. Sahlins makes no reference to Durkheim's work in his first paper although the omission is made good in his book published seven years later. See 'The segmentary lineage', *American Anthropologist* LXIII, 1961, p. 325.

15. See E. Gellner, *Saints of the Atlas* (Weidenfeld and Nicholson: London, 1969); also his *Muslim Society* (Cambridge University Press: Cambridge, 1981). The pioneering anthropological work is E.E. Evans-Pritchard, *The Sanusi of Cyrenaica* (Clarendon Press: Oxford, 1949).

16. F. Barth, *Political Leadership among Swat Pathans* (Athlone: London, 1959).

17. M.D. Sahlins, 'The segmentary lineage', *American Anthropologist* LXIII, 1961, p. 322.

18. M.D. Sahlins, *Tribesmen* (Englewood Cliffs, 1968), p. 20.

19. M. Godelier, *Perspectives in Marxist Anthropology* (Cambridge University Press: London, 1977), translated from French: *Horizons, trajets marxistes en anthropologie* (Maspero: Paris, 1973).

20. M. Godelier, *Perspectives in Marxist Anthropology* (London, 1977), p. 70.

21. M. Godelier, *Perspectives in Marxist Anthropology* (London, 1977), p. 87. This argument, as indeed Godelier's whole approach, leans heavily on Engels.

22. M. Fortes and E.E. Evans-Pritchard (eds), *African Political Systems* (London, 1940), p. 8.

23. See J.P. Digard, 'On the Bakhtiari' in *The Conflict of Tribe and State in Iran and Afghanistan*, R. Tapper (ed.) (Croom-Helm: London, 1983), pp. 331–6. Digard asks, 'Moreover, how can it be maintained that a segmentary structure is *inherently* contradictory with a class structure, when, as a matter of *fact*, these two forms of organization co-exist and "function" simultaneously in several societies, including the Bakhtiari?' (p. 332).

24. M. Fortes and E.E. Evans-Pritchard (eds), *African Political Systems* (London, 1940), p. 8.

25. N.K. Bose, *Tribal Life in India* (Delhi, 1971).

26. B.K. Roy Burman, 'Transformation of tribes and analogous social formations', *Economic and Political Weekly* XVIII, 27, 2 July 1983, pp.

1172–4; see also his 'The post-primitives of Chota Nagpur' in UNESCO, *Trends in Ethnic Group Relations in Asia and Oceania* (UNESCO: Paris, 1979), pp. 102–41.

27. M.H. Fried, *The Notion of Tribe* (Cummings Publishing Co.: Menlo Park, 1975).

28. M. Godelier, *Perspectives in Marxist Anthropology* (London, 1977).

29. M.H. Fried, *The Notion of Tribe* (Menlo Park, 1975), Chapter 2.

30. Writing about the Kamar and the Gond who have close cultural affiliations, Fürer-Haimendorf observed in 1951: 'The Kamars consider the Gonds as their social superiors, but nevertheless they do not countenance unrestricted social intercourse with their Gond neighbours. Sexual relations with a Gond is sufficient ground for excommunication and a woman who eats food cooked by Gonds is at once expelled from the tribal community. A man, on the other hand, may eat Gond food, but Kamars and Gonds do not freely intermingle at feasts and ceremonies' (C. von Fürer-Haimendorf, Foreward in S.C. Dube, *The Kamar* (Universal Publishers: Lucknow, 1951), p. v).

31. M.H. Fried, *The Notion of Tribe* (Menlo Park, 1975), p. 30.

32. T. Trautman, *Dravidian Kinship* (Cambridge University Press: Cambridge, 1981).

33. On this, however, there is some difference of opinion. See, for instance, the three-part article by L. Dumont, 'Marriage in India: the present state of the question'. *Contributions to Indian Sociology* 5, 1961, 7, 1964 and 9, 1966.

34. E.E. Evans-Pritchard, *The Nuer* (Oxford, 1940), Chapter 4.

35. M.H. Fried, 'On the concepts of "tribe" and "tribal society" ' in *Essays on the Problem of Tribe*, J. Helm (ed.) (American Ethnological Society: Washington, 1968), p. 15.

36. E. Colson, *The Makah Indians* (Manchester University Press: Manchester, 1953), p. 62.

37. E. Colson, 'Contemporary tribes and the development of nationalism' in *Essays on the Problem of Tribe*, J. Helm (ed.) (Washington, 1968), p. 202.

38. J.W. Anderson, 'Khan and Khel: dialects of Pakhtun tribalism' in *The Conflict of Tribe and State in Iran and Afghanistan*, R. Tapper (ed.) (London, 1983), p. 121.

39 The most illuminating contemporary discussion is in E. Gellner, *Muslim Society* (Cambridge, 1981); see also his *Saints of the Atlas* (London, 1969).

40. D. Brooks, 'The enemy within: limitations on leadership in the Bakhtiari' in *The Conflict of Tribe and State in Iran and Afghanistan*, R. Tapper (ed.) (London, 1983), p. 338.

41. This remark is controversial, but here I follow D.D. Kosambi, *An Introduction to the Study of Indian History* (Popular Prakashan: Bombay, 1956), especially Chapter 1.

42. N. Ray, *Nationalism in India* (Aligarh Muslim University: Aligarh, 1973); N.K. Bose, *Tribal Life in India* (Delhi, 1971).

43. N. Ray, *Nationalism in India* (Aligarh, 1973), p. 123.

44. For an alternative formulation of the distinction see S. Bouez, *Réciprocité et hiérarchie* (Société d'ethnographie: Nanterre, 1985), pp. 14–15.

45. D.D. Kosambi, *An Introduction to the Study of Indian History* (Bombay, 1956), p. 8.

46. D.D. Kosambi, *An Introduction to the Study of Indian History* (Bombay, 1956), pp. 26–30.

47. B.K. Roy Burman, 'The post-primitives of Chota Nagpur' in UNESCO, *Trends in Ethnic Group Relations in Asia and Oceania* (Paris, 1979), p. 26.

48. Among the better known are H.H. Risley, *The Tribes and Castes of Bengal*, 2 vols (Bengal Secretariat Press: Calcutta, 1892); E. Thurston, *Castes and Tribes of Southern India*, 7 vols (Government Press: Madras, 1909); W. Crooke, *The Tribes and Castes of the North-western Province and Oudh*, 4 vols (Calcutta, 1896); R.E. Enthoven, *The Tribes and Castes of Bombay*, 3 vols (Government Central Press: Bombay, 1920–2).

49. D.D. Kosambi, *An Introduction to the Study of Indian History* (Bombay, 1956), p. 25; italics where capitalization in original.

50. I. Habib, 'Caste in Indian History', being the first of two Kosambi Memorial Lectures delivered in Bombay in February 1985, ms.

51. I. Habib, 'Caste in Indian History', p. 12.

52. N.K. Bose, 'The Hindu method of tribal absorption', *Science and Culture* VII (1941), pp. 188–94.

53. N.K. Bose, *The Structure of Hindu Society*, trans A. Béteille (New York, 1975.

54. For a recent description of the melange of tribes and castes in Assam see A. Cantlie, *The Assamese* (Curzon Press: Philadelphia, 1984). On the Khasi, see P.R.T. Gurdon, *The Khasis* (Macmillan: London, 1914), and for a more recent work, H. Bareh, *History and Culture of the Khasi People* (Published by the author: Calcutta, 1967).

55. F. Barth, *Political Leadership among Swat Pathans* (London, 1959). See also F. Barth,'The system of social stratification in Swat, North Pakistan' in *Aspects of Caste in South India, Ceylon and North-west Pakistan*, E.R. Leach (ed.) (Cambridge, 1960), pp. 113–46.

56. E. Colson, *The Makah Indians* (Manchester, 1953), p. 11.

57. E. Colson, *The Makah Indians* (Manchester, 1953), p. 1.

58. B.K. Roy Burman, 'Transformation of tribes and analogous social formations', *Economic and Political Weekly* XVIII, 27, 2 July 1983.

59. B.K. Roy Burman, 'The post-primitives of Chota Nagpur' in UNESCO, *Trends in Ethnic Group Relations in Asia and Oceania* (Paris, 1979), p. 112.

60. G.S. Ghurye, *The Scheduled Tribes* (Popular Book Depot: Bombay, 1959).

61. R. Tapper, 'Introduction' in *The Conflict of Tribe and State in Iran and Afghanistan*, R. Tapper (ed.) (London, 1983), pp. 46–7.

62. K.S. Singh, *Tribal Society in India* (New Delhi, 1985), especially Chapter 6.

63. G.S. Ghurye, *The Scheduled Tribes* (Bombay, 1959), articulates the nationalist point of view forcefully.

64. For a succinct account of the Constitutional position, see M. Galanter, *Competing Equalities* (Oxford University Press: New York, 1984), pp. 147-53.

65. This case is described in K.S. Singh, *Tribal Society in India* (New Delhi, 1985), p. 80.

66. A. Béteille, *Individualism and the Persistence of Collective Identities* (University of Essex: Colchester, 1984).

Chapter 4 : Caste and politics in Tamilnadu

1. R.W. Nicholas, 'Factions: a comparative analysis', *Political Systems and the Distribution of Power*, ASA Monographs 2 (London and New York, 1965).

2. P.R. Brass, *Factional Politics in an Indian State: The Congress Party in Uttar Pradesh* (Berkeley and Los Angeles, 1965).

3. See A. Béteille, *Caste, Class and Power: Changing Patterns of Stratification in a Tanjore Village* (Berkeley and Los Angeles, 1965).

4. E.A. Shils, 'Primordial, Personal, Sacred and Civil Ties', *British Journal of Sociology* 8, 1957, pp. 130-45.

5. Cf. M.N. Srinivas, *Caste in Modern India and Other Essays* (Bombay, 1962), p. 5.

6. See A. Béteille, *Castes: Old and New, Essays in Social Structure and Social Stratification* (Bombay, 1969), Chapter 5.

7. S.F. Nadel, 'Dual Descent in the Nuba Hills' in *African Systems of Kinship and Marriage*, A.R. Radcliffe-Brown and D. Forde (eds) (London, 1950), p. 337.

8. J.H. Hutton, *Caste in India*, 3rd edn (Bombay, 1961), pp. 205-6.

9. See A. Béteille, *Caste, Class and Power* (Berkeley and Los Angeles, 1965), especially Chapter 3.

10. M.N. Srinivas, *Caste in Modern Indian and Other Essays* (Bombay, 1962), p. 5.

11. See A. Béteille, *Castes: Old and New* (Bombay, 1969), Chapter 5.

12. M.N. Srinivas, *Caste in Modern India and Other Essays* (Bombay, 1962), p. 5.

13. For the concept of merging series, see J. Goody, 'The Fission of Domestic Groups among the LoDagaba' in *The Developmental Cycle in Domestic Groups*, J. Goody (ed.) (Cambridge, 1958), p. 60.

14. A. Béteille, *Caste, Class and Power* (Berkeley and Los Angeles, 1965), Chapter 3.

15. A lineage is itself often internally segmented.

16. See A. Béteille, *Castes: Old and New* (Bombay, 1969), Chapter 1.

17. The Brahmins in Tamilnadu constitute between 3 and 4 per cent of the total population.

18. The Poondi Wandiyars, the Kapisthalam Muppanars and the Ukkadai Thevars.

19. Quoted in C.V. Subba Rao, *Life and Times of Sir K.V. Reddi Naidu* (Rajahmundry, 1957), pp. 17-19. I am grateful to Miss G. Uma for having drawn my attention to this book and for having provided me with other interesting material on the non-Brahmin movement.

20. E.K. Gough, 'The social structure of a Tanjore village' in *Village India*, McKim Marriott (ed.) (Chicago, 1955); 'Caste in a Tanjore village' in *Aspects of Caste in South India, Ceylon and North-west Pakistan*, E.R. Leach (ed.) (Cambridge, 1960).

21. D. Sivertsen, *When Caste Barriers Fall* (New York, 1963).

22. A. Béteille, *Caste, Class and Power* (Berkeley and Los Angeles, 1965).

23. E.K. Gough, 'The social structure of a Tanjore village' in *Village India*, McKim Marriott (ed.) (Chicago, 1955), p. 38.

24. This was written when the Congress was in power; it applies even more to the present situation.

25. S. Harrison shows the tie-up between the Communists and the DK in his book, *India: The Most Dangerous Decades* (Bombay, 1960), pp. 182-90.

26. D. Sivertsen, *When Caste Barriers Fall* (New York, 1963), p. 126.

27. R. Dahl, *Who Governs?* (New Haven, 1961).

28. Quoted in C.V. Subba Rao, *Life and Times of Sir K.V. Reddi Naidu* (Rajahmundry, 1957), pp. 17-23.

29. C.V. Subba Rao, *Life and Times* (Rajahmundry, 1957), p. 30.

30. C.V. Subba Rao, *Life and Times* (Rajahmundry, 1957), pp. 30-9.

31. C.V. Subba Rao, *Life and Times* (Rajahmundry, 1957), p. 53.

32. R.L. Hardgrave Jr., *The Dravidian Movement* (Bombay, 1965), p. 19.

33. R.L. Hardgrave Jr., *The Dravidian Movement* (Bombay, 1965), p. 21.

34. Quoted in Subba Rao, *Life and Times* (Rajahmundlkry, 1957), p. 19.

35. K.B. Krishna, *The Problem of Minorities* (London, 1939), pp. 154-5.

36. R.L. Hardgrave Jr., *The Dravidian Movement* (Bombay, 1965), p. 16.

37. M.N. Srinivas, 'The social system of a Mysore village' in *Village India*, McKim Marriott (ed.) (Chicago, 1955).

38. M.N. Srinivas, 'The social system of a Mysore village' in *Village India*, McKim Marriott (ed.) (Chicago, 1955), p. 18.

39. M.N. Srinivas, 'The social system of a Mysore village'.

40. In this sense, Kumbapettai, Thyagasamudram and Sripuram are exceptional rather than general.

41. L.I. Rudolph and S.H. Rudolph, 'The political role of India's caste associations', *Pacific Affairs* XXXIII, 1, 1960, pp. 5-22.

42 *The Mail*, 13 February, 1962.

43. C.V. Subba Rao, *Life and Times* (Rajahmundry, 1957), p. 107.

44. A. Béteille, *Caste, Class and Power* (Berkeley and Los Angeles, 1965).

45. *The Mail*, 9 June 1961.

46. This case was reported in detail in the September and October 1957 issues of *The Hindu*; see, in particular, the issue of 15 September 1957, 16 September 1957 and 22 September 1957.

47. M.N. Srinivas, *Caste in Modern India and Other Essays* (Bombay, 1962), p. 75.

48. E.K. Gough, 'The social structure of a Tanjore village' in *Village India*, McKim Marriott (ed.) (Chicago, 1955).

49. M. Weber, *The Religion of India* (New York, 1958).

50. I am grateful to Mr E.A. Ramaswamy for the important information on Coimbatore where he is making an intensive study of textile workers' unions.

51. E.R. Leach (ed.), *Aspects of Caste in South India, Ceylon and North-west Pakistan* (Cambridge, 1960), p. 6.

52. E.R. Leach (ed.), *Aspects of Caste* (Cambridge, 1960), p. 7.

53. E.R. Leach (ed.), *Aspects of Caste* (Cambridge, 1960), p. 7.

54. See A. Béteille, *Castes: Old and New* (Bombay, 1969).

55. P.R. Brass, *Factional Politics in an Indian State* (Berkeley and Los Angeles, 1965).

56. L.I. Rudolph and S.H. Rudolph, 'The political role of India's caste associations', *Pacific Affairs* XXXIII, 1, 1960, pp. 5-22.

57. R.A. Dahl, *Who Governs?* (New Haven, 1961), p. 34.

58. P.R. Brass, *Factional Politics in an Indian State* (Berkeley and Los Angeles, 1965).

59. S.M. Lipset, *Political Man* (London, 1963), p. 31.

Chapter 5 : The politics of 'non-antagonistic' strata

1. In talking about Bailey in the following pages, I shall confine myself to the views expressed by him in this paper which is probably his most comprehensive general statement on caste. These seem to me to be at variance with some of his earlier views which I think would support the basic argument of this chapter.

2. There is an interesting discussion in R.W. Nicholas 'Factions: a comparative analysis', *Political Systems and the Distribution of Power*, ASA Monograph 2 (London, 1965).

3. For an interesting discussion see S. Ossowski, *Class Structure in the Social Consciousness* (London, 1963), pp. 110-18.

4. At this level the caste system is above all a system of ideas and of values, a formal system, comprehensive and rational, a system in the intellectual sense of the term.

5. Our first task consists in grasping this intellectual system, this ideology.

SOURCES

Aron, R., *La Lutte de classes* (Paris, 1964).
Bailey, F.G., 'For a sociology of India', *Contributions to Indian Sociology* III, 1959.
Béteille, A., 'A note on the referents of caste', *European Journal of Sociology* V, 1964.
Dahrendorf, R., *Class and Class Conflict in Industrial Society* (London, 1959).
Dumont, L., *Homo hierarchicus* (Paris, 1966).
Frykenberg, R.E., *Guntur District, 1788-1848* (Oxford, 1965).
Frykenberg, R.E., (ed.), *Land Control and Social Structure in Indian History* (Madison, Wisc., 1969).
Lange, O. (ed.), 'Political Economy of Socialism' in *Problems of Political Economy of Socialism*, O. Lange (ed.) (Delhi, 1962).
Leach, E.R., *Political Systems of Highland Burma* (London, 1954).
Leach, E.R., 'What we should mean by caste' in *Aspects of Caste in South India, Ceylon and North-west Pakistan*, E.R. Leach (ed.) (Cambridge, 1960).
Lockwood, D., 'Some remarks on "the social system"', *British Journal of Sociology* VII, 1956.
MacPherson, C.B., *The Real World of Democracy* (Oxford, 1966).
Mannheim, K., *Ideology and Utopia* (London, 1960).
Marcuse, H., *Soviet Marxism* (New York, 1961).
Mayer, A.C., 'Change in a Malwa Village', *Economic Weekly*, 24 September 1955.
Metcalfe, T.R., 'From Raja to landlord: the Oudh Talukdars, 1850-1870' in *Land Control and Social Structure in Indian History*, R.E. Frykenberg (ed.) (Madison, Wisc., 1969).
Nemchinov, V.W., 'Changes in the class structure of the Soviet Union', *Transactions of the Third World Congress of Sociology* VIII (London, 1957).
Nicholas, R.W., 'Factions: a comparative analysis', *Political Systems and the Distribution of Power*, ASA Monograph 2 (London, 1965).
Ossowski, S., *Class Structure in the Social Consciousness* (London, 1963).
Ossowski, S., 'Old notions and new problems: interpretations of social structure in modern society', *Transactions of the Third World Congress of Sociology* III (London, 11956).
Srinivas, M.N., *Social Change in Modern India* (Berkeley, 1966).
Wesolowski, W., 'Les notions de strates et de classe dans la société socialiste', *Sociologie du Travail* IX, 1967.

Chapter 6 : Networks in Indian social structure

1. E.E. Evans-Pritchard, *The Nuer* (Oxford, 1940).
2. E.E. Evans-Pritchard, *The Nuer* (Oxford, 1940).

3. This procedure, it may be noted, delimits only the 'formal' structure. The understanding of the 'informal' or operative structure requires additional tools. The delimitation of the formal structure is, however, an essential preliminary to the delineation of the informal structure.

4. McKim Marriott (ed.), *Village India* (Chicago, 1955).

5. E.E. Evans-Pritchard, 'Kinship and the local community among the Nuer' in *African Systems of Kinship and Marriage*, A.R. Radcliffe-Brown and D. Forde (eds) (Oxford, 1950), p. 365.

6. E.E. Evans-Pritchard, *The Nuer* (Oxford, 1940), p. 264 (our italics).

7. This process was grasped, with rare perception, by Emile Durkheim in *The Division of Labour in Society* (1893) (The Free Press: New York, 1933). Durkheim showed how the segmental structure with its sharply defined outlines gave place to the organized structure with its interpenetration of groups with the change from mechanical to organic solidarity (pp. 177-90, 256-75).

8. This is not to deny that networks existed in traditional society also. Their role in contemporary India has, however, become more important. For a brief discussion on networks in traditional India see p.

9. The village was (and still is) clearly divided into three territorial segments: the *agraharam* (where Brahmins live), the non-Brahmin streets and the *cheri* (inhabited by untouchables).

10. See J.A. Barnes, 'Classes and committees in a Norwegian Island parish', *Human Relations* VII, I, 1954, pp. 39-58.

11. J.A. Barnes, 'Classes and Committees', *Human Relations* VII, I, 1954, pp. 39-58.

12. I. Karve, 'What is caste? (1) Caste as extended kin', *The Economic Weekly*, Annual Number, January 1958.

13. This is not contradicted by the fact that the network of formal kinship relations (based upon genealogical ties rather than effective exchange of obligations) expands with an expansion of the limits of endogamy.

14. M.J. Levy Jr., *The Structure of Society* (New Jersey, 1952), pp. 88ff.

15. F.G. Bailey, 'Politics and society in contemporary Orissa' in *Politics and Society in India*, C.H. Philips (ed.) (Londonl, 1963).

16. I. de Sola Pool, 'The mass media and politics in the modernization process' in *Communications and Political Development*, L.W. Pye (ed.) (New Jersey, 1963).

17. See, for instance, M. Singer, 'The Social Organization of Indian Civilization', *Diogenes*, Winter 1964.

Chapter 7 : The future of the Backward Classes

1. Comprising the Scheduled Tribes, the Scheduled Castes and the Other Backward Classes; the Denotified Tribes, who constitute a small minority,

are not considered separately here. For a general account, see Lelah Dushkin, 'The Backward Classes', *The Economic and Political Weekly* 29 October, 4 and 18 November, pp. 1665-9, 1695-1706, 1729-38.

2. Karl Mannheim, *Ideology and Utopia* (New York, 1936).

3. Gunnar Myrdal, *Value and Social Theory* (London, 1958).

4. Marc Galanter, 'Equality and "Protective Discrimination" in India', *Rutgers Law Review* XVI, 1, 1961, pp. 42-74.

5. A. Béteille, 'Question of Definition' in *Tribal India, Seminar* 14, 1960, pp. 15-18.

6. B.S. Guha, 'Indian Aborigines and Who They Are', in *The Adivasis* (Delhi, 1955), p. 31.

7. Government of India, *Report of the Backward Classes Commission* (New Delhi, 1956), p. 48.

8. The author is grateful to Mr L.P. Singh, Home Secretary, Government of India, for supplying this information.

9. M.N. Srinivas, 'Sanskritization and Westernization' in *Society in India*, Aiyappan and Bal Ratnam (eds) (Madras, 1956).

10. M.N. Srinivas, *Religion and Society Among the Coorgs of South India* (Oxford, 1952).

11. M.N. Srinivas et al., *Caste: A Trend Report and Bibliography* (Oxford, 1959), p. 140.

12. M.N. Srinivas, 'The Dominant Caste in Rampura', *American Anthropologist* 61, 1, 1959, pp. 1-16.

13. M.N. Srinivas, 'Sanskritization and Westernization' in *Society in India*, Aiyappan and Bal Ratnam (eds) (Madras, 1956).

14. J.H. Hutton, *Caste in India* (Bombay, 1961), p. 205.

15. J.H. Hutton, *Caste in India* (Bombay, 1961), p. 205.

16. J.H. Hutton, *Caste in India* (Bombay, 1961), p. 206.

17. F.G. Bailey, *Politics and Social Change: Orissa in 1959* (Berkeley, 1963), p. 51.

18. Government of India, *Report of the Commissioner for Scheduled Castes and Scheduled Tribes for the Year 1961-62* (New Delhi, 1963), p. 6.

19. The author is grateful to his colleague, Mr G.S. Aurora, for the information on the Meenas.

20. M.N. Srinivas, 'Sanskritization and Westernization', in *Society in India*, Aiyappan and Bala Ratnam (eds) (Madras, 1956).

21. Harold R. Isaacs, 'A Reporter at Large, The Ex-Untouchables' I, *The New Yorker* (December, 1964), pp. 138-40.

22. Courtesy Mr L.P. Singh.

23. Harold R. Isaacs, 'A Reporter at Large, The Ex-Untouchables' I, *The New Yorker* (December, 1964), pp. 138-40.

24. Harold R. Isaacs, 'A Reporter at Large, The Ex-Untouchables' II, p.75.

25. Martin Orans, *The Santal, A Tribe in Search of a Great Tradition* (Detroit, 1965), p. 101.

26. Myron Weiner, 'The Politics of South Asia' in *The Politics of the Developing Areas*, Almond and Coleman (eds) (Princeton, 1960), p. 192.

27. F.G. Bailey, *Politics and Social Change: Orissa in 1959* (Berkeley, 1963).

28. *The Weekly Mail*, 18 February 1962.

29. L.P. Vidyarthi, 'The historical March of the Jharkhand Party: A Study of Adivasi Leadership in Tribal Bihar', *Sociological Bulletin* 1, 2, 1964, p. 5.

30. N.K. Bose, 'Change in Tribal Cultures Before and After Independence', *Man in India* 44, 1, 1964, p. 5.

31. N.K. Bose, 'Change in Tribal Cultures Before and After Independence', *Man in India* 44, 1, 1964, p. 7.

32. F.G. Bailey, *Politics and Social Change: Orissa in 1959* (Berkeley, 1963), p. 41.

Chapter 8 : Equality as a right and as a policy

1. R. Dworkin, 'Reverse Discrimination', in R. Dworkin, *Taking Rights Seriously* (Duckworth: London, 1977), pp. 223-39.

2. For a discussion of equality as conceived in terms of the 'anti-discrimination' principle, see O.M. Fiss, 'Groups and the Equal Protection Clause' in *Equality and Preferential Treatment*, M. Cohen, T. Nagel and T. Scanlon (eds) (Princeton University Press: Princeton, 1977), pp. 84-154.

3. R.H. Tawney, *Equality* (1931) (Unwin: London, 1964).

4. The most consistent exposition of this point of view is in F.A. Hayek, *The Constitution of Liberty* (Routledge: London, 1960), but see also R. Nozick, *Anarchy, State and Utopia* (Basil Blackwell: Oxford, 1974), and M. Friedman, *Capitalism and Freedom* (University of Chicago Press: Chicago, 1962).

5. B. Sivaramayya, 'Equality and inequality: the legal framework' in *Equality and Inequality: Theory and Practice*, A. Béteille (ed.) (Oxford University Press: Oxford, 1983), pp. 28-70.

6. The classic formulation of this linkage is in A. de Tocqueville, *Democracy in America*, 2 vols (Knopf: New York, 1956), but see also A. Béteille, 'Individualism and Equality', *Current Anthropology* 27, 2, April 1986, pp. 121-34 (see Chapter 9).

7. A very good historical account is to be found in J.R. Pole, *The Pursuit of Equality in American History* (University of California Press: Berkeley, 1978).

8. R. Dworkin, 'Reverse Discrimination' in R. Dworkin, *Taking Rights Seriously* (Duckworth: London, 1977), p. 232.

9. R. Dworkin, 'Reverse Discrimination', p. 227.

10. This was the position consistently adopted in the Constituent Assembly by B.R. Ambedkar, Chairman of the Drafting Committee and independent India's first Minister of Law. See A. Béteille, *Individualism and the Persistence of Collective Identities* (University of Essex: Colchester, 1984).

11. L. Dumont, *From Mandeville to Marx* (University of Chicago Press: Chicago, 1977); L. Dumont, *Essais sur l'individualisme* (Seuil, 1983); S. Lukes, *Individualism* (Basil Blackwell: Oxford, 1973); A. Béteille, 'Individualism and Equality', *Current Anthropology* 27, 2, April 1986, pp. 121-34. (see chapter 9).

12. L. Dumont, *Homo hierarchicus* (Paladin: London, 1972); N.K. Bose, *The Structure of Hindu Society* (Orient Longman: Delhi, 1975). See also the Kale Memorial Lecture by M.P. Rege, *Concepts of Justice and Equality in the Indian Tradition* (Gokhale Institute: Pune, 1985).

13. B. Sivaramayya, *Inequalities and the Law* (Eastern Book Co.: Lucknow, 1984), p. 5.

14. I have discussed some of the ambiguities of the official classification in my Commonwealth Lectures, 'Positive Discrimination and Social Justice', delivered in the University of Cambridge, April - May, 1985.

15. Tara Patel (ed.), *Removal of Untouchability in Gujarat* (Gujarat University: Gujarat, 1973); I.P. Desai, *Untouchability in Rural Gujarat* (Popular Prakashan: Bombay, 1976). See also M.J. Moffatt, *An Untouchable Community of South India* (Princeton University Press: Princeton, 1979).

16. R.G. Karmarkar, *The Protection of Civil Rights Act, 1955* (N.R. Bhalerao: Pune, 1978), p. v.

17. J. Woodburn, 'Egalitarian societies', *Man* 17, 1982, pp. 431-51.

18. See my 'Equality of Opportunity and the Equal Distribution of Benefits', *Arthavijnana* 27, 2, 1985, pp. 96-114.

19. The empirical material on the association between caste and occupation is uneven. See V.S. D'Souza, *Inequality and its Perpetuation* (Manohar: New Delhi, 1981); J. Sarkar, *Caste, Occupation and Change* (B.R. Publishing Corporation: Delhi, 1984).

20. R.H. Tawney, *Equality* (Unwin: London, 1964), p. 103.

21. O.M. Fiss, 'Groups and the Equal Protection Clause', in *Equality and Preferential Treatment* (Princeton, 1977), pp. 84-154.

22. They speak of 'goals' rather than 'quotas'. For a balanced account, see R.A. Rossum, *Reverse Discrimination* (Marcel Dekker: New York, 1980).

23. The only quotas specified by the Constitution are those relating to sears in Parliament and in the state Legislatures, but these are subject to a time limit.

24. For a detailed discussion see M. Galanter, *Competing Equalities* (Oxford University Press: Oxford, 1984).

25. R. Dworkin, 'Why Bakke Has No Case' *New York Review of Books*, 10 November 1977.

26. M. Weiner et al., *India's Preferential Policies* (University of Chicago Press: Chicago, 1981).

27. R. Dworkin, 'Reverse Discrimination' in R. Dworkin, *Taking Rights Seriously* (Duckworth: London, 1977), p. 225.

28. B. Sivaramayya, *Inequalities and the Law* (Lucknow, 1984), p. 36.

However, other interpretations of the relationship between Articles 14 and 16 may be found in the State of Kerala vs. N.M. Thomas, AIR, 1976: SC 490.

29. *Constituent Assembly Debates: Official Report*, vol. 7, 1950, p. 702.

30. AIR, 1976: SC 527.

31. AIR, 1976: SC 536.

32. B. Sivaramayya, *Inequalities and the Law* (Lucknow, 1984), p. 89.

33. A. Béteille, *Individualism and the Persistence of Collective Identities* (Colchester, 1984).

34. Karnataka Backward Classes Commission, *Report*, Government of Karnataka (Bangalore), 1975.

35. B. Sivaramayya, *Inequalities and the Law* (Lucknow, 1984), pp. 88-91.

Chapter 9 : Individualism and equality

1. Dumont (1972, p. 42), for instance, writes: 'As opposed to modern society traditional societies ... know nothing of equality and liberty as values ... known nothing, in short, of the individual'.

2. This is the title of the French edition; the English edition, published simultaneously, is called *From Mandeville to Marx*. The subtitle has roughly the same meaning in both editions.

3. This began to change from the middle of the nineteenth century onwards. The first major step was the Caste Disabilities Removal Act of 1850.

4. This view was widely expressed in the press when large concessions were announced in Gujarat and Madhya Pradesh on the eve of the elections in 1985 and, earlier, in Bihar in 1977.

5. Anti-reservation agitation and riots began in Gujarat and Madhya Pradesh in March 1985 and continued with great severity in Gujarat for several months.

6. These issues have in the last few years been discussed extensively in the national press, especially in *The Times of India*.

7. A recently retired judge of the Supreme Court writes: 'It was in the nineteenth century that the demand for civil rights came to be articulated by the Indians. The birth of the Indian National Congress provided the platform to give expression to the desire for civil rights which then meant equality with the Englishmen' (Reddy, 1976, pp. 10-11). See also Ganguli (1975).

8. Cf. Ballhatchet (1979, p. 6): 'Competitive examinations for the Indian Civil Service began in 1855, and an Indian candidate, Satyendranath Tagore, was successful in 1863. The Civil Service Commissioners reacted in characteristic fashion by manipulating the marking scheme so as to impede subsequent Indian candidates'.

SOURCES

Arnold, M., 'Equality' in *Mised Essays* (John Murray: London, 1903), pp. 48-97.

Ballhatchet, K., *Race, Sex, and Class Under the Raj* (Vikas: New Delhi, 1979).

Bankimchandra Chatterji, (1382 Bengali calendar) Bankim Rachanabali (in Bengali) (Sahitya Samsad: Calcutta, n.d.), vol. 2.

Béteille, A., 'Homo hierarchicus, Homo equalis', *Modern Asian Studies* 13, 1979, pp. 529-48.

Béteille, A., *The Idea of Natural Inequality* (London School of Economics: London, 1980).

Béteille, A., *The Backward Classes and the New Social Order* (Oxford University Press: Delhi, 1981).

Béteille, A., *Individualism and the Persistence of Collective Identities* (University of Essex: Colchester, 1984).

Béteille, A., *Equality of Opportunity and the Equal Distribution of Benefits* (Kale Memorial Lecture, Gokhale Institute of Politics and Economics, Poona, 1986).

Béteille, A., *Positive Discrimination and Social Justice* (Commonwealth Lectures, Cambridge University), ms., n.d.

Burckhardt, J., *The Civilization of the Renaissance in Italy* (1860) (Random House: New York, 1954).

Coleman, J.S., 'Equality of opportunity and equality of results', *Harvard Educational Review* 43, 1, 1973, pp. 129-37. *Constituent Assembly Debates: Official Report*, vol. 7 (New Delhi, 1950).

Duby, G., *The Three Orders* (University of Chicago Press: Chicago, 1980).

Dumont, L., *Homo hierarchicus* (Paladin: London, 1972).

Dumont, L., *From Mandeville to Marx* (University of Chicago Press: Chicago, 1977).

Dumont, L., 'On value', *Proceedings of the British Academy* 66, 1980, pp. 207-41.

Dumont, L., *Essais sur l'individualisme* (Seuil: Paris, 1983).

Durkheim, E., 'Individualism and the intellectuals' (1898) trans S. Lukes and J. Lukes, *Political Studies* 17, 1969, pp. 114-30.

Dworkin, R., 'DeFunis vs Sweatt' in *Equality and Preferential Treatment*, M. Cohen. T. Nagel and T. Scanlon (eds) (Princeton University Press: Princeton, 1977).

Elias, N., *The Court Society* (Basil Blackwell: Oxford, 1983).

Fiss, O.M., 'Groups and the equal protection clause' in *Equality and Preferential Treatment*, M. Cohen, T. Nagel and T. Scanlon (eds) (Princeton University Press: Princeton, 1977), pp. 84-154.

Friedman, M., *Capitalism and Freedom* (University of Chicago Press: Chicago, 1962).

Galanter, M., *Competing Equalities* (Oxford University Press: London, 1983).

Galton, F., Hereditary Genius (1869) (Watts: London, 1950).

Ganguli, B.N., *Concept of Equality* (Indian Institute of Advanced Studies: Simla, 1975).

Glazer, N., *Affirmative Discrimination* (Random House: New York, 1975).

Goldman, A.H., *Justice and Reverse Discrimination* (Princeton University Press: Princeton, 1979).

Government of India, *Report of the Backward Classes Commission (Mandal Commission)* 4 (New Delhi, 1981).

Hayek, F.A., *The Constitution of Liberty* (Routledge: London, 1960).

Hayek, F.A., 'Individualism: true and false' (1946) in *Individualism and Economic Order* (University of Chicago Press: Chicago, 1980), pp. 1-32.

Holmstrom, M., *Industry and Inequality* (Cambridge University Press: Cambridge, 1984).

Huizinga, J., *The Waning of the Middle Ages* (Edward Arnold: London, 1924).

Huxley, T.H., 'On the natural inequality of man', *The Nineteenth Century* no. 155, 1890, pp. 1-23.

Joseph, K. and J. Sumption, *Equality* (John Murray: London, 1979).

Letwin, W. (ed.), *Against Equality* (Macmillan: London, 1983a).

Letwin, W., 'The case against equality' in *Against Equality*, W. Letwin (ed.) (Macmillan: London, 1983b).

Lévi-Strauss, C., *Structural Anthropology* (Basic Books: New York, 1963).

Lucas, J.R., 'Against equality', *Philosophy*, October 1965, pp. 296-307.

Lukes, S., *Individualism* (Basil Blackwell: Oxford, 1973).

Macfarlane, A., *The Origins of English Individualism* (Basil Blackwell: Oxford 1978).

Maine, H.S., *Lectures on the Early History of Institutions* (1875) (John Murray: London, 1914).

Maine, H.S., *Ancient Law* (1861) (Oxford University Press: Oxford, 1950).

Malinowski, B., *Crime and Custom in Savage Society* (Routledge: London, 1926).

Nozick, R., *Anarchy, State and Utopia* (Basil Blackwell: Oxford, 1974).

Ossowski, S., *Class Structure in the Social Consciousness* (Routledge: London, 1963).

Pollock, F. and F.W. Maitland, *The History of English Law Before the Time of Edward I* (1895) (Cambridge University Press, 1968), vol. 1.

Rawls, J., *A Theory of Justice* (Oxford University Press: London, 1973).

Reddy, P. Jaganmohan, *Social Justice and the Constitution* (Andhra University Press: Waltair, 1976).

Rossum, R.A., *Reverse Discrimination* (Marcel Dekker: New York, 1980).

Simmel, G., 'Individual and society in eighteenth- and nineteenth-century views of life' (1917) in *The Sociology of Georg Simmel*, K. Wolff (ed.) (Free Press: Glencoe, 1950), pp. 58-84.

Simmel, G., *On Individualism and Social Forms*, D.N. Levine (ed.) (University of Chicago Press: Chicago, 1971).

Sivaramaÿya, B., 'Equality and inequality: the legal framework' in *Equality and Inequality*, A. Béteille (ed.) (Oxford University Press: Delhi, 1983).

Srinivas, M.N., *India 2000 A.D.: The Next Fifteen Years* (Austin: University of Texas Press, 1986).

Tocqueville, A. de, *Democracy in America*, 2 vols (1835-40) (Knopf: New York, 1956).

Tripathi, P.K., *Some insights into Fundamental Rights* (University of Bombay: Bombay, 1972).

Williams, B., 'The idea of inequality' in *Philosophy, Politics, and Society*, 2nd series, P. Laslett and W.G. Runciman (eds) (Basil Blackwell: Oxford, 1962).

Chapter 10 : Individual and person as subjects for sociology

1. There is a long line of prominent American sociologists who have written about the self, from G.H. Mead, *Mind, Self and Society* (University of Chicago Press: Chicago, 1934) to E. Goffman, *The Presentation of Self in Everyday Life* (Doubleday: 1959).

2. For a recent critical account see A. Bharati, 'The self in hindu thought and action' in A.J. Marsella, G. DeVos and F.L.K. Hsu (eds) *Culture and Self*, (Tavistock Publications: London, 1985), pp. 185-230.

3. E. Durkheim, *The Division of Labour in Society* (1893) (Macmillan: London, 1984.

4. E. Durkheim, *The Elementary Forms of Religious Life* (1912) (Allen & Unwin: London, 1915), p. 270.

5. M. Mauss, 'A category of the human mind: the notion of person, the notion of "self"' in his *Sociology and Psychology* (1938) (Routledge: London, 1979), pp. 57-94.

6. N. Luhmann, 'The individuality of the individual: historical meanings and contemporary problems' in T.C. Heller et al. (eds), *Reconstructing Individualism*, (Stanford University Press: Stanford, 1986), p. 313.

7. Two of his most influential pupils, Evans-Pritchard, Professor of Social Anthropology at Oxford (1946-70) and Fortes, Professor of Social Anthropology at Cambridge (1950-73) both became increasingly critical of Malinowski, if not hostile to him, although Malinowski's intellectual influence was very strong on them, particularly on Evans-Pritchard. For derogatory and hostile remarks made by the former in print, see E.E. Evans-Pritchard, *Social Anthropology* (Cohen and West: London, 1951), pp. 93-6, and *A History of Anthropological Thought* (Faber and Faber: London, 1981), pp. 197-200; what was put down in print was mild compared to what was said in coversation. Fortes was more guarded, but far from flattering in his references to Malinowski in M. Fortes, *Kinship and the Social Order*,

(Routledge: London, 1969), pp. 4-5.

8. See the Introduction by Lévi-Strauss in M. Mauss, *Sociologie et Anthropologie*, (Presses Universitaires de France: Paris, 1960), pp. ix-lii. See also the introduction in L. Dumont, *Essais sur l'individualisme* (Seuil: Paris, 1983), pp. 11-30, especially pp. 11-18.

9. Malinowski is not so much as mentioned in a recent Oxford symposium on the person: M. Carrithers, S. Collins and S. Lukes (eds), *The Category of the Person* (Cambridge University Press: Cambridge, 1985), whereas the editors took pains to make a fresh English translation of Mauss's essay on the person to serve as the opening chapter in the volume.

10. Meyer Fortes has left a brief but vivid account of Mauss on that occasion. See M. Fortes, 'The Concept of Person' in his *Religion, Morality and the Person* (Cambridge University Press: Cambridge, 1987).

11. See M. Mauss 'A category of the human mind: the notion of person, the notion of "self"' in his *Sociology and Psychology* (London, 1979), pp. 57-94 and M. Carrithers, S. Collins and S. Lukes (eds), *The Category of the Person* (Cambridge, 1985).

12. E. Durkheim, *The Division of Labour in Society* (London, 1984).

13. E. Durkheim, 'Individualism and the Intellectuals' (1898), trans S. Lukes and J. Lukes, *Political Studies* 17, 1969, pp. 114-30.

14. M. Mauss, 'A category of the human mind' in M. Mauss, *Sociology and Psychology* (London, 1979).

15. The point was made forcefully in his celebrated Marett Lecture, 'Social anthropology: past and present', republished in E.E. Evans-Pritchard, *Essays in Social Anthropology* (London, 1951). See also 'The position of women in primitive societies' in his *The Position of Women in Primitive Societies and Other Essays in Social Anthropology* (Faber and Faber: London, 1965), pp. 37-58; and his *Theories of Primitive Religion* (Clarendon Press: Oxford, 1965).

16. Durkheim, *The Division of Labour in Society* (London, 1984), p. 84.

17. M. Mauss, *The Gift* (1925), (Routledge: London, 1954), p. 3.

18. Compare C. Geertz, *Works and Lives* (Polity Press: Cambridge, 1988) on Evans-Pritchard: 'On the Akobe as the Isis, men and women are brave and cowardly, kind and cruel, reasonable and foolish, loyal and perfidious, intelligent and stupid, vivid and boring, believing and indifferent, the better the one than the other' (p. 71).

19. B. Malinowski, *Crime and Custom in Savage Society* (Kegan Paul, Trench & Trubner: London, 1925), p. 127.

20. B. Malinowski, *Crime and Custom in Savage Society* (London, 1925), p. 57.

21. B. Malinowski, *Crime and Custom in Savage Society* (London, 1925), p. 57.

22. E.R. Leach, 'The epistemological background to Malinowski's empiricism' in *Mind and Culture*, R. Firth (ed.) (Routledge: London, 1957), p. 127.

23. E.R. Leach, 'The epistemological background to Malinowski's empiricism'

in *Mind and Culture*, R. Firth (ed.) (London, 1957), p. 127.

24. G. Bateson, *Naven* (1936) (Wildwood house: Aldershot, 1980), p. 31.

25. G. Bateson, *Naven* (Aldershot, 1980), p. 124.

26. E.E. Evans-Pritchard,'The Nuer of the Southern Sudan' in M. Fortes and E.E. Evans-Pritchard (eds), *African Political Systems* (Oxford University Press: Oxford, 1940), p. 296.

27. E.E. Evans-Pritchard, *The Nuer* (Clarendon Press: Oxford, 1940), p. 90.

28. E.E. Evans-Pritchard, *The Nuer* (Oxford, 1940), p. 171.

29. E.E. Evans-Pritchard, *Nuer Religion* (Clarendon Press: Oxford, 1956).

30. G. Lienhardt, 'Self: public, private' in *The Category of the Person*, M. Carrithers, S. Collins and S. Lukes (eds) (Cambridge, 1985), pp. 141-55.

31. M. Mauss, 'A category of the human mind' in M. Mauss, *Sociology and Psychology* (London, 1979), p. 62.

32. K. Bhattacharyya, 'The status of the individual in Indian metaphysics' in *The Status of the Individual in East and West*, C.A. Moore (ed.) (University of Hawaii Press: Hawaii, 1968), p. 47.

33. K. Bhattacharyya, 'The status of the individual', p. 47.

34. K. Bhattacharyya, 'The status of the individual', p. 48.

35. P.T. Raju, 'Indian epistemology and the world and the individual' in *The Status of the Individual in East and West*, C.A. Moore (ed.) (Hawaii, 1968), p. 134.

36. Rabindranath Tagore, *Nationalism* (Macmillan: London, 1917).

37. Radindranath Tagore, *Personality* (Macmillan: London, 1917).

38. N.K. Bose, *My Days with Gandhi* (Nishana: Calcutta, 1953); see also his *Selections from Gandhi* (Navajivan Publishing House: Ahmmedabad, 1957).

39. M. Mauss, 'A category of the human mind' in M. Mauss, *Sociology and Psychology* (London, 1979), p. 90.

40. Jawaharlal Nehru, *The Discovery of India* (1946) (Asia Publishing House: Bombay, 1961), pp. 247-8.

41. J. Nehru, *The Discovery of India* (Delhi, 1961), p. 252. Nehru also pointed to the significance of the *sannyasi* or renouncer as an alternative to the individual-in-society. On this see also N.K. Bose, 'Return of the Individual', *Man in India* 34, 3, 1954.

42. A. Macfarlane, *Marriage and Love in England 1300-1840* (Basil Blackwell: Oxford, 1986); also his *The Origins of English Individualism*, (Basil Blackwell: Oxford, 1978).

43. Niharranjan Ray, *Nationalism in India*, (Aligarh Muslim University: Aligarh, 1973), pp. 142ff.

44. Jayaprakash Narayan continued his advocacy of a return to village self-government into the post-independence period. He presented his case in a widely circulated but unpublished tract, *A Plea for the Reconstitution of Indian Polity* (c. 1960).

45. *Constituent Assembly Debates: Official Report*, vol. 7 (New Delhi, 1950), p. 39.

46. M.K. Gandhi, *Varnashramadharma*, (Navajivan Publishing House: Bombay, 1962).

47. P.V. Kane, *History of Dharmasastra* 2nd edn. (Bhandarkar Oriental Research Institute: Poona, 1974), vol. II, part I, p. 7.

48. N.K. Bose, *The Structure of Hindu Society* (1949) (Orient Longman: Delhi, 1975), p. 137.

49. M.K. Srinivas, *Social Change in Modern India* (University of California Press: Berkeley, 1966).

50. A. Béteille, *The Backward Classes and the New Social Order*, (Oxford University Press: Oxford 1981).

51. E. Durkheim, *The Division of Labour in Society* (London, 1984).

52. A. Béteille, *Individualism and the Persistence of Collective Identities* (Third Fuller Bequest Lecture) (University of Essex: Colchester, 1984).

53. N.K. Bose, 'Calcutta: A premature metropolis', *Scientific American* 213, 3, 1965, p. 102.

54. *Constituent Assembly Debates: Official Report*, vol. 7 (New Delhi, 1950), 701.

55. In the case of the Scheduled Tribes, as against the Scheduled Castes (and also the Other Backward Classes), the preservation of language, religion and culture is an additional consideration.

56. M. Galanter, *Competing Equalities* (Oxford University Press: Oxford, 1984). I have discussed these in my unpublished Commonwealth Lectures, *Positive Discrimination and Social Justice* (University of Cambridge, 1985).

57. A. Béteille, 'Equality as a right and as a policy', *LSE Quarterly* 1, 1, 1987, pp. 75-98 (see Chapter 8).

58. For arguments relating to the United States, see O.M. Fiss, 'Groups and the equal protection clause' in *Equality and Preferential Treatment* M. Cohen, T. Nagel and T. Scanlon (eds) (Princeton University Press: Princeton, 1977), pp. 84-154. See also R. Dworkin, 'Reverse Discrimination' in his *Taking Rights Seriously* (Duckworth: London, 1977), pp. 223-39.

59. A. Béteille, 'Equality of opportunity and the equal distribution of benefits', *Artha Vijnana* 27, 2, 1985, pp. 96-114.

60. Firstly, the Scheduled Castes as a proportion of the total population increased between 1951 and 1981 from 14.4 to 15.75 per cent, and the Scheduled Tribes from 5.4 to 7.76 per cent, mainly as a result of the inclusion of new groups. Secondly, new lists of the Other Backward Classes have been made and enlarged in both North and South India.

Index

16/1683 - 10/2000